INVASION '51

INVASION '51

The Birth Of Alien Cinema

by Sean Kotz

BearManor Media

2022

Invasion '51: The Birth of Alien Cinema

© 2022 by Sean Kotz

Published in the United States of America by:

BearManor Media
1317 Edgewater Dr #110
Orlando FL 32804

bearmanormedia.com

Printed in the United States.

Typesetting and layout by John Teehan

Cover by Phillip Payne

ISBN—978-1-62933-994-8

Table of Contents

Dedication

To Carmen, the love of my life,
who makes everything possible
and worthwhile.

Acknowledgements

I WOULD LIKE TO acknowledge the help and support of several people beginning with Bill Kaffenberger, a fine writer, researcher and scholar whose interest in the idea helped me bring this to publication. Also, my friend Phillip Payne, who designed this cover and has been a co-conspirator on several art projects over the years. I met both gentlemen through our shared love of Richmond's Hall of Fame horror movie host, the Bowman Body (a. k. a. Bill Bowman) who brought these films to a generation of kids.

Additionally, several people contributed their time and expertise via correspondence and made critical contributions to solving mysteries and providing insight with regard to these three films: Dr. Nahum Arav, Professor of Physics, Virginia Tech; Arianne Ulmer Cipes; Billy Gray; Jay Graybeal, chief curator at the Army Heritage and Education Center; writer (and brother from another mother), Phil Hore; Capt. Benjamin Hughes, USAF; Mallory Porter and Margot Stipe of the Frank Lloyd Wright Foundation; Patrick Russ, orchestrator and arranger; Matthew J. Seelinger, Chief Historian, U. S. Army Foundation; Warren Sherk, Associate Director, Special Collections at Academy of Motion Picture Arts and Sciences; Margo Stipe, Frank Lloyd Wright Foundation; and Douglas Walla, curator of Paul Laffoley's legacy.

Also, this book could not have been completed without the aid and resources of libraries, particularly the staff of Radford City Public Library, Radford University Library and Virginia Tech's Newman Library and their Special Collections.

Preface

ON DEC. 2, 1950, Louella O. Parsons, famed Hollywood insider and Motion Picture Editor for the International News Service, opened her brief production notice for *The Man from Planet X* with a stray observation: "I'll this say for these moon epics—'Rocketship XM' and 'Destination Moon'—they clean up at the box office. Apparently, people like to hear about far away places and unknown quantities" (7). It would prove a much more prognostic statement than she could have known.

As she wrote that, not only *The Man from Planet X* but also *The Thing from Another World* and *The Day the Earth Stood Still* were all in development and would change the cinematic landscape forever. All three are alien invasion films, a critically important subgenre with no exact precedent in cinema. The concept of aliens preexisted, of course. Extraterrestrials with superior technology, development and intellect populated pulp magazines though these never had mainstream attention. People might well have had some experience with H. G. Well's *War of the Worlds* which began as a serialized story, saw publication as a novel and later famously manifested as a 1939 Halloween radio drama orchestrated by Orson Welles (no relation to the author). But in terms of silver screen aliens landing in Washington D. C. (or Scotland... or the Arctic), that had never been done.

This book charts the evolution and production history of these three films in detail, analyzes them as cinematic art and discusses their cultural legacy. Each film takes a slightly different approach to the basic idea, each blueprinted its own subgenre, and each conditioned our subsequent concept of aliens and alien contact ever since. If extraterrestrial (or perhaps interdimensional or ultraterrestrial) contact lies in our future, cinema set our expectations in motion back in 1951.

For the most part, *Invasion '51* avoids cumbersome academic theory and cinematic terminology, but it does assume the reader is an intelligent and interested party looking for something more than amusement. When necessary, applied concepts get brief explanation. There's detail, analysis and exploration, but the goal is clarity and accessibility for anyone interested in the subject matter, academic or otherwise. Students and scholars may find much to draw on, but hopefully the readership is full of former kids who stayed up late and pulled in close to the TV to see something weird and wonderful.

Klaatu barada nikto, my friends. Klaatu barada nikto…

WORK CITED

Parsons, Louella O. "Stars Cast for Movie about Lotta Crabtree." *San Francisco Examiner*. 2 Dec. 1950. p. 7.

The Context For Contact

A **VERY SPECIFIC** historical Petri dish cultured the "alien invasion" film in 1951. Real (and imagined) acts of Soviet espionage threaded their way into the American subconscious in the years immediately following World War II. Hand in hand with the "Red Scare" was the culture shift that came with the sudden realization that nuclear weapons made complete destruction possible. And in the skies, trained, combat-experienced pilots not only saw UFOs and tracked them on radar, but in at least one case, a flyer died chasing one. As a result, "flying saucers" frequently commanded front page headlines and the Air Force had to take them seriously (as well as work out some plausible explanations). Meanwhile, Tinseltown whirled in turmoil. The studio system was collapsing, Senator Joseph McCarthy's authoritarian witch hunts had shaken even Humphrey Bogart to the core, and Americans were suddenly passing on a trip to the movies in favor of a little glowing box soon to bring Hollywood its greatest threat since the depression... a wacky redhead named Lucille Ball.

Understanding that interplay of forces anchors a solid appreciation for why *The Thing from Another World*, *The Day the Earth Stood Still* and *The Man from Planet X* captured so many imaginations and propelled a whole new genre. The movies needed something to appeal to a new audience in a new world of cold war nuclear politics and rapidly changing technology and values. And it couldn't be kid stuff. The times had changed and so had the terrors that watermarked them, so the movies had to change too.

"Cold enough for you?"

Beginning with the explosion of "Little Boy" over Hiroshima on August 9, 1945, Americans lived for four years in a paradoxically uneasy peace of mind. The U.S. had "The Bomb," which offered substantial assurance against attack, but also waited for the other proverbial shoe to drop. It hit the floor in the late summer of 1949 when the Soviet Union tested its first successful nuclear weapon. The unpleasant realities of fruitful Soviet espionage and the rise of McCarthy's authoritarian scapegoating fomented potent social and political fears against a backdrop of expanding suburbs, a booming post-war economy, and the national optimism of the world's dominant superpower.

Of course, it's not exactly a news flash to connect the Cold War to mid-century science fiction films, but late '40s geopolitics and the new science of mass destruction created anxieties significantly shaping alien invasion fantasies in specific ways. The years between the bombs proved an incubation period for suspicion, paranoia and xenophobia that predictably found expression in cinema, particularly science fiction, a short time later.

Two principal fears guided American post-war anxieties: nuclear warfare and communist takeover (whether by infiltration or as a function of warfare.) The latter manifested overtly in espionage films like *The Woman on Pier 13* (a.k.a *I Married a Communist*, 1949) and *I Was a Communist for the FBI* (1951) which typify the "Red Scare" subgenre with secret meetings, family disintegration and sexual seduction connected to communist ideology.

But science fiction had a capacity to tap annihilation and infiltration paranoia simultaneously. Consider the giant ants in *Them!* (1954), for example. As a result of nuclear testing, they grow enormous and thus embody the now familiar mutation motif of the early nuclear age. As a cooperative collective with no concept of individualism, the ants reflect a popular image of robotic and relentless communism—a swarming hoard expanding secretly underground. Additionally, they symbolize invasive, militaristic colonization as "the only other creatures besides man who wage war," as Dr. Harold Medford (Edmund Gwenn) explains during a flickering 16 mm instructional reel embedded in the film. The day *Them!* opened nationwide, June 19, every paper in the U.S. had the same front page news about war, invasion and communism in Guatemala. You might put down the paper to escape into the cool, dark cavern of the theater, but beware. Inside a symbolic war and infiltration drama waged to clutch at the recesses of your psyche.

Having said that, *Them!* is a rarity in its dual symbolism since giant monster films tend to stick to the "Nature Runs Amok" theme in which abuse of nature leads to unintended and disastrous consequences. Indeed, that is the surface theme in *Them!* with connection to the Red Scare requiring a bit more from the viewer to pick up on consciously. And while giant movie monsters surged in the 1950s, they were hardly new. Giant apes and dinosaurs smashed cities well before *Them!*

But alien invasion was an entirely new genre in 1951, at least in terms of feature films, and offered another layer of fear for development. Cinematic aliens, no matter how bizarre, generally had human qualities and motives, if not always humanoid forms. That allows for conquest and domination themes in which the outer space menace stands in for the Soviet Union and communism much more directly. Subsequently, alien invasion films commonly point to humanity's array of social, political and even personality disorders exemplified by a will to dominate, conquer or simply destroy. They also provide a mythology instructing socially endorsed behavior in the face of the unknown through heroism and archetypes of "alienness." In other words, these films work to define values, especially mid-century American values, and give audiences three distinct (and lasting) ways to understand the alien: adversary, superior, and enigma.

One of the most pervasive fears appeared as an "infiltration" strategy, patterned on well publicized acts of Soviet espionage. The concept of communists infiltrating society and government institutions felt reasonable in the wake of a decade of high-profile espionage and collusion cases. Seemingly average citizens like Alger Hiss, Julius and Ethel Rosenberg, and Elizabeth Bentley (whose testimony before the House Un-American Activities Committee particularly shocked the public) embodied the power of propaganda to "turn" a person against their country. The concept of a seeping, underground campaign to create traitors and sympathizers inspired Harry Truman to issue Executive Order 9835 in 1947 (only a few months before the first major national UFO flap) known as the "Loyalty Order." In short, it authorized an investigation of all civilian federal employees to clip out Soviet influence and infiltration (Truman). The willingness of Americans to endorse such surveillance on other Americans bespeaks the level of paranoia of the times.

In alien invasion films, this fear of communist takeover frequently means the aliens practice some form of mental control to induce personality changes and mindless submission of individual will—first in one's family and neighbors, and eventually in figures of authority. As we shall see, mental control acts as the prime tool for the alien in *The Man from Planet X*, initiating a major genre theme. For example, *Invaders from Mars* (1953), *Invasion of the Body Snatchers* (1955), *It Conquered the World* (1956), and *Invisible Invaders* (1959) all read easily as communist influence films following that general pattern. And while this can seem like overblown paranoia today, in the 1940s and '50s, a pattern of infiltration surged in U.S. headlines and propaganda to justify it.

While the term "alien invasion" might instantly conjure up dramatic large scale attack scenes from films like *War of the Worlds* (1953) or *Earth Vs. The Flying Saucers* (1956), more commonly, alien invasion cinema of the 1950s tends to feature some sort of alien "advanced guard" or "scout" unit. This can range in size from a hidden base (a la *Killers from Space*, 1954) to a single creature, as seen in *The Thing from Another World* and *The Man from Planet X*. Symbolically, this reflects the fear of individual communist operatives hedging their way into society to undermine it. Narratively speaking, this gives the heroes both a manageable threat and a timeline for discovery, strategy and action. And generally, it takes coordinated community action to stamp out the surrogate commies, a compact between citizens, soldiers, scientists and leaders.

Another Cold War anxiety of the times--cultural and/or human annihilation--first found voice in alien invasion films as well. The prospect of two opposing nations with the capacity for nuclear war made such a thing literally possible for the first time. On September 9, 1949, about 10 days after the first test in the U.S.S.R., American intelligence informed President Truman that abnormal levels of radioactive air turned up in the Pacific Northwest, indicating a successful Soviet atomic weapon test. It changed things over night:

> Moscow's success in building a nuclear bomb was a monumental development made all the more alarming for U.S. strategists by the fact that it occurred one-to-four years sooner than analysts had expected. The White House chose to preempt possible Kremlin triumphalism by announcing the finding to the world on 23 September 1949, a move that evidently came as a shock to the Soviets who had no idea the U.S. had the capability to isolate and identify the signs of a nuclear blast. ("Detection")

The sci-fi response to this new reality might be called the "Warning from Space" motif, in honor of the 1956 Japanese film of that name, in which aliens raise such concerns (though deploying a nuclear weapon ultimately saves Earth from a planetary collision). In these films, aliens become alarmed over the sudden explosion of human technology and our inevitable entry into the interstellar community. Our penchant for warfare and expansion (and expansion through warfare) sometimes leaves the aliens in the position of the good guys and humans needing some paternal direction (or restriction). As we will see, *The Day the Earth Stood Still* is the first and arguably the best of this sub-genre.

HOT OFF THE PRESSES: "PILOT IS BAFFLED BY 'FLYING SAUCERS'"

It's a good bet readers have heard of Kenneth Arnold. If not, he is the flyer referenced in the Hartford Courant's headline, "Pilot Is Baffled by 'Flying Saucers'" from June 26, 1947. Two days before, Arnold had spotted "nine bright, saucer-like objects flying at 'incredible speed'" between Mt. Rainier and Mt. Adams ("Pilot" 1). It was one of many headlines (styled differently at each paper) recounting the UFO sighting that ignited the 1947 summer flap and would play heavily into depictions of Hollywood spacecraft in the coming years.

The Boise Idaho resident spotted the objects during a short flight from Chehalis to Yakima (in Washington state) on the 24th. Arnold took a slight detour, looking for a crashed Marine C-46 worth $5000 reward money. He never found the plane but a string of bright, nearly blinding, objects caught his attention which he reported upon landing in Yakima before flying to Pendleton, Oregon, for an airshow. Word of the "air mystery" arrived before Arnold landed and the pot was already stirring.

If Arnold had been headed for an auto show, fire safety convention or nearly anything else, it's unlikely his sighting would have even been recorded. But airshows, of course, are filled with pilots and enthusiasts whose knowledge of and interest in aircraft constitutes a point of pride. It's not hard to imagine a hot debate over Arnold's objects breaking out there. Were they "ours" or "theirs"? Was he mistaken? Or crazy?

In any case, the stir in Pendleton the next day brought Kenneth Arnold to *The East Oregonian* newspaper offices, presumably to set matters straight. He spoke with reporter Bill Bequette and his editor, Nolan Skiff, who put it on the AP wire before noon on June 25th. Clearly, reasonable concern over national security motivated Arnold's report--not personal publicity--and no one expected the story to go very far despite the chatter in town. However, in the slow news week, accounts of Arnold's sighting ran from coast to coast, birthing the "flying saucer."

Arnold ultimately disdained the term "flying saucer." It was used derisively soon after his report and he resented the ridicule. (He wouldn't be the last to feel that way.) The specific term did not appear in the first reports, but it seems to have originated somewhere along the AP wire service and wound up in quotation marks. Arnold would dispute ever using the term "flying saucer" throughout his life, claiming his initial statements were simply misinterpreted. On April 7, 1950 (nearly three years later), CBS news broadcasted an interview between Arnold and famed newsman Edward R. Murrow. To clear things up, Arnold told him:

> These objects more or less fluttered like they were, oh, I'd say, boats on very rough water or very rough air of some type, and when I described how they flew, I said that they flew like they take a saucer and throw it across the water. Most of the newspapers misunderstood and misquoted that too. They said that I said that they were saucer-like; I said that they flew in a saucer-like fashion (Murrow).

Indeed, the initial report used the phrase "'saucer-like'" aircraft flying in formation, not "flying saucer" (Wright). The same day, however, an interesting report published in the *Medford Mail Tribune* had Arnold telling Jack Whitman (whomever he was), "They were shaped like saucers and were so thin I could barely see them" ("Amateur Aviator" 1).

In any case, Arnold gave the press the raw material to coin the term even if he never actually said "flying saucer" himself. This was not necessarily an intentional distortion of his experience. In 1947, reporters used note pads to keep up with their sources requiring a certain amount of memory for quoting and interpreting a subject. Also, physical space (i.e., available column inches) dictated how much detail might go into a report, especially one coming off a news wire. Many AP, UP an INS reports got clipped or embellished depending on the space available. On June 25, the article was just an oddity suitable for leftover space. Condensing "nine saucer-like aircraft flying in formation'" into the catchy, compact and visual phrase "flying saucer" would have been considered practical rather than unethical. So, it is not surprising that within 24 hours of the *East Oregonian* article, *The San Francisco Examiner*, *The Philadelphia Inquirer*, *The Minneapolis Star*, *The Montgomery Advertiser*, *The Baltimore Sun*, *The Daily Oklahoman*, and many other papers ran headlines citing "Flying Saucers."

"ARMY DECLARES FLYING DISK FOUND!"

Over the next three weeks, a remarkable phenomenon took place: for a brief time, "flying saucers" graced newspaper headlines daily in the United States (and elsewhere) and garnered serious and extensive attention. Regular people stepped forward after Arnold's sighting to report their own experiences, most of which seem sincere. Strange lights and unidentified flying objects were suddenly newsworthy, and it almost became fashionable to have a local sighting. The whole nation collectively considered the possibility of extraterrestrial life and visitation for the first time.

By the same token, many of the clichés associated with the phenomenon seemingly developed in this period too. Ministers warned of the end times, pranksters sought attention, satirists and know-it-alls blamed alcohol and overactive imaginations, and the whole thing played out in black and white with few reasonable answers. To borrow the front-page headline from the Hazelton Pennsylvania *Plain Speaker* on July 07, "'Flying Saucers' Reported Seen in 38 States But No Clue To What Air Travelers Really Are."

The phenomenon reached a fevered pitch between July 6 and 12, with the now infamous Roswell crash report marking the peak. Undoubtedly, something physical crashed and left debris on the J. B. Foster Ranch (though what crashed remains debated to this day). Ranch manager Matt Brazwell collected the material and brought it to the sheriff in Roswell. In turn, it went to Major Jesse Marcel, now famous for his photo holding pieces of a weather balloon in the *second* official release that snuffed the story.

However, UFO fans fixate on the *first* release from Public Information Officer 1st Lieutenant Walter Haut as evidence of a cover up. On July 8, a day already ladled with flying saucer reports and commentary across the country, many West Coast papers (due to later filing times) ran a story like the one commanding all-capped one-inch bold headlines seen in the *Spokane Daily Chronicle*: "ARMY DECLARES FLYING DISK FOUND."

With little else to go on, papers quoted Haut (misidentified as Warren Haught... or Haudht in true saucer craze fashion) who potently stated, "The many rumors of the flying discs became a reality yesterday when the intelligence office of the 509ᵗʰ (atomic) bomb group of the Eighth air force, Roswell army airfield, was fortunate enough to gain possession of a disk..." (1).

Officially, the "Roswell Incident" has been chalked up to a crashed surveillance balloon from Operation Mogul designed to detect nuclear blasts. The Army needed to keep Mogul a secret and offered an eagerly received official weather balloon cover story. In those days, people trusted the government, and thus, the fervor soon deflated, so to speak, especially since most of the country heard the debunking story first rather than the original report. In other words, the explanation assured commonsense normality and vented the tension that came with flying saucers—just what the public wanted to hear.

Haut distanced himself from Roswell for decades, but in the 1990s, he gradually became more vocal. In a signed and witnessed affidavit released after his death, Haut claimed to have seen an egg-shaped craft in a hangar and a pair of bodies with exposed heads "larger than normal and the contour of the canvas suggested the size of a 10 year old child" (Haut, 2002 Sealed Affidavit). The value of that statement depends on the reader. For UFO crash proponents, Haut was one of several genuine voices trying to reveal the truth when he was finally able. For skeptics, he was the self-invested co-founder of the International UFO Museum and Research Center.

After the Roswell Incident was dismissed in the press, it essentially laid dormant until the 1980s, a testament to both the role and power of the press in 1947. For our purposes here, that's important. In the 1940s (and for a long time after), most people got their news and information from their local paper. News reporting was generally respected as a professional career *and* a pillar of democracy, the so called "Forth Estate." As we will see, news reporting—specifically getting vital information to the public--plays a significant role in *The Thing from Another World*, *The Man from Planet X*, and *The Day the Earth Stood Still*.

SIGNS OF A GRUDGE

Even though the Roswell weather balloon story soothed the public with a rational answer, it did little to stop the saucers themselves. No doubt the

U. S. military took the issue seriously, launching a series of investigations into the phenomenon. In many ways, their hand was forced by the death of Captain Thomas F. Mantell of the Kentucky National Guard's air wing. Mantell and two other pilots were dispatched to chase down a "flying saucer" spotted over Kentucky, Ohio and Tennessee on January 7, 1948. Most of the country learned about the incident two days later in an Associated Press report describing the event as a "fruitless chase" ("Flyer Killed" 2). Mantell, an experienced aviator decorated for his service in WWII, pursued the object in his P-51 Mustang after two others broke off due to fuel and air supply issues. He appears to have lost consciousness past 25,000 feet flying without oxygen (Randle 6).

Project Sign, the first official inquiry into the UFO phenomenon, chartered in December of 1947, began in earnest on January 23, 1948 (just two weeks after the Mantell crash). By February 1949, the investigation name changed to *Project Grudge*, and so did the mission, according to Air Force Captain Edward J. Ruppelt's 1956 book, *The Report on Unidentified Flying Objects*:

> With the new name and the new personnel came the new objective, get rid of the UFO's [sic]. It was never specified this way in writing but it didn't take much effort to see that this was the goal of Project Grudge. This unwritten objective was reflected in every memo, report, and directive. (57).

Project Grudge terminated with an announcement concluding that flying saucers essentially were not real on December 27, 1949 (remember that date, readers). However, Grudge became the more famous, or perhaps infamous, *Project Blue Book* in 1951, with Ruppelt at the helm until 1953. (*Blue Book* ran through 1969). Readers should note that Ruppelt's 1956 version, published two years after his Air Force retirement, expresses seemingly open-minded consideration of the flying saucer conundrum and frustration with the dismissive agenda. However, the extended 1960 version concludes that UFOs are not extraterrestrial or even extraordinary, disappointing many UFOlogists.

Like the Arnold sighting, Roswell and everything before and after, official and interpretive material on *Sign*, *Grudge* and *Blue Book* abounds elsewhere. For the purposes of this discussion, the projects demonstrate the intensity of the flying saucer phenomenon leading up to the alien invasion films of 1951. The undercurrents of legitimate fear and mystery swelled and surged in the years just prior to the explosion of invasion films. Without that potent underlying anxiety, these films might easily have been a fad, like the breakdancing movies of the 1980s.

THE SHAKY STATE OF THE FILM INDUSTRY IN 1950

The U. S. film industry faced storm clouds everywhere in 1950, a major factor in pushing out new and exciting science fiction films.

In the 1930s, "roughly eighty million people went to the movies every week, with weekly attendance peaking at ninety million in 1930 and again in the mid-1940s" (Denby 29-30). These are staggering figures considering U.S. population reached around 123 million in 1930 and 140 million in 1945 according to the US Census Bureau's Historical National Population Estimates. In other words, somewhere around 70 percent of Americans found their way to the theater weekly in the first year of the Great Depression (though figures declined through 1934) and again during the war years.

During WWII, the tail end of Hollywood's Golden Age, Americans sought escapist relief and films were one of the few pleasures not rationed. Films offered a community experience as well, important for morale and public engagement. Plus, the value was substantial. Moviegoers could enjoy a feature (and often two) for about 25 cents, plus a cartoon, news reels, and serials. Even in very rural areas, small towns still had at least one theater, generally near the center of town with other activities close by.

But in the years following World War II, there was another drop in cinema attendance as the country reset itself culturally. A relatively new technology, television, began to take hold in 1950, cutting into attendance numbers with each passing year. In 1950, only about 9% of Americans owned televisions. By 1951, that number more than doubled to 23%, in no small part due to the watercooler conversation offered by a dazzlingly talented redhead named Lucille Ball. By the middle of the decade, nearly 65% of all U.S. households had at least one TV set ("Number of TV Households") and the movie industry struggled again.

Meanwhile, in Washington, D. C., the House UnAmerican Activities Committee (HUAC) begin pushing its McCarthyist tentacles into Hollywood almost as soon as the war was over. On July 29, 1946, William "Billy" Wilkerson, owner, publisher and editor of *The Hollywood Reporter*, an influential trade magazine, printed a list of Hollywood 'communists and communist sympathizers.' This propelled an investigation ultimately resulting in the notorious blacklist and the so-called "Hollywood 10," a group composed mostly of writers, including Dalton Trumbo, the author of the highly patriotic, *30 Seconds Over Tokyo*. The group were indicted and sentenced for not cooperating (Baum and Miller). All indications suggest the group actually were members of the Communist Party but that was not illegal in itself and they had no nefarious plans to subvert American democracy. Trumbo, an uncredited writer on *Rocketship XM* in 1950, would later win two Oscars for writing with *Roman Holiday* (1953) and *The Brave One* (1956), both under assumed names in virtual exile.

The situation quickly exploded when Jack Warner of Warner Bros. went to D.C. to get ahead of the accusations and stumbled and bumbled his way through intense questioning drawing more scrutiny, this time directed toward A list screen personalities. As a response:

> A group of stars, including Humphrey Bogart, Lauren Bacall, Danny Kaye and Larry Adler, flew to Washington to protest and ended up on the famous blacklist... When they came back from Washington, many of the group changed their minds. Bogart was the first to do so. "That trip was ill-advised, even foolish," he declared ... "I have absolutely no use for communism." He was then free to go on to make *Key Largo*. (Freedland).

The upshot of all this was a sense of unease, paranoia and destabilization in Hollywood as well as a renewed distrust in middle America for "artist types." Tinseltown still remembered what happened to Fatty Arbuckle during the moralist witch hunts of 1922 that ultimately lead to the Production Code, only this time, a person might be unemployable or even jailed merely for thoughts, words or personal associations. Ironically, the industry that helped US patriotic propaganda so visibly during the war, now once again symbolized corruption, this time as a political nest of socialist vipers, contributing to the flood of "Red Scare" movies that displaced horror and arguably delayed science fiction for half a decade.

Another blow came with a Justice Department decision in 1948 regarding *United States v. Paramount, 334 U.S. 131*. Back in 1938, the Department filed an antitrust suit against Hollywood's studios alleging that Paramount, 20 Century Fox, Warner Bros., RKO, MGM, Universal, Columbia and United Artists engaged in price setting and conspired to monopolize film distribution through theater ownership and secret deals. Ten years later, the Supreme Court demanded changes and the studios submitted to the terms of the "Paramount Consent Decrees." In essence, this broke up the long-standing vertical integration of the studios that insulated them from competition. It also:

> outlawed various motion picture distribution practices including block booking (bundling multiple films into one theatre license), circuit dealing (entering into one license that covered all theatres in a theatre circuit), resale price maintenance (setting minimum prices on movie tickets) and granting overbroad clearances (exclusive film licenses for specific geographic areas). (United States Department of Justice)

None of this impacted theater attendance directly, but it deeply affected the profitability and organization of Hollywood at a critical time. In turn, that put pressure on producers to create more "sure fire" film products to keep the coffers full.

SOLUTIONS

Moments of crisis tend to inspire innovation. In the 1950s, as a response to these challenges, drive-in theaters blossomed, Technicolor expanded rapidly, and Cinerama and 3-D motion pictures emerged to varying degrees of success. But another innovation was a new type of cinema itself, the serious, adult science-fiction feature. Cold war tensions were an itch that could be scratched in the new genre and no matter how entertaining television was, the small screen left much to be desired for thrill seekers. While these innovations may be seen as somewhere between faddish and desperate today, they continued the long path of spectacle and immersion that had drawn the public to the theater since Euripides gave the world Apollo's fiery sun-chariot and its team of golden dragons. Science-fiction cinema offered just such sensationalism for hungry audiences, much to the delight of producers and distributors.

In short, the time was right for the invasion film.

Works Cited

"Amateur Aviator Reports Seeing 'Saucer' Planes." *Medford Mail Tribune,* 26 June 1947, p.1.

Baum, Gary and Daniel Miller. "The Hollywood Reporter, After 65 Years, Addresses Role in Blacklist." *The Hollywood Reporter,* 19 Nov. 2012. https://www.hollywoodreporter.com/features/blacklist-thr-addresses-role-65-391931

Denby, David. "Has Hollywood Murdered the Movies." *The New Republic,* 4 Oct. 2012, p. 29-30.

"Detection of the First Soviet Nuclear Test, September 1949." *National Security Archives.* https://nsarchive.gwu.edu/briefing-book/nuclear-vault/2019-09-09/detection-first-soviet-nuclear-test-september-1949

"Flyer Killed After Futile Chase of 'Flying Saucer.'" *Los Angeles Times,* 9 January 1948, p. 2.

"'Flying Saucers' Reported Seen in 38 States But No Clue To What Air Travelers Really Are." *The Plain Speaker,* Hazelton Pennsylvania, 7 July 1947, p. 1.

Freedland, Michael. "After the Purge." *The Guardian,* 9 Aug. 2005. https://www.theguardian.com/film/2005/aug/09/features.features11

"Historical National Population Estimates." U.S. Census Bureau. https://www2.census.gov/programs-surveys/popest/tables/1900-1980/national/totals/popclockest.txt

Haut, Walter. "2002 Sealed Affidavit of Walter G. Haut." *Roswellproof.com* http://www.roswellproof.com/haut.html

Murrow, Edward R. "Transcript of Ed Murrow-Kenneth Arnold." Interviewed by Edward R. Murrow. *CUFOS Associate Newsletter,* Feb.-Mar. 1984. Project1947.com. http://www.project1947.com/fig/kamurrow.htm

"Number of TV Households in America" (chart). *The American Century.* https://americancentury.omeka.wlu.edu/files/original/60e94905a0e02050a5b78f10b1b02b07.jpg

"Pilot is Baffled by 'Flying Saucers.'" *The Hartford Courant*, 26 June 1947, p. 1.

Randle, Kevin. "An Analysis of the Thomas Mantell UFO Case." *NICAP. org*. http://www.nicap.org/docs/mantell/analysis_mantell_randle.pdf

Ruppelt, Edward J. *The Report on Unidentified Flying Objects*, Kindle Edition, p. 57.

Them! Directed by Gordon Douglas, performances by James Arness, Joan Weldon, James Whitmore, Warner Bros., 1954.

Truman, Harry S. Executive Order 9835. *National Archives. Harry S. Truman Library*. https://www.trumanlibrary.gov/library/executive-orders/9835/executive-order-9835

United States Department of Justice. "The Paramount Decrees." https://www.justice.gov/atr/paramount-decree-review, 7 Aug. 2020.

Wright, Phil. "The Sighting." *The East Oregonian* (Pendleton, Oregon). June 16, 2017. Updated Dec. 13, 2018.

2 Cinematic Science Before 1951... Mad and Otherwise

TODAY, WE FIXATE on cinematic genre as a primary definer, creating not just subgenres, but sub-subgenres to describe film niches in exhaustive detail. However, sci-fi, fantasy, horror and mystery were all considered styles in the "thriller" mode during Hollywood's Golden Age. It is hard to find what we might recognize now as a straight-up science fiction film during that period. *Invisible Ray* (1936) comes to mind, but so much of the genre has since been labeled "horror" that it is easy to forget *Frankenstein* (1931), *Dr. Jekyll and Mr. Hyde* (1932), and *The Invisible Man* (1933) are science fiction first. Understanding this era helps put meaning and perspective on how and why alien invasion cinema treats science and scientists differently and where the two eras overlap.

In essence, a traditional horror film has an irrational (i.e., supernatural) problem requiring an irrational solution. For example, a ray of sunlight destroys the vampire; a silver bullet slays the werewolf... but why? The answers lie in the symbolism beneath these myths, but not in rational logic. In science fiction, the problem has a rational cause—one that can be understood by scientific inquiry. And science is generally the solution to the problem as well, even if it also constitutes the origin. The two intermingle in the classic "mad scientist" film to some degree, but any film featuring a problem created by experimentation with the natural physical world has at least one foot in science fiction.

CRAZY AM I?

The basic mad scientist archetype (with its roots in 18th Century litera-ture) took hold in "thriller" cinema after World War I in no small part because science became agent of death in the war. Nearly every promising invention and advance from the previous two decades, from chemistry to airplanes, from assembly lines to automobiles—even radio and film—had become instruments of horrific and unparalleled warfare.

It's not surprising, then, that mad science was the beating heart of many successful genre films after the war, first in Germany (for example, *Metropolis* in 1927) and later in the U. S., especially after the exodus of German film talent to American shores with the rise of Hitler. *Franken-stein* (1931), *Dr. Jekyll and Mr. Hyde* (1932), *Island of Lost Souls* (1932), *The Invisible Man* (1933), and *Mad Love* (1935) all feature brilliant but misguided men 'tampering in God's domain.' In the 1940s, that tradition continued with a rather bizarre but common incarnation of the archetype in several "ape" movies where Bela Lugosi, Boris Karloff and John Car-radine would inject murky serums to transform apes into humans and the other way around. Because of the dark nature of their anti-hero scientists, we may think of them as horror films first, but these stories cannot hap-pen without the technology (however speculative) to propel the plot.

The 1950s, however, would treat science and scientists, especially in the first half of that decade, radically differently. The cinematic mad scien-tist typically falls into one of three categories--Promethean, Faustian, or Nemesissian. Prometheus, a Greek Titan credited with creating humanity from clay, brings fire to his creation, enabling mankind to flourish inde-pendently of the gods. Essentially, his intentions are good, but he creates irreversible problems. The cinematic Promethean mad scientist can be seen in Henry Frankenstein and Dr. Jekyll. They seek to do something great for humanity, but their egos and moral failings unleash horrors.

Faustian scientists have a dark heart underneath their ambition and like the mythical Faust, their egos drive them to apply intellect for self-service and pleasure. Dr. Gogol (Peter Lorre) in *Mad Love* (1935) exem-plifies this. He is a brilliant scientist and surgeon but he uses his powers to break up a happy marriage so he might have the woman he desires.

The Nemesissian scientist (from the Greek goddess of retribution, Nemesis) is an outcast who hates the world, particularly other scientists who ridicule and typically bar him from the scientific community. In other words, his motive is ultimately revenge to balm his wounded pride.

Dr. Moreau (Charles Laughton) in 1932's *Island of Lost Souls* typifies this mode. He sees nothing wrong with creating a society of half-men, half-animals if he can prove his theories to a world that rejects him on moral grounds.

In any form, the "mad scientist" reflects a general fear of science despite our cultural dependency on it. Frankly, most people do not understand science and since it tends to call religion and cultural tradition into question, science creates enemies. Conscious and subconscious cultural fear of genius, newness, and difference (i.e., "otherness") embodied in a single individual all get exercised (and occasionally exorcised) in the anti-heroes and outright villains of mad science cinema.

THE SCIENTIST/HERO OF THE NUCLEAR AGE

The cinematic image of both science and the scientist shifted dramatically after World War II to an "Edisonian" model, named after Thomas Edison. The popular image of Edison in his time as a "Great Man" applying his talents to better the world gives us the term. Interest in science as a tool for problem solving and improving the world came from the uniquely American experience of the war. U. S. technical ingenuity enabled naval invasions on both fronts. U. S. air power crippled the Nazi war machine and ensured successful campaigns in Western Europe without the mass of ground troops the Russian front required. Radar, sonar, and techno-espionage were critical. And of course, the nuclear bombs dropped in Japan to end the war signaled a utilitarian application of science to end a horrible conflict. From the American point of view, science saved the world in WWII and mastery of it subsequently made U.S. scientists protagonists, not mad villains.

In the early 1950s, Edisonian scientists were far more common on screen than ever before, a trend that started with the three alien invasion films of 1951. It became a routine plot point found in many science fiction films, particularly giant monster films, to call in one of America's great minds to sort out both the cause of and solution to the problem. For example, consider Professor Tom Nesbitt (Paul Christian) in Warner Bros.' 1953 feature, *The Beast from 20,000 Fathoms* (the film that would inspire *Gojira*). Nesbitt's research team tests a nuclear bomb in the arctic, accidentally releasing a gigantic dinosaur, the Rhedosaurus, that eventually makes its way to New York City to cause havoc. Along the way he meets with a pair of paleontologists, Dr. Thurgood Elson (Cecil Kelloway), and his assistant, Lee Hunter (Paula Raymond), to identify and neutralize the threat. The film ends with the Nesbitt and a soldier launching a nuclear isotope into an open wound on the creature. Thus, even when science creates a problem (like nuclear contamination embodied in a fictional dinosaur) it also gives us the tools to overcome that problem and many others.

Pot Shot Rockets

The first two legitimate space travel films in the sound era were *Rocketship-XM* and *Destination Moon*, released almost exactly one month apart in the early summer of 1950. In their time, both were something of a novelty simply as serious science-fiction. Considering the volume of sci-fi stories in pulp magazines with rocket travel, and the cinematic suitability of such tales, it seems interplanetary sci-fi should have blossomed sometime in the first 50 years of commercial cinema, but that is not the case.

In the silent period, a few space travel films hit European screens, including the first sci-fi movie, *La Voyage Dans La Lune* (*A Trip to the Moon*) by Georges Méliès in 1902. Méliès also produced a follow up of sorts called *Le Voyage à travers l'impossible* (*An Impossible Voyage*), taking travelers to the sun instead of the moon. The titles indicate the frivolity of both films, and in truth, there is lots of fiction (fantasy really) but no real science.

The first full length space travel science fiction film, a British production of H. G. Wells' *First Men in the Moon*, appeared in 1919, but is now considered lost. In 1929, Fritz Lang directed *Frau im Mond* (*Woman in the Moon*), a dramatic film with moments rivaling his first masterpiece, *Metropolis* (1927). Based on a novel written by Lang's wife, Thea Von Harbou, called *Rocket to the Moon*, it presumes a breathable lunar atmosphere but has touches of realism including a multi-staged rocket and the effect of G-force. Most importantly, perhaps, it creates a trope borrowed by *Destination Moon* and other films—the idea of abandonment. In this case, a shortage of oxygen means one person must stay behind. However, rather than abandon her love, another character, Friede, stays behind as well. Ironically, Lang would leave Von Harbou in Germany. He brought his genius to America in 1936; she remained to aid the Nazi propaganda machine.

There were space opera serials like *Flash Gordon* (starring Olympian Buster Crabbe) in the 1930s featuring ungainly rocket ships resembling futuristic city busses and hammy "aliens" decked out like a summer theater production of *Julius Caesar*. These cliffhanger formats ran between cartoons and features as filler for a cheap thrill. Like the examples mentioned above, *Flash Gordon* depicts the idea of humans going out into space, but no real invasion motif emerges directly. In the second sequel, *Flash Gordon Conquers the Universe* (a.k.a. *Purple Death from Outer Space* from 1940), spaceships from planet Mongo target humans with a deadly plague, but most of the action takes place off Earth without an invasion.

Technically speaking, the first film to depict an alien arrival on earth may be the 1920 German film, *Algol*, but that is highly debatable. "Algol" is both the name of the "alien" and a known star cluster (then thought to be one star) with a peculiar common name—the Demon Star. Algol, identified by scientists as Beta Persei, appears to blink as its three stars eclipse one another and derives its name from same Arabic word that gives us the term "ghoul." In Greek descriptions, the star cluster signifies the writhing snake-filled head of Medusa in the hands of her slayer, Perseus.

Algol opens with a model observatory scanning the night sky and title cards explaining the pulsating star in ominous terms. It then turns to coal miner Robert Herne (Emil Jennings) and his initial encounter with the title character (played by John Gottowt, who would later portray Prof. Bulwer, the Van Helsing counterpart in *Nosferatu*, 1922). Argol gives Herne a machine capable of tapping the power of the Demon Star to produce unlimited energy, allowing him to rise from his humble station to a world master in a year, when Argol returns to savor the ruin of Herne's life and Earth's coal-based economy.

So, is this a true alien invasion film? No, not likely. Argol does not arrive in a spaceship or give the appearance of an alien in any way and instead plays a role akin to Mephistopheles in legend of Faust. In fact, there's no real evidence that Argol actually hails from the star (at least not as a product of scientifically engineered travel) and his demonic qualities of false gifts, temptation and devilish *schadenfreude* (all classic German religious themes) take center stage. The bulk of the film, in fact, explores rising post-war themes of class, labor, power, and corruption common in other Weimar era cinema and the star offers little more than an intriguing plot device to initiate the movie.

One serial, *The Purple Monster Strikes* (1945), and its sequel, *Flying Disc Man from Mars* (1950) merits a little attention here. They are exactly as good as those titles make them sound and boast some genuinely ridiculous moments. However, the basic plot has "The Purple Monster" (his self-styled moniker) scouting Earth for a Martian invasion. He comes to steal plans for a space plane that enables controlled landings… because Martian technology has apparently peaked at crashing capsules in the desert. The Purple Monster is foiled, of course, but five years later a Martian named "Moto" arrives as the titular *Flying Disc Man from Mars* wearing the same costume. Naturally, Earthlings vanquish him as well. The impact of both serials registers between forgettable and forgotten, but they show that alien visitation (and invasion) plots found some traction immediately after the war.

There are various reasons for the dearth of space travel in the movies prior to 1950. In part, rockets were essentially rather exotic technology for most people until WWII. The V1 and V2 attacks--and the subsequent appropriation of German scientists by the United States and Soviet Union to win the space race--changed all of that, of course. Also, convincing special effects were not particularly easy or cheap and since mainstream interest in science-fiction was comparatively low, there was little reason to roll the dice on a picture deemed outlandish from the outset. That too would change.

EXPEDITION '50

For a brief period, then, mad science took a back seat to progressive, Edisonian science, beginning with three films that came out in 1950: *The Flying Saucer*, *Rocketship XM* and *Destination Moon*. One could be forgiven for instinctively thinking *The Flying Saucer* was the first space alien contact film, but it is not. Its futuristic technology makes it science fiction, but the origin of the exotic device is decidedly terrestrial. The film feels very much like a serial and tells the story of Mike Trent (played by Mikel Conrad, the film's writer, producer and director). Trent is a wealthy young Alaskan playboy recruited to investigate Soviet spies in The Last Frontier. They are after a real flying saucer invented by Dr. Lawton (Roy Engel), an American scientist. After a series of twists, turns and betrayals, the saucer is finally stolen but explodes before the Russians can lay their hands on it when Lawton detonates a bomb. Oh… and Trent finds love in the arms of the secret agent he's been helping all along, Vee Langley (Pat Garrison), in the event readers must resolve the formula checklist.

Conrad did what he could to stir up intrigue for his film. While in development under the working title, *The Secret of the Flying Saucers*, a United Press release quoted Conrad saying "I have found a saucer. I'm not telling how." He further claimed footage of a real flying saucer lay locked in a bank vault. "I have scenes of the flying saucer landing, taking off, flying and doing tricks. The saucer is not created in miniature or by trick photography. It is a mechanical manmade object" ("'Flying discs' Coming" 19) Obviously, they had no such thing, but hyperbole was not out of bounds in Hollywood by any means. Even the press release doubts the claim but as documented by Robbie Graham in *Silver Screen Saucers*, it almost backfired. Conrad went under investigation for two months by the United States Air Force Office of Special Investigations. Despite declaring that there were no such things, the Air Force sure was taking an interest in the claim.

The film has its fans, but *The Flying Saucer* has gotten little attention as part of the sci-fi canon. Some of this reflects the general production quality and predictability of the plot and characters, but in the end, it really is a cold war spy movie. Of note, however, is the film's scientist. Dr. Lawton is clearly a "good guy" who doesn't want the fruits of his genius to fall into the wrong hands. If nothing else, it represents an Edisonian departure for the cinema scientist that will evolve in the coming years.

Rocketship XM and *Destination Moon* are better, more important contributions to the genre. Both are exploration films, projecting humanity outward into space (as opposed to hosting an interstellar visit). In the case of *Destination Moon*, the drama comes from the difficulty of space travel itself (essentially a technically driven "character vs. nature" format) and practical problem solving. Hailed as a scientifically accurate film, it feels like a documentary at times but its technicolor opulence and convincing space suits served it well. Lives are risked (but not lost) and the primary problem leading to the climax is limited fuel and excess weight, similar to the limited oxygen problem in *Frau im Mond*. In both films, one person must stay behind but in the case of *Destination Moon*, the problem resolves with science, not love.

In *Destination Moon*, a film within the film featuring Woody Woodpecker provides wisecracking comic relief to soften the blow of rocket science for the general audience. Suspension of disbelief is particularly important in science fiction, and in 1950, people simply did not believe we could ever get to the moon (and to this day, a surprising number of people don't think we ever did.) Woody literally calls it "comic book" stuff and parades around in confident disbelief—until he gets a firsthand demo. By the end of the short, he's putting in his two bucks to back the project. This insertion reveals how novel and unbelievably futuristic space exploration seemed in 1950. Forty-three years later, *Jurassic Park* would use the same explanatory cartoon device to bolster the premise of extracting DNA from dinosaur blood in amber encased mosquitos, something otherwise incomprehensible for the average viewer.

Today, *Destination Moon* doesn't generally hold the attention of even well-primed audiences despite its quality, but in its time, reviews called it thrilling. This is the first heady space exploration movie and its legacy includes films like *2001: A Space Odyssey* (1968), *Gravity* (2013) and *The Martian* (2015). But despite that distinguished lineage, space exploration as a self-sustaining plot doesn't ring many bells.

Rocketship-XM launched a more familiar formula. The crew of the ship, four men and one woman (a staple ratio for future films) goes off to the moon but gets diverted to Mars. Once they land, the crew discover a fallen civilization, wiped out by a nuclear blast, enabling a rather preachy but legitimate message point. Its remaining inhabitants (humanoid, of course) have devolved to little more than boulder-hurling mutated throwbacks. Ultimately, those who escape the "savages" crash to earth with the fuel expended. This nihilism, bold in cinema of any sort, is counterbalanced with the promise of a new mission.

Rocketship-XM came out four weeks before *Destination Moon* and was rushed through production to be the first of its kind, a common practice in Hollywood then and even today. (The following year, *The Man from Planet X* would pull the same stunt on *The Thing from Another World*.) Famously grilled on *Mystery Science Theater 3000*, the significantly lower budget results in several earmarks of cheap sci-fi. But in terms of its influence, the *Rocketship-XM* formula of humans arriving on other planets and facing adversaries has a more vibrant legacy than practical space exploration films. We crave monsters because, for better or worse, humans (and perhaps particularly post-WWII Americans) define ourselves by overcoming adversity and fear. Cheesy offerings abound like *Angry Red Planet* (1960) and *Planet of the Dinosaurs* (1977), but *Alien* (1979) also blossoms in that genre tree.

Another factor playing into off-world contact films (and their relative success) is the Western history of colonialism and expansion, rationalized with concepts like the "Civilizing Mission" and "Manifest Destiny." The Civilizing Mission held that European culture was inherently superior and justified the conquest and enslavement of non-European peoples with the premise that "civilizing" these places was part of the "White Man's Burden." Frequently this tied into (or originated with) religious conversion to Christianity. Manifest Destiny was an American extension of the civilizing rationale. It held that the United States was destined to expand westward, displacing other powers (namely France and Spain) and acquiring native territories. Democracy and Christianity philosophically rationalized the frequently brutal and unjust practices that came with that expansion.

This might seem a trendy socio-political read on the surface, but that background helps make sense of why stories like *Rocketship-XM* would evolve in the United States. As a social and political construct, America conceived itself consciously and unconsciously as an extension of European culture and a literal byproduct of exploration. Exploration and expansion not only went unquestioned as an inherent good, it seemed part of the American DNA. Consider too that the U. S. had just spent four years orchestrating and executing invasions in the Mediterranean, the Pacific and Atlantic in WWII, justified by principle and necessity in a war against tyranny. The United States' claim to world superiority in 1950 (inherent in its combination of democracy, nuclear power and even movies themselves) seemed self-evident and self-justifying at home. Space exploration merely constituted the next step in the American mythology.

In that context, U.S. audiences could conceptually accept expansion into space as a new Manifest Destiny (or perhaps an entitlement) with ease but conceive facing a superior spacefaring culture only later. For many, the idea of aliens itself was radical and reflected a long history of positing humans as the universal center of a divine plan. But the simple fact that *Rocketship-XM* and *Destination Moon* came before any alien invasion films reveals the general public's framework in 1950. If humans go out to space, it gives us control and implies a technical mastery if not superiority. If they come here, that's the opposite story and it takes getting used to.

As a final note, an intriguing moment occurs in *Rocketship-XM* (1950) when the project director, Dr. Ralph Fleming (played by Morris Ankrum, a regular in Martian themed sci-fi films) addresses the press. After asking for cooperation from the news reporters, Fleming actually thanks them for ignoring the UFO phenomenon saying, "I'm sure that we can all recall the wild tales of the flying discs, the flying saucers, spaceships and who knows what imaginative creations. The press is to be commended for discounting in most instances these premature rumors." There is absolutely no practical reason for this statement. It doesn't play into the plot and there are no space traveling aliens in the film to make it ironic. It may represent the general attitude of the American public at the time or reflect the official government position that these things simply did not exist.

WORKS CITED

"'Flying Discs' Coming to Screen; Real Thing Producer Says." *The Tribune* (Scranton, PA). 14 September 1949.

Graham, Robbie. *Silver Screen Saucers: Sorting Fact from Fantasy in Hollywood's UFO Movies*. White Crow Productions Ltd. Kindle Edition.

Rocketship X-M. Directed by Kurt Neuman, performances by Lloyd Bridges, Osa Masen, and John Emery, Lippert Pictures. 1950.

3

The Thing From Another World

IN 1951, The *Man from Planet X*, *The Thing from Another World*, and *The Day the Earth Stood Still* would arrive within six months of one another and give shape to our primary models for alien contact. The most common model--the hostile invader—got its first true cinematic attention in *The Thing from Another World*, a fast-paced, witty and somewhat claustrophobic story of a small U. S. military contingent and scientific expedition grappling with a deadly extraterrestrial. While *The Man from Planet X* was technically screened for limited audiences a few weeks before *The Thing*, most American theater patrons would have had a chance to see this movie first and shudder in the presence of its far more deadly and aggressive alien.

The Thing (as it was originally called) had a long term, large scale impact as a critical and popular success due in part to its freshness. Its basic premise of an alien invader set to take over the world establishes key elements we've now come to expect in alien adversary film: (a) an unknown entity (i.e., the creature); (b) analysis as a key to defeating the alien; (c) a combination of military and scientific personnel to combat it; (d) an underlying love story; and of course, (e) dramatic special effects. In the context of cinematic science fiction, *The Thing from Another World* was unlike anything seen before and spring-boarded a string of sci-fi thrillers to come.

The story, however, was not new. John W. Campbell's 1938 novella, *Who Goes There?*, generally gets credit as the source material, but its origins trace to H. P. Lovecraft's serialized story, *At The Mountains of Madness*. This tale was first rejected by Lovecraft's primary publisher, *Weird*

Tales, in 1931, but eventually saw publication in *Astounding Stories* in 1936. The core elements of story and its creatures are so striking that director Guillermo Del Toro called *Who Goes There?* "a direct rip off of *At the Mountains of Madness*" in Frank Woodward's 2008 documentary, *Lovecraft: Fear of the Unknown* (1:12:30).

The Lovecraft novella features the discovery of an ancient race of extraterrestrials, "the Elder Things," by a scientific team in Antarctica. These non-anthropomorphic creatures (classic Lovecraftian style) have pillar shaped bodies like cacti with five lower limbs, wing-like structures and a starfish-like "head" with five eye stalks and five feeding stalks. These nearly indestructible beings can hibernate for eons, reproduce like plants and have some degree of psychic power—qualities found in various later cinematic and literary incarnations of the Thing.

But by the time the scientists discover the Elder Things, they have fallen victim to the shoggoths, a genetically engineered slave race of amorphous and initially mindless beings. Their protoplasmic formlessness allows them to take any necessary shape to perform a task and adapt to any condition but also makes them incomprehensible and terrifying for humans. The Elder Things once bent the shoggoths to their will, but they eventually evolved a consciousness of their own.

However, *Who Goes There?* directly inspired the film. The tale appeared first as a 12-part serial in *Astounding Science Fiction,* a pulp magazine. Pulp mags were relatively "popular" as a subway genre but definitely not mainstream and struggled for credibility and financial stability. Magazines like this began in large scale in the 1930s and remained on newsstands for decades. (In fact, *Astounding Science Fiction* still publishes as *Analog* as of 2022). But in the highly conformist society of the times, such magazines with their gaudy and lurid covers came over as material for oddballs, juveniles and eggheads. The specific connections to this version of the story get attention below, but for the moment, it's important to note that like *Frankenstein* (1931), *The Thing from Another World* had a literary origin… just not a literary pedigree… and to this day, comparatively few people know the source material.

However, producer Howard Hawks had no intention of recreating the horror classics of the past. According to George E. Turner's 2020 retrospective on the film for *American Cinematographer,* Hawks said in a press release,

It is important that we don't confuse the Frankenstein-type of film with the science-fiction picture. The first film is an out-and-out horror thriller based on that which is impossible. The science-fiction film is based on that which is unknown, but given credibility by the use of scientific facts which parallel that which the viewer is asked to believe.

In other words, you can't just sew body parts together and expect them to function after a jolt of electricity. You could, however, discover a frozen space creature, thaw it out, and spend the next 24 hours fighting to save humanity. This devotion to science-fiction as a more realistic context for inducing terror may help explain why the film's flying saucer crashes on November 1, the day *after* Halloween. Hawks thus consciously sought to leave Gothic horror behind, though as we will see, his film and creature never shook the Frankenstein connection fully.

WILL THE REAL DIRECTOR PLEASE STAND UP?

Essentially, Howard Hawks understood the next wave of genre thrillers needed to offer something for a more world-wise and science literate post-WWII viewership. After facing the real-life horrors of Nazism, kamikazes and nuclear warfare, the time demanded a new, more relevant type of scare—one with global implications. Simply put, the old horror approach would no longer cut it. The Gothic chillers that had so successfully thrilled audiences of the 1930s had wandered into absurdity by the mid-40s, offering little beyond pure escapism. By the time *Abbot and Costello Meet Frankenstein* hit the screens in 1948, cinema's first iconic monsters had devolved into undisguised jokes and it would take the talents of Terrence Fisher, Jimmy Sangster, Peter Cushing and Christopher Lee at Hammer Studios to revive them meaningfully a decade later.

Even though Howard Hawks would never produce or direct another science fiction film, he was on to something big. Best known as a director of screwball comedies, war dramas and Westerns, Hawks saw the potential for his unique style in sci-fi when he bought the screen rights to *Who Goes There?* However, Hawks did not direct the movie—or at least he did not take a director's credit. The honor went to film editor Christian Nyby as a type of 'thank-you" for taking over the edit of *Red River* (1948), winning an Oscar in the process. According to Nyby, the original editors were making a mess of the film and he worked on *Fighter Squadron* during the day and *Red River* after 6 p.m. until it was done (Gentry).

Unfortunately for Nyby's legacy, he rarely gets any credit for *The Thing*'s success and groundbreaking influence. Part of the problem may have been the quality of the film itself. "It was too big of a success for my own good," Nyby told interviewer Jim Davidson in 1992. "Nobody believed a first time director could have such a big hit. They gave Howard all the credit" (43). It also put him in a strange position when offered B movie opportunities since, "after producing such a successful picture, being relegated to cheap schlock would be admitting that Howard Hawks directed *The Thing*'" (qtd. in McCarthy 481).

It is easy to believe Hawks directed it for several reasons. *The Thing from Another World* displays the distinctly stylized characterizations, overlapping dialog, democratic group dynamic and strong female leads trademarking Hawk's career. The film's personality driven interactions, plot tensions, quick decisions (with varied results) and sexual chemistry also echo Hawks' previous directorial efforts like *The Road to Glory* (1936), *Bringing Up Baby* (1938) and *The Big Sleep* (1946). "Hawks prepared the script and supervised the production," wrote Robin Wood, noting the undeniable mode of the film. "No one who has seen it can doubt that in all essentials it is a Hawks film" (Wood 107).

But, while Hawks' presence and stylistic touch resonates in *The Thing*, the often repeated (and rarely questioned) claim he was "the real director" merits debate. Much of it relies on stories from cast and crew. For example, associate producer Ed Lasker (whose wealth and friendship got him into Hawk's Winchester Pictures), swore Nyby never directed at all. Lasker even claims to have told Nyby to wait until Hawks arrived on the one day he was late to the set. Kenneth Tobey admitted to Nyby directing one scene but represented that as a tumbling disaster with actors falling over themselves without a clue of what to do (McCarthy 480).

According to Nyby, the daily dynamic between he and Hawks was not commonplace and may explain why Tobey felt Hawks actually directed the film. "The script was just sort of a map of where he [Hawks] was going and he would fill it in as he went along" (Davidson 42). Each morning, "we would sit down with the actors and write the scene we were going to shoot. I'd get out there and shoot the scene—the sequence and then the close ups. We'd finish that and do another one. That's the way the whole picture went" (42). Script-boy Richard Kienen confirmed the unorthodox and chaotic approach of Hawks rewriting each scene as they went with all cast members in the room. "It was weird for the actors because they never knew when they would be gotten by the Thing, so they never knew when they came to work if it would be their last day" (qtd. in McCarthy 480). Hawks' commanding presence dominated production, not just rewriting scenes but blocking them, rehearsing them and making changes. This, from an actor's point of view, exemplifies direction.

However, in a 1997 *Los Angeles Times* tribute to Nyby, Henry Furhmann (who calls Nyby "my Uncle Chris") interviewed Nyby's son (also a director) and other cast members who painted a clearer picture of the film behind the scenes. Nyby, a first-time director, worked under a mentor he idolized, getting support and attention along the way in creating Hawks' vision for the film. Star Robert Cornthwaite (Dr. Carrington) put it this way: "Chris always deferred to Hawks, as well he should. Hawks was giving him the break, after all" (Furhmann). However, in the end, Cornthwaite considered Nyby the director.

This lands with the account of William Self who played Lt. Barnes, the hapless soldier who throws an electric blanket on the ice block and triggers everything. In an interview with Tom Weaver published in *Eye on Science Fiction*, Self explains the director/producer relationship he witnessed:

> Nyby... generally ran the rehearsal, and Hawks stood on the sidelines with his arms folded and watched and listened. Then Chris would go over to Howard and they would have their private conversation, and Chris would come back and talk to *us*. A lot of things would stand, but other things he would say, "Well, let's try this" or "Let's try that" or "Why don't you come here instead of there? Hawks was directing the picture from the sidelines. (272)

The trademark overlapping dialog technique adds more fuel to claims that Hawks directed the film. That effect was actually accomplished in editing and Nyby explained that Hawks liked working with him because he liked cutting that way, beginning with the film *To Have and To Have Not* (1944). "We used what was called a push-pull track.... If you were astute, careful and patient enough, you could match those tracks so that you could overlap the dialog and get the stuff synchronized" (Davidson 43). Early in the process, Nyby told Hawks he wanted to use the same method with *The Thing from Another World* and Hawks agreed. In other words, it was Nyby's idea.

Ultimately, Christian Nyby found the recurring question of the "real" director irritating to say the least. As recounted in the *Times* article, he once told *Cinefantastique* magazine: "This is a man I studied and wanted to be like. You would certainly emulate and copy the master you're sitting under, which I did. Anyway, if you're taking painting lessons from Rembrandt, you don't take the brush out of the master's hands" (Fuhrmann).

But no matter how "hands on" Hawks was, his official title of producer came down to his contract with RKO. Howard Hughes, who owned a controlling share of RKO, mismanaged the company so badly that it fell to the bottom of the major studios list. When things got rough, he asked Hawks to return to the studio and help bolster the sagging company. This must have been satisfying for Hawks who had once been a favored son of RKO but was cut free by Sam Briskin in 1938 after a blow up over the now iconic screwball comedy, *Bringing Up Baby*. Indifferent to studio admonishments, Hawks ran up a production bill of over a million dollars in the throes of the Great Depression for a B picture to please his own standards... all while drawing $2500 a week (Jewell 137). Worse yet, its star, Katherine Hepburn, was singled out as "box office poison" in the infamous theater owners' ad on May 3 in the *Hollywood Reporter* (Othman 6). The film eventually made its money back after an international release and a pair of domestic re-releases in the 1940s, but it was considered a flop in its time.

Hawk's arrangement with Hughes in 1950 treated him as an independent filmmaker, requiring three movies. He'd direct two with a director's fee of $175,000 each and one he'd produce for $125,000, from which the director's salary of $50,000 would be paid (McCarthy 469). He did not, however, pay Nyby anywhere near that, pocketing $44,040 for himself (475), no doubt reinforcing the story that Hawks directed the film.

Being a producer (rather than a director) on a risky project functioned as a bit of a safety mechanism as well since public scrutiny for the success or failure of a film first goes to the director. As a producer, Hawks could stay involved, even control things, and yet keep a theoretical distance from the film which might well have flopped. Today, sci-fi movies attract top talent and command impressive budgets with little concern since they typically guarantee huge returns. But in 1950, when production began, science-fiction feature films were uncommon and risky. And in this case, Hawks decided early on that there would be no "star power" to draw ticket sales, increasing that risk.

At this point in his career, Hawks could probably have gotten anyone he wanted for the roles. He had paired some of the screen's best romantic duos including Cary Grant and Kathrine Hepburn, and Humphrey Bogart and Lauren Bacall, but it's difficult to imagine either pair matching wits with a menace from outer space. Hawks felt the film would play much better and more believably with regular Joes (and one regular Josephine) solving the problems. "There are no stars or familiar faces in the picture," Hawks said, "because, to give the story the impact it deserves, we want audiences to accept the characters as actual people, not actors" ("Five Unknowns," 12). There's even a line subtly acknowledging this choice when Lt. MacPherson (Robert Nichols) prepares to use a flare gun to ignite the Thing. Ned Scott (Douglas Spencer) asks, "You know how to shoot that thing don't ya?" to which MacPherson replies "I saw Gary Cooper in *Sergeant York*." Cooper won the 1941 Best Actor Academy Award for that film, directed by Hawks, and no doubt Hawks could have talked the perennial box office magnet into the male lead if he wanted him… but he didn't.

OUR CAPTAIN HAS SOME FUNNY IDEAS

That role went to Kenneth Tobey who played Captain Pat Hendry, leader of an Air Force flight crew stationed in Anchorage, Alaska. Tobey had a kind of every day good looks with a wave of red hair and rough-hewn features offset by a warm smile. Originally from Oakland, California, Tobey served in the Pacific as a B25 tail gunner, an experience that clearly factored in his portrayal of Pacific Theater vet Capt. Hendry. He worked on and off Broadway in New York for many years until his friend Gregory Peck coaxed him out to Hollywood. Tobey, Peck and Warren Stevens had bunked together in 1940 while working at the Barter Theater in Abingdon, Virginia and became fast friends ("Third Pal" 9). For a while he even lived with Peck and his family while he searched for film work, which he got in bits and pieces.

Despite press claims that his role in in *The Thing* was his first, Tobey played small roles in nearly a dozen earlier films including *I Was a Male War Bride*, a Howard Hawks smash hit, where Tobey landed a last minute role as an unnamed naval sentry. While filming the movie, Hawks supposedly told the genial actor "Someday I'm going to make a picture with unknowns. If you are still unknown, Ken, I'll want you as the lead"

(Zeitlin 75). According to the story, when the call came for a screen test, Hawks made him take it as a formality, but had already made the decision. Given Hawks' clear pride in discovering new talent throughout his career, this story likely rings true.

In any case, Kenneth Tobey might have been vaguely familiar to some viewers, but he didn't exactly have Gary Cooper levels of visibility, and thus fit Hawks' need for an "unknown." After *The Thing*, however, Tobey would have a long career in television and film, frequently playing military and police officers. Fans of Ray Harryhausen's stop-motion monster pictures, for example, will remember him from *The Beast from 20,000 Fathoms* and *It Came from Beneath the Sea*. Tobey died in 2002 at the age of 85, but his career concluded in the no-budget sci-fi spoof released three years later, *The Naked Monster*, reprising his role as Col. Pat Hendry, a retired monster hunter with one last beast to slay.

In *The Thing from Another World*, Tobey demonstrates a kind of idealized mid-level command style in his portrayal. Capt. Hendry seems as comfortable with the rank and file as with his officers. He takes good-natured ribbing and has his own wry sense of humor but has no trouble tightening the ropes of command. When interacting with the scientists, particularly Dr. Carrington (Robert Cornthwaite), he asks questions and trusts their judgment—until it becomes dangerous. He compensates for any comparative deficiency in intelligence with a hefty dose of practical wisdom. In one of the most telling expressions of his character, he listens to the suggestions of his crew, particularly the crew chief (Dewey Martin) known only as "Bob." Hendry takes responsibility for the blunders but gives credit where it is due. As a result, he has the respect of his men and the audience.

The opening scene introduces Hendry playing cards with his co-pilot, Lt. Eddie Dykes (James Young), and navigator, Lt. Ken MacPherson (Robert Nichols). Reporter Ned Scott, a.k.a. "Scotty" (Douglas Spencer) comes in and shakes off the cold as Dykes and MacPherson needle their captain over a drunken night with a date whom we will eventually meet. Hendry takes it for a while and just as he's ready to fire back, he's called away to see General Fogerty (David McMahon). But despite the warmth and distraction of the club, Hendry snaps to, dons his coat and marches off to see the general without a grumble, letting the audience see his devotion to duty.

This opening scene carefully constructs an indeterminate impression of the captain, making him interesting to watch. It is hard to know if he's somewhat incompetent or just a nice guy with a taste for whiskey and women who lets his officers have a little fun at his expense. This ambiguity directs our attention to his decision making and lays in an underlying tension at each stage nicely. Ultimately, however, Hendry's character will acquit himself repeatedly in the coming action with a clear sense of responsibility and decisive action "above and beyond the call of duty."

CUT FOR AN AMBUSH

In this opening scene, we also get a quick introduction to some of our major figures in classic Howard Hawks tumbling dialog style. Bits of character and backstory fall out, setting the stage for the well-woven romance within. Moreover, it provides a symbolic look at the film to come. In many ways the story will be a multiplayer poker game complete with bad hands, lucky cards, gambles, bluffs and strategy, with Hendry at the center of the action playing the cards he's dealt. He will not only match wits with "The Thing" (James Arness), but simultaneously contend with the Arctic elements, a frustrated reporter, Dr. Carrington and even his love interest, Carrington's secretary, Nikki Nicholson (Margaret Sheridan).

When Hendry gets his orders from Fogerty to investigate the crash of "an airplane of unusual type," there are subtle indications that he's a practiced poker player. For instance, after Fogerty repeats the base rumors of a budding romance between the captain and the secretary, he says Hendry can maroon Scotty up there… but not to get ideas about getting marooned himself. Fogerty tells him, "And I'd like it if you didn't smash a landing ski this time," which Hendry calls "an unavoidable accident." This suggests Hendry intentionally broke a landing ski to extend a previous stay in Nikki's company but managed to walk the line of duty successfully. The simple exchange sets up the romantic subplot and portrays Hendry as a likably crafty officer simultaneously. It might even give us insight on Fogerty's anxiety and outrage when communications are cut off with the expedition later in the film.

Once he arrives at the base, Hendry goes immediately to see Nikki and determine how badly he may have messed things up. In her office, he comes over as angry since she's not only abandoned him in Seattle but a pinned a note on him appraising his legs (turning the tables on a traditional sexual evaluation of women). The scene implies that they may have slept together for a few rounds of dialog since he seemingly woke up without pants and but despite his "making like an octopus," she apparently managed to drink him under the table and he slept alone. Again, we are left to wonder about his judgment, wherewithal, and competence.

But in a parallel scene in the same room later, we see just how wily a poker player Capt. Hendry can be. He has just laid down the law with Carrington and decided to keep the Thing frozen until further orders. In the mess hall, Nikki admires how he handles the situation and he suggests they start over. She offers him a much-deserved drink in her office if he can behave so he suggests she tie him up to keep his inner octopus at bay. In fact, he not only suggests but insists and offers to bring the rope. Once they've had a couple drinks, he pries the full story of their previous encounter from her and finally gets a kiss. More importantly, she confesses her genuine interest saying, "Why if you weren't tied up I'd never tell you how much I liked you." At that moment, she finds herself lighting his cigarette from his untied hands, much to her dismay.

It is a remarkable scene simply for the sexual chemistry and bondage implications, but beneath it lies the key to Capt. Hendry's character. He's not likely to get fooled twice and will gladly allow his adversaries to assume a false advantage. He suggests she bind him specifically because it will put her at ease enough to speak her emotions... and because he knows he can get out. The scene tells us Hendry is a strategist and much more cunning than he appears. He uses the expectations and assumptions of others to his advantage. In the end, that very quality will undo the invader when Hendry and his crew lure the Thing into a trap using the creature's own assumption of having the upper hand.

In the early drafts, Hendry comes over as a brooding, lecherous and even bullying suitor, not the crafty egalitarian leader we see in the film. In the August 28, 1950 draft, Hendry (then called Henry) is simply not a nice guy. He's more unabashedly interested in sex and clearly bitter when Nikki rejects what she calls "promiscuous lovemaking" (Lederer). (In those days, the phrase "love making" could pass on screen as general courtship, though the sexual connotation would register as well.) His aggressive character exudes in lines like these from the first draft:

> Pat, last time you were here, I spent three days wrestling with a typical air corps wolf. It was like playing puss-in-the-corner with Bluebeard or somebody. You even invaded my bedroom, claiming you were looking for a lost pocketknife. Now, I'm

fond of you, Pat, but this time, if you don't keep your hands to yourself, we're through.

Through the rest of the scene in this first draft, he shows a sense of entitlement and has lines like, "You don't want to talk about what I thinking," and "All dames are alike." Worse yet, in a later scene, he actually hits her in the stomach as she tries to conceal Carrington's notes and she thanks him for it since she does not have the will to betray her boss's orders.

While Edward Lederer's first draft defaults to machismo clichés (Nikki even identifies her pursuer's thought process as a "stupid cliché"), it is, after all, just a draft. The final film, in contrast, thankfully gives the audience much more sophisticated characters, dialog and relationships. Lederer probably realized his Bluebeard captain and fainting secretary (yes, she does faint) were cardboard stand ins and eventually went on to sculpt Nikki into arguably the most intelligent and independent woman in sci-fi film until Ellen Ripley appeared in *Alien* in 1979.

A VERY INTERESTING TYPE...

Hendry's love interest in the film, Nikki Nicholson is played by Margaret Sheridan, a talented actress with an intriguing path straight to a lead role. She was not quite 25 when she took the part, her first in any film, but Sheridan portrayed her pivotal character with tremendous maturity, flair and ease. Hawks discovered her in 1945, spotting her picture in a magazine. He tracked her down, and after a brief interview, put her on contract. Hawks prepared her to play Tess Millay in *Red River*, but she became pregnant right before production began. Known as "Margaret O'Sheridan" around that time, it seems she went on contract without working for anyone for several years. During that time, she resumed her work as a fashion model, a vocation the film references early on when Lt. Dykes (James Young) refers to a "pin-up girl" among the scientists.

Hawks fully expected her to star in another film sooner rather than later, but she held him off for half a decade. After a few empty rumors of her coming to the screen after the birth of her daughter, Hawks temporarily dropped her contract. However, his partner, Edward Lederer, resigned her for Hawks' Winchester Pictures around 1948, reflecting the well-placed faith the director had in her future (Scott, Drama-Arts 1).

Hollywood gossip columnist Hedda Hopper reported in March of 1949 that Sheridan secured a lead opposite Montgomery Clift in *The Sun Also Rises* (28), but almost 10 years passed before that film saw the screen with an entirely different producer, director and cast. Three months later, Winchester announced that Hawks was planning a film called *Morning Star* (again never produced) as a vehicle for Sheridan and none other than Gary Cooper. A snippet went out outlining a story about a group of scientists in New Mexico planning an interplanetary rocket trip. "As they are about to launch, a green-haired dish from Venus lands on earth to help guide them through space" (Hopper 55). Sheridan, apparently envisioned as the "green haired dish," seems pegged here as a Hawksian screwball comedy heroine. The plot, however, seems to be closer to a serious romance between a Venusian guiding angel, posing as a Russian refugee, and a handsome scientist whose love will unite two worlds.

Fortunately, however, the role of Nikki Nicholson brought Margaret Sheridan to the screen instead. Robert Wood called Nikki an archetypal "Hawksian woman, the equal of any man, yet intensely feminine" (107). Nicholson is independent, smart, witty, personable, courageous and seeks control of her destiny. She sets the ground rules for her relationship with Captain Hendry and, significantly, she never screams, even when under direct attack (unlike most '50s monster movie heroines). This makes her important not only in *The Thing from Another World* but in sci-fi film as a whole. She's the first of what will be called "a new breed of woman" four years later in *It Came from Beneath the Sea*.

Most importantly, Nicholson (not the scientists or soldiers) figures out how to defeat the seemingly unstoppable Thing with a quick answer to a simple question. What do you do with a vegetable? "Boil it. Stew it. Bake it. Fry it." As the most clearly free-thinking character in the film, Nikki arrives at the solution instantly. Unlike the other principal characters, she does not stay intellectually chained to a power hierarchy (including gender expectations). Carrington is a vassal of pure science, and his team defers to him for far too long. Similarly, Hendry holds to his martial obligations, and his men follow suit. Even the reporter, Scotty, must submit to the Air Force and laments the imagined tirades his unseen editor will have for him. But Nikki, guided more strongly by her own moral compass and reasoning skills, becomes the critical player in the equation.

Her turning point comes as Dr. Carrington reveals he's made the connection between the seed pods in the creature's hands and its need for blood. After handing Nikki his notes, he takes his colleagues to a back-room "nursery" where nearly two dozen multi-lobed plants pulsate as they take nourishment from draining blood plasma bottles. Carrington's face hints at self-satisfaction as his colleagues show their wonderment. When asked how many units of plasma they have left, he ominously replies "Enough, I hope." In other words, Carrington intends to grow the plants to full size—even after he's acknowledged the danger in the previous scene.

Nikki seems to be the only character who registers Carrington's intentions. While the scientists gather around the table, the camera subtly isolates Nikki, first in the background and then with interior framing created by the hanging bottles and apparatus. As the scientists ponder the Thing's regenerative powers and the seedlings' rapid growth rate, Nikki's face registers distress with each horrific detail as she closes her eyes in an attempt to block it out psychologically. When Dr. Wilson (Everett Glass) describes the sound revealed by his stethoscope as "almost like the wail of a newborn child that's hungry," Nikki closes her eyes again, soothes her temple and asks Dr. Carrington if she may leave. In the shot, the self-satisfied Carrington looms large in the left foreground, and Wilson recedes behind him. The camera now isolates Nikki even more prominently with the apparatus and again in a doorway—a frame within a frame within the frame of the screen itself—focusing our attention on her, constricting and trapping her until she exits.

In the next scene, just as she's finished typing Carrington's notes, Hendry enters and asks about the missing plasma. She's covered the notes to conceal them and has an opportunity to protect Carrington's interests (he's specifically asked that no one see them), but she does not. Nikki tells Hendry, "You better take a swing at my chin and take a look at those notes... I should be trying to stop you." In theory, she owes Carrington loyalty, but Nikki understands the grave and global nature of letting him proceed and that only Hendry has the muscle and authority to stop it. Thus, she independently reasons that the Thing can overtake the planet and breaks ranks, saving not just the team but humanity itself.

The next time we see her, she's entered the men's barracks area and has exchanged her plaid flannel (seen on members of the science team) for a jacket with a military cut. Here she delivers her solution to cook the Thing and the men quickly respond to the suggestion. As the crew chief moves to prepare the kerosene, she seamlessly takes over tracking the Thing with the Geiger counter. She has effectively joined the fight and in a careful gesture typical of the film, from here on out, she's abandoned

the tight professional hair bun signifying her position as Carrington's secretary and will not be seen near him again. Likewise, later in the film,
Nikki notices the Thing cuts off the heat before the others. She also alerts
Hendry when Carrington cuts the generator and shows up with a gun in
an effort to save the monster. To say this independent agency and courage
represents a forward-thinking departure for a female lead in 1951 is a true
understatement.

Sheridan would appear in only six films over a short career, mostly
between 1951-54, and a few television shows. Sci-fi film buffs have pon-
dered and lamented this over the years, especially since her career seemed
poised for lift off. Since her well-publicized marriage to pilot William Pat-
tison dissolved abruptly just a few months after the film came out, speculation sometimes falls there. She'd been painted as the exemplar of domestic
bliss in numerous publicity articles mentioning the "stork visit" that kept
her out of *Red River*. And within a week of *The Thing's* national release,
Modern Screen (a name-dropping dreamy Hollywood insider magazine)
published Sheridan's wistful personal account of a vacation in Tahoe with
Robert Mitchum's family—but not her husband. In the ironically titled,
"I Found Romance in the Mountains," Sheridan assured the world of her
"wonderful husband," but between the lines, spending 11 to 18 days alone
each month and waiting for letters didn't sound all that blissful (Sheridan 36, 114-5). It is a small stereotypical jump to think the divorce de-
termined her professional trajectory, but Sheridan probably just didn't
care for stardom. She made choices both before and after *The Thing from
Another World* to turn down the glitz and glamour. Instead, she had two
more children in a new marriage, and concentrated on charity work until
dying of lung cancer in 1982. Perhaps she had more of Nikki in her than
apparent to Hawks as he tried to engineer his next star.

IF YOU WERE FOR SALE, I COULD GET A MILLION BUCKS

The role of Dr. Arthur Carrington went to another relative newcomer,
Robert Cornthwaite, who, like Kenneth Tobey, would be typecast into a
steady career. Amazingly, Cornthwaite played Dr. Carrington at just 34
years old, a testament to the makeup artistry of Lee Greenway and hair
stylist Larry Germain who produce a convincingly middle-aged scientist in this picture. Cornthwaite would work into his 80s (again, like Tobey) with several dozen film and TV credits—cast frequently as a scien-

tist, doctor or the occasional judge, coroner or reverend. He worked for Hawks again in 1952's *Monkey Business* as Dr. Zoldeck and played Dr. Pryor in *War of the Worlds* a year later. And he too would appear in *The Naked Monster,* reprising Dr. Carrington. In a hilarious phone exchange with Hendry says he wants to take the monster out for brunch and discuss "nature and Schopenhauer and the Unified Field Theory."

Dr. Carrington supplies a fascinating take on the new screen scientist. Though not quite the Edisonian hero of future films, Carrington is certainly not a "mad scientist" in the traditional sense either (see Chapter 2 for a discussion of the mad scientist archetype). Initially, he's quite grounded, measured and thoughtful. But as he loses sleep and the stress mounts, his manner becomes progressively irrational. Nonetheless, the film makes his overwrought exhaustion and clouded but genuine scientific curiosity clear, never painting him as inherently crazy, delusional or reckless. In that context, Carrington's name implies that he carries too much... and perhaps cares too much as well.

Consequently, rather than suggest the dangers of science in the classic mad scientist trope, he more clearly represents the dangers of asking too much of science. Carrington is the exact opposite of Nemesissian, Faustian and even Promethean mad scientists driven by ego. Carrington, in contrast, is generally moved by a "pure" science to understand and advance, a constant theme of his dialog. He frequently vacillates between self-righteous and pleading tones, lobbying for science as the only solution and intellect as the only rationale for existence. We never know his specific discipline, but we know he participated in the Bikini nuclear tests. This may add to his underlying psychology. Carrington boasts about splitting the atom but the Pacific war veterans in his company mock the "accomplishment." For Carrington, fission ultimately must be a good thing—it simply must be to rationalize his life's work.

This abstract idealism creates a dangerous circular logic he's unable to see critically. "Knowledge is more important than life, Captain," he tells Hendry. "We've only one excuse for existing - to think, to find out, to learn." Thus, if intellect serves humanity and science expands and expresses intellect, then science must always be the answer to any problem. Once he's concluded the Thing has a superior intellect, Carrington can only see it as a pathway upward for humanity... even if the Thing kills everyone on the planet. He's devoted to this mantra like a religious fanatic—or a child who refuses to face practical truths that unhinge the ideals he holds dear. If he were to ever divorce science from morality or even acknowledge the limits or potential evils of science, his whole psyche would crumble... which it nearly does.

This bullheaded insistence upon his "faith," even in the face of human annihilation, may surface because of his exhaustion but it reveals an underlying character weakness. Nikki puts it best when she advises Hendry regarding Carrington's behavior:

> Pat, would you remember something? He's tired. He hasn't slept since you found that thing. And he's not thinking right. I know him and he doesn't think the way we do anyway. But he's found something no one can understand. Until he can solve it, he'll ...You know, like a kid with a new toy...

That "kid" characterization becomes a central film motif. Hendry compares the scientists obsessing over the Thing to "nine-year-olds drooling over a new fire engine." Carrington later suggests the soldiers are behaving the same way, "like frightened children." But as Hendry points out, they are frightened for good reason. Additionally, the costuming intentionally cultivates the image of Carrington as adult child. His light gray turtleneck sweater stands out against a neat dark blazer featuring ostentatious but purely ornamental metallic buttons and a little gold crown emblem over the heart. He also sports a pair of slightly oversized wool trousers. Visually, he carries an air of absurd self-importance, like a child whose mommy just dressed him and told him how grown up he looks.

This also plays into the larger theme of reproduction in the film. Hendry and Nikki play romantic tag for a while, but in the end, they are destined for marriage and future "dependents." Contemporary mores and the restrictions of the Production Code prohibit any real sexual implications between them, but their give-and-take surges with physical attraction. Other references to sex come from Lt. Dykes' war tales. He hopes to die and go to Accra, where it is "105 in the shade and the women wore hardly anything at all. Very intelligent of them." The Thing causes a stir reminiscent of being "stuck on Beulen Island with the old 97th Bomber Group. An Army nurse came ashore and caused just about the same disturbance as this guy from Mars has around here." Linking sex starved soldiers to intellectually driven scientists demonstrates Carrington's obsession with science and shows that intellectual temptation has as many dangers as desires of the flesh.

Compare that to the alien's asexual reproduction, a trait Carrington openly admires, identifying it as the evolutionary cause of its superior intellect. "Its development was not handicapped by emotional or sexual factors," he muses. Then, after laying the foundation for intelligent plants on earth (and instantly sending Hendry and his men into a private discussion), Carrington reveals the discovery of seed pods, "The neat and unconfused reproductive technique of vegetation. No pain or pleasure as we know it. No emotions. No heart. Our superior. Our superior in every way." In other words, Carrington envies the Thing's independence from reproductive biology and all its messy social and emotional entanglements. Carrington, the middle-aged little boy, is sexually stunted, petulantly devoted to intellect in lieu of a normal development and subsequently, dangerously blinded by it.

Interestingly enough, this scene initiates Carrington's relentless quest to "communicate" with this asexual superior. Carrington, a Nobel Prize winner with a handful of intellectual peers globally, even has trouble connecting to the scientists around him. His desire to commune with the Thing (whom Scott jokingly calls "our boyfriend") seems obsessive, desperate and almost submissively lovelorn. If he could establish communication, it would compensate for his human disconnection and vindicate his intellect. Ironically, the concept of intellect without emotion stimulates his most impassioned speeches and again, we might see him as something of a religious zealot who has exchanged human sexuality for a divine intercourse.

If *The Thing from Another World* signifies the rise of a nuclear age mythology, Carrington stands as the symbol of the post-war quandary new science presents. In traditional mythologies, the fit heroes balance head and heart, using rationality to temper emotion and emotion to inspire rational action. That's exactly what Hendry and Nikki do when they put their personal desires aside to fight the menace. Carrington outclasses them both intellectually but, like a prepubescent child, he lacks wisdom and cannot see the dangers of his one-sided approach. Carrington idealistically (and delusionally) believes the mind inherently overcomes emotions, and since he can't admit he's wrong, he can only double down on science as the solution to every problem. That general quality can be seen in the mad scientist of the 1930s and '40s whose work leads only to destruction and casts doubt on intellectuals as dangerous. But as the 1950s began, America's scientific geniuses had not only won the last war but were instrumental in maintaining both peace and superiority. Thus,

Carrington's work and mission is never in question—only his ability to manage the responsibilities. And in the end, despite his shortcomings, Carrington still garners praise in Scotty's final report.

THE THING FROM ANOTHER WORLD

But what of Carrington's substituted love interest—the Thing?

As most fans of the film love to mention, James Arness, best known as Matt Dillon in the long running TV series *Gunsmoke*, played the title role. He'd served in WWII, earning a Purple Heart for a leg wound at Anzio that kept him from returning to combat. Billed as Jim Arness in *The Thing from Another World*, the rising star was the first person signed. Winchester Pictures paid him $750 per week with "$1,000 petty cash voucher in advance and a salary extension clause of eight days beyond the completion date as an inducement not to take any other jobs before the starting date of November 18" (Turner, "Thing"). The contract kept him on hand so the costume department could develop and fit the one-of-a-kind rubber headpiece.

Popular Hollywood legend holds that embarrassment regarding the role kept Arness from attending the premiere and he "refused to discuss it," especially once his career took off (Turner, "Thing"). Another story has it that he ate alone in the commissary because his makeup upset to the cast and crew (Johnson 164). But according to a 2005 interview with Arness by Glenn Lovell in the *Sarasota Herald Tribune*, he embraced the part:

> I'd always been told Arness hated the role, which was played in platform boots and sponge-rubber appliances. Lee Greenway, the film's makeup artist, once told me that Arness was so embarrassed by the way he looked, he ate alone on the set.
>
> "Not true!" says Arness, finally setting the record straight. "I started in movies in 1946, and lost a lot of parts because of my height [6-foot-7]. When Howard Hawks put me in 'The Thing,' it was a great break for me at the time, because I was struggling to get any kind of job whatsoever, and that picture got a tremendous amount of publicity... and got me other work afterward." (Lovell)

After *The Thing from Another World*, Arness's career did, in fact, take off. He captured over a dozen credited film parts before landing his epic starring role in *Gunsmoke* in 1955, including FBI investigator Robert Graham in *Them!* (1954) for Warner Brothers, a he-man romantic lead and his only other sci-fi appearance.

The monster makeup design took about two months and several incarnations partly because Lee Greenway did not sketch his ideas but preferred to sculpt them on a live model, taking each proposed design to Hawks directly for approval by driving to his home in Beverly Hills. According to Al Taylor and Sue Roy in *Making a Monster*, while stopped at a red light, a woman looked over from another car and fainted on the spot. John Johnson identifies it as "the version which was finally approved" (163).

The screen design featured a slightly bulbous but generally squared off foam rubber skullcap, coupled with platform boots pushing the actor to at least seven feet tall. The skin had a greenish tone and tubes fashioned like veins carried colored water beneath the latex skin. With each breath, a football bladder attached to a specially designed belt pushed air through the tubes making the water surge. Another vein/tube ran down the back, venting the headgear to keep it cool. In a San Bernardino test screening, close ups of the creature supposedly caused viewers to pass out (Taylor and Roy), and ultimately, they decided to remove them and keep the creature's appearance somewhat ambiguous. Similarly, they decided to blur the focus with post-production effects when Arness was onscreen. Fortunately, however, modern prints feature the creature in clear focus, though the close ups vanished long ago.

Technically speaking, Arness was not the only actor to play the Thing in the film. In the fire scene, stuntman Tom Steele wore a special asbestos version of the costume (Turner, "Howard Hawks'" 84). And at the end of the movie, when they electrocute the Thing, the filmmakers employed four figures to achieve the shrinking affect. Arness began the scene and after a few seconds, stuntman Teddy Mangean stepped in. Then, four-foot two-inch actor Billy Curtis followed him. Finally, a 12-inch model represented the last stages of the dying creature. Initially, Kenneth Strickfadden, the electrical genius who engineered the voltage effects in *Frankenstein* (1931), came in to work with Donald Steward, but they soon abandoned practical effects. The head of RKO's camera effects department, Linwood Dunn, provided the solution. Overlaying a gray film on the main edit, Dunn etched in the electrical bolts frame by frame and then blurred the image "putting them slightly out of focus and printing through a piece of organdy gauze to disperse the light and give the edges a glowing effect" (Turner, "Thing").

That "What-is-it"

By design, filmgoers had no real idea what to expect with this new breed of science fiction film which would prove a far cry from the previous year's *Destination Moon*. *The Thing from Another World*'s unique marketing teased the mystery of the monster with question marks. "Natural or Supernatural?" "How did it get here?" and "Will it destroy us all?" blazed across ads that teased the film's characters recoiling in fear and wonder— but no clear monster. One ad even features a child in a highchair: "Her life can be counted in seconds… as long as THE THING is at large!" ("Her Life" 5).

As J. P. Telotte notes in "What is This Thing? Framing and Unframing the Science Fiction Film," that's not what the target audience might well have expected. Coming from the pulp sci-fi magazine world, where exotic cover art monsters from outer space pulled in readers, a rendering of the movie menace in all its potential glory seems a natural. In fact, posters for *The Man from Planet X* and *The Day the Earth Stood Still* would both mirror pulp covers, but *The Thing* relied on a corpuscular dripping red text that implied terror and promised mystery rather than definition.

Hawks played this angle of intrigue consistently through the production and promotion. Somewhere around November 1, 1950 (incidentally the same day and month the action begins in the film), Hawks showed off a block of ice 15 feet long and six feet wide with a body frozen in it at the RKO sound stage. A few days later, "Prowling the streets was a grotesque figure with a huge misshapen head, five foot arms and extra long legs" ("Howard Hawks" 13). But all this was apparently planned specifically so he could deny what people had seen was actually "the Thing" to drum up interest.

The promotions department would cook up other ideas as the film grew closer to cultivate public interest. *The Dayton Daily News* ran a seven-day contest to guess what the Thing is with clues provided by the distributors. Participants would send in a clipped form from the paper with winners judged on accuracy and timeliness by a pair of RKO representatives, the paper's "Amusements" editor, and the manager of the RKO

Keith's Theater. And there was serious money involved--$100 for first place with other cash prizes available.

Incidentally, the top prize ultimately went to Fred Breitkreitz who remembered *Who Goes There?* While it seems the paper sought "intelligent vegetable" as the answer, Mr. Breitkreitz provided a lengthy description based on the source material: "'The Thing' may be described as a sentient, extraterrestrial being, capable of infiltrating into and controlling another animal and of utilizing the mass so gained to become a larger animal, or subdivide, each subdivision becoming a separate entity" (Barton A-7). He goes on to clarify the term "animal" as relative and the use of electricity to destroy it. One gets the feeling the winner would be blissfully at home in today's "nerd culture."

Cincinnati and Dayton both got a visit from "The Thing" promotional truck, a solid black mobile ballyhoo wagon with "The THING is inside!" blazoned in green letters on the side panels. The Messmore and Damon Company created the rolling promotional device which went from town to town on a schedule. Messmore and Damon specialized in large scale animatronic displays like "The World A Million Years Ago," a traveling dinosaur exhibit tied in with *The Lost World* (1925). The curious would enter the vehicle to get a brief and disorienting glimpse of a replica of the title character. According to the April 18 issue of *Exhibitor*, 3000 people came to venture into the vehicle in these two Ohio cities:

> Entering the truck, a person walked warily through pitch darkness until a foot hit a treadle switch. In an instant, the interior was suffused in green, then a return to darkness, and when the person came out he had an eerie tale to tell of what he saw. No two persons told the same version of what they saw. ("Branches Cincinnati" NT-1)

The Thing truck, as it became known, stirred up business across the country. In Boston, supposedly 16,000 people experienced the gimmick ("The Thing is Inside" NT-2). What specifically awaited inside for curious thrill-seekers is apparently lost to time.

Other promotions in various cities hyped the film in unique ways. In Richmond, Virginia, radio station WLEE and DJ Harvey Hudson (now in the Virginia Broadcasting Hall of Fame) offered free tickets to the person who came by the station with the most unique "thing" ("Richmond" NT-4). The June 20 issue of *Exhibitor* reported that the Criterion Theater in

New York City did exceptional business with an ambulance parked outside, a gag done in many places, often with a nurse (or at least someone in a nurse costume) in attendance. The same issue also reported:

> The campaign worked out for "The Thing" at the RKO Proctor's Newark by H. R. Emde, Newark division manager, included the use of a large flat truck with a box 10 feet long, five feet high, and four feet wide, painted with copy reading: "This box contains 'The Thing,' which starts at RKO Proctor's." The truck was sent around bustling areas one week in advance. In the lobby, there was a large board on an easel with chains, bent steel, locks, revolver, rifle, and a sign reading—"These are the items which failed to hold 'The Thing." A stencil in front of the box office caught the eye. Another attention getter was a cage set out on the sidewalk with a sign, "Reserved for 'The Thing." ("Newark" NT-3)

And in Fort Worth, Texas, the Interstate Theater offered a free summer pass a girl who could sit through the midnight showing of *The Thing* without leaving, presumably alone ("San Antonio," NT-3).

The most amazing promotion was probably in Erie, Pennsylvania, where theater manager Andrew Gibson arranged for a plane to circle the city with pre-recorded PA announcements about the film while "belching chemical clouds of flame and smoke." The grand finale came when:

> [T]he plane, which had been wired with flash bulbs, gave off a blinding glare over the center of the city, and disappeared into the night with all lights off. Police, radio and TV stations, and newspapers, which had all been previously briefed, were bombarded with phone calls. Radio and TV stations made special announcements, to relieve switch board congestion, and all the time was free. ("Erie" NT-4).

So... What Is It?

Physically, despite Hawks' desire to separate the two, the Thing bears a noticeable resemblance to Universal's Frankenstein monster, especially in the relatively flat head and gigantic size. Also, Arness spends much of his screen time smashing things as he growls and moans making the connection natural. Not surprisingly, the physical similarities to Boris Karloff's monster did not escape critics and promoters latched on to that, making "if you liked that you're gonna love this" sales pitches audiences would grasp. Thus, even if Hawks' publicity distanced his creature from the Universal Studios creature, Frankenstein's visually iconic monster made a functional comparison, good copy, and great business.

Reviews and promotional ballyhoo surrounding the film demonstrate the interlocking monster images. *Harrison's Reports*, a trade magazine, wrote "the story deals with a strange invader from another planet, a Frankenstein-like man whose body is composed of vegetable matter and who lives on animal and human blood" (54). A glowing review from *The Philadelphia Inquirer* commented "The Thing itself appears only briefly and looks rather like our friend the Frankenstein's monster" ("Shocker" 32). Bob Thomas's AP syndicated Hollywood column reported that "it harks back to the finest tradition of the early *Dracula* and *Frankenstein* efforts (2)… while the Scottsboro Ritz theater promised it was "more terrifying than *Frankenstein*. More frightening than *Dracula!*" ("Ritz" 1). In fact, ads across the country mocked the towering Frankenstein monster and blood-drinking Dracula as "sissies" and "boy scouts." The Indiana Theater in Kokomo even promised an appearance from 'Frankenstein' himself at a midnight showing of *The Thing from Another World* in an ad advising parents to only bring children after sundown if "equipped with diapers and rubber pants" ("Shocking!" 5).

At least one review, however, found the image disappointing. Sara Hamilton, writing for *Photoplay*, said "Unfortunately, the Frankenstein-ish appearance of this refugee destroys much of the illusion. A 'Thing' in less human form would have deepened the horror to our way of thinking" (28). Hamilton, of course, saw the edited version without the pulsating closeups that sent tests audiences into a tizzy.

Hamilton might have been happier with the concept found in Lederer's first draft which more closely mimicked the creature described in *Who Goes There?* In Chapter 2 of the novella, the team debates thawing the creature intentionally, weighing potential problems like alien bacteria and viruses (which gets a verbal nod in the film). A physicist, Norris, vehemently opposes thawing it: "How the hell can these birds tell what they are voting on? They haven't seen those three red eyes, and the blue hair like crawling worms. Crawling—damn, it's crawling there in the ice right now!" When the team gets their first look, "three mad, hate-filled eyes blazed up with a living fire, bright as fresh-spilled blood from a face ringed with a writhing, loathsome nest of worms, blue, mobile worms that crawled where hair should grow" (Campbell). Elsewhere, the creature possesses taloned feet and makes a horrible mewing sound as it attempts to transform into a dog.

Clearly, however, recreating the literary monster would present serious practical problems and seems unreasonable in 1951, especially since the required cinematic action would render a floppy rubber suit comically disastrous on screen (as it does in many films). However, Lederer's early draft of the screenplay echoes the source material's vision. First, we get a description from "Ken," a character who transforms into Bob in the final version. He leaves his guard post, spooked by what he sees, describing it as follows: "It's got crazy hands. No ears, and a lot of eyes. They're all open! I turned a flash on it - and it looked like it was moving" (Lederer, scene 20). Three scenes later, Barnes goes on watch, drinking whiskey and talking to the Thing in ice to relieve the stress. In the original draft, McAuliffe (MacPherson in the final film), has accidentally put a pick into the creature's head during excavation (reflecting the source material) and the script suggests a visible green ooze as Barnes shines his flashlight to get a better look:

> . . . the ice is now almost transparent. Through it, only partially distorted, can be seen an unearthly horror. It has a bulbous head, a tiny suck-hole for a mouth, multiple eyes, no ears. Its arms are extra-long, ending in thorny clusters, rather than hands. It stares malevolently through the ice. (Lederer, scene 23).

This draft demonstrates an ambitious creature concept for the time and seemingly they planned something grand from the outset with a $10,000 effects budget (Turner, "Thing"). But when all was said, they settled for a more conventional (and manageable) look, the final cost was closer to $40,000 (Johnson 164).

Other problems prevented a faithful representation from the novella as well. Blair, the biologist who examines the cells, determines that the Thing reproduces with a plasma that absorbs and imitates life forms, but the original creature remains intact and hidden. In other words, the literary monster retains its physical form while using the raw matter of its victims to mimic them. (John Carpenter's 1982 version of the story takes this plot point on well, as does the 2011 prequel, also called *The Thing*.) That quality of mass reproduction transformed into the seed pod device, present in the early draft, as a practical necessity and viable alternative.

However, all film versions (thus far) lack the literary monster's most frightening ability. Campbell's monster not only reads minds but also absorbs personalities and histories, giving it a complete tool kit for fooling inquisitive human adversaries and a significant advantage. In *Who Goes There?*, Norris even claims the creature invades his dreams while in the ice. Removing this quality reduces the threat level in the film but it streamlines the narrative. Ultimately, the psychic power is reduced to a reference in the final version of the film. As the showdown draws close, Lt. McPherson (Robert Nichols) says, "This is no joke. What if he can read our minds?" Lt. Dykes (James Young) replies, "He's going to be awful mad when he gets to me."

The Hawks' film did add a new and significant dimension to the Thing—radioactivity—something no monster had embodied before. The crew uses a Geiger counter to discover and later track the invader as it batters the Arctic outpost. By detecting the radiation, the characters have some forewarning, one of their few tactical advantages. However, forewarning engenders foreboding as they await impending attack. This quality creates some of the tensest moments in the film and connects nuclear radiation with impending dangers always lurking in the back of the American mind in 1951.

NEW WORLD MONSTER

In terms of character, the Thing reflects the enigma cultivated in the ad campaign. It never speaks, no definitive clues to its mission exist and everything must be deduced from actions and interactions. Notably, this marks a new direction for science-fiction as opposed to its Gothic horror predecessors. Audiences see the Frankenstein monster constructed, watch as Dracula feeds on Renfield and witness Lon Chaney attacked by a wolf. We know who and what those monsters are. But in *The Thing*, and much subsequent sci-fi, the audience occupies a position within the quest to understand the alien, the ultimate unknown. Part of the power of *The Thing from Another World* comes from following along with the scientists as they gradually discover the intellectual carrot's indifference to bullets, vegetable-like cells, asexual reproduction and need for human blood.

Because our understanding relies entirely on deduction (and a few assumptions), it leaves the theoretical possibility that the Thing may have arrived on Earth with no intention of staying or conquering, here only because of an accident. After all, if you want to plant seeds, the Arctic wastes aren't exactly the Garden of Eden. A remote area in the Amazon Basin, the Congo or Southeast Asia makes more sense. Furthermore, as Carrington says, "It's a stranger in a strange land. The only crimes were those committed against it. It woke from a block of ice, was attacked by dogs and shot by a frightened man." Perhaps the panicked reaction of Barnes plugging six slugs into it before the first 'hello' sets an unnecessary conflict into motion.

Perhaps… but not likely. Even if that were the case, the Thing makes no attempt to communicate with the humans. Dr. Carrington's supposition that operating a spacecraft unequivocally equates to moral superiority or uncluttered, emotionless logic is highly suspect as well. Its culture might merely have a few hundred years head start, but as we see from human history, advanced technology does not automatically yield advanced morality or even thinking. If anything, the Thing's motivations seem just as reactionary and anger-motivated as human behavior. Thus, even if the circumstances occur by chance, the film gives us an adversary who behaves monstrously and shows a will to kill.

Of course, we know from the press releases that Hawks' intended to create a monster, but a new one for a new time. As he said repeatedly, Hawks specifically wanted something different from Universal's Frankenstein monster, though the two compare at some levels. Both come to us as nameless terrors essentially indestructible by conventional means. Through eight films, Frankenstein's monster is burned, crushed, submerged, shot, crushed again in an explosion, buried in molten sulfur, gassed, burned again, frozen, carried away by a flood, smothered by quicksand, and burned once again. That's a lot to tolerate (even in the absurd reality of sequelization). Additionally, electrocution, which kills the Thing, actually revives Frankenstein's monster, perhaps making it an even tougher customer. The only way to destroy it, as noted by Dr. Waldman (Edward Van Sloan) in the original film is to reverse its creation through vivisection--which fails when the monster wakes up.

Universal's monster, unloved and unwanted, a horrifying nightmare hodgepodge of human parts with a damaged brain, reflects the externalized horrors of post-WWI trauma. As Scott Poole successfully demonstrates in his book, *Wasteland: The Great War and the Origins of Horror*,

WWI turned science into mass murder and subverted the hopefulness engendered with two decades of remarkable invention in the 1890s and early 1900s. The war left a "Lost Generation" with broken minds and patchwork bodies wandering like the Frankenstein's monster through dead interior landscapes. As Poole puts it in *Wasteland*: "The war shattered the nineteenth-century consensus about death. The double became an image of mortality that could be tortured and mangled. The terror would become fully incarnated in Dr. Frankenstein's stitched-together horror" (Poole). In that sense, he became the ultimate symbol of horror after the WWI. Gruesome to look upon, fearful to tangle with and caught in a man-made expression of living death, the Frankenstein monster is a true horror.

But, even on its most murderous rampage, Frankenstein's monster can only destroy individual humans—not humanity itself.

For several reasons, then, the Thing echoes as an atomic age nightmare. Frankenstein's monster cannot take over the planet and doesn't have the will to do so. It is not highly intelligent (in fact its brain is either damaged or deranged in each version) and it cannot self-replicate. It won't enslave or farm us as food for its progeny, or even impact more than a relative handful of people. Hence, the Frankenstein horror carries weight in the imagination of an individual face off. (In fact, some films like *Bride of Frankenstein* and *Ghost of Frankenstein* demonstrate that a moderate number of angry villagers with torches and pitchforks can subdue and imprison him.) Therefore, like Dracula, Hyde, Imhotep, the Wolfman and other contemporaries, Frankenstein's monster represents personal rather than global fears.

In contrast, the post-WWII psychological zeitgeist of impending atomic warfare created a new audience needing new stories to manage new fears. Total annihilation suddenly manifested as a genuine possibility and the Thing's capacity (and desire) to destroy humanity embodies those fears perfectly. The problem was no longer that you might meet a monster in the dark symbolizing the tragedies of the past, a la *Frankenstein*. The new and much bigger problem demanded a monster reflecting the tragedy of the future—complete and utter destruction of everyone everywhere.

And that's exactly what Hawks taps when declaring *The Thing* is not a "*Frankenstein*-type film." In interviews and press releases, Hawks drilled the realism of the thesis from the outset, insisting "It's not hokum or fantasy… The story is based on a theory propounded by a reputable scientist" (Quigg, 4-B). Horror films of the '20s and '30s could not produce such a creature because people could not imagine one. By the 1950s, they could not stop imagining one.

LOOKING FOR A STORY

Without newspaperman Ned Scott, played by Spencer Douglas, *The Thing from Another World* might be yet another fad film. He garners some of the movie's choicest lines (not to mention both the first and the last) and he's arguably the best conceived supporting role of the genre. But what makes Scott so critical is his position between the past and the future, trying to decipher and manage both in a brave "new world of gods and monsters," to borrow from Dr. Pretorius (Ernest Thesiger) in *The Bride of Frankenstein* (1935).

Throughout the movie, Scotty dances between interpreting an abstract intellectual elite (Dr. Carrington) and negotiating a reactionary, somewhat unimaginative Cold War military mentality (Captain Hendry). He admires and appreciates Carrington, but can see the scientist embodies an impractical, potentially dangerous, abstraction. Similarly, Scotty's combat reporting relates him to Hendry and his men but resents the by-the-book mindset that both destroys the saucer and locks down his story. He's conspicuously devoted to his own abstraction, of course, his sacred duty of finding and delivering the truth to the people. Scotty's relentless drive originates in his own ideal standard, "the Constitution of the United States. For your information, it's called freedom of the press." Consequently, Scott stands as the high priest of the people's democratic right to know, advocating for post-war mainstream America itself to the point of symbolizing it.

Newspapers reigned supreme in 1951, playing a vital role in American culture that grew through the 1970s without a serious drop off until the early 1990s with the rise of cable news and the internet. In 1940, just before America entered WWII, U.S. weekday newspaper circulation was around 41 million but by 1950 that number had jumped to almost 54 million according to the Pew Research Center ("Newspaper Fact Sheet"). WWII made papers integral to daily life and small towns all over the country depended on them to follow the crusade against foreign fascism... and later, domestic communism. Consequently, for about forty years, prominent reporters became minor culture heroes. From Dorothy Thompson and Edward R. Murrow to Woodward and Bernstein, news reporting was a trusted and esteemed profession deemed critical to democracy. Thus, Ned Scott represents that powerful, vital relationship between global affairs and individual Americans.

Scotty bears a strong resemblance physically and in demeanor to America's most famous war correspondent, Ernie Pyle, who died tragically just a few days before the war's end in the Pacific Theater. Audiences of the time would likely see the connection from the outset. Pyle covered the war in Britain, North Africa, Italy, France (he landed at Omaha Beach) and Asia. Right before the showdown in *The Thing from Another World*, when Hendry tells him he doesn't belong there, Scott replies, "I didn't belong at Alamien or Bougainville or Okinawa. I was just kibbitzing!" It's apparently a throwaway line of bravado, but he covers both fronts too and ends with the very place Pyle died, surely no accident.

Scotty is not just the first person to speak in the film but the first we see. *The Thing* opens with a high angle shot of the newsman trudging through windswept snow reminiscent of another sci-fi/horror classic, *The Invisible Man*. As we soon find out, he braves all this "looking for a story." When Scotty enters the Officers Club in Anchorage, he's paradoxically both anonymous under his clothing and obvious in his civilian dress. Yet, he's an outsider who fits in seamlessly. He nonchalantly greets his wartime buddy Lt. Dykes and even takes over Capt. Hendry's poker hand when he's called away. We quickly sense Scotty probably knows no other life besides chasing stories in far off and dangerous places. "Eight o'clock at night and the general yelling for his troops. Sounds like the old days," Scotty remarks with a smile, letting us know he's no stranger to combat zones, and he's probably never really left the war behind. Thus, in a scene lasting around two minutes, we get a potent exposition of his character reflecting the military integration of Ernie Pyle.

Additionally, like Pyle, Scotty also bears a love/hate relationship with the military. Pyle criticized the military for its policies regarding reporting and restricting information, and stood up for the regular G.I., playing a critical role in securing combat pay as a correlative to flight pay (Gould and Horowitz 214). Likewise, Scott punches out from the common man's corner, distrustful and downright oppositional to military authority. This emerges even in the first scene when he laments that "Fogerty's nursing his secrets like a June bride" (yet another marriage and reproduction reference, incidentally.) Pyle's appreciation for military brass was similarly suspicious. Instead, he tended to report the war from the common soldier's perspective. His most famous piece, "The Death of Captain Waskow," exemplified his direct, but detailed style and tinges of it can be felt in Scotty's praise and warning at the end of the film.

Scott's role as the voice of America begins when the film takes to the air. As they approach the Arctic base, the drama's primary stage, Scotty's reaction says a great deal about U.S. post-war attitudes regarding science. Gazing down on the instillation, a mid-century miracle of human ingenuity at the top of the world, Scott remarks, "Hey, the taxpayers ought to see this." In 2021, that line would likely come over as cynical, suggesting a waste of federal resources. But in 1951, the phrase indicates patriotic pride. Such an installation validated America's worth and leadership at the international table, demonstrating not just intellectual but also economic and political power.

Scotty next asserts himself when the team arrives at the crash site asking questions in true reporter style: "What could melt that much ice?" and "Dr. Chapman, could an airplane melt that much ice?" The questions (and there are plenty) bespeak a well-conceived character asking on behalf of his fictional readership. More importantly he asks for the audience, playing a critical role by verifying enough of the science to validate the fiction. His genuine curiosity reflects both the average person's lack of knowledge and desire for understanding. Such a thing might seem ridiculous in mid-20th Century America without confirmation, so it serves a role for the filmmakers, establishing plausible circumstances for a later suspension of disbelief.

The ensuing alien recovery sequence positions Scotty to speak for the nation as their eyes and ears on the scene. He's ecstatic when he shouts, "We've found a flying saucer!" And when muzzled by Hendry, he's equally passionate in justifying his right to tell the world. This sets in motion an interior conflict between the people's rights versus the government's authority—a tenuous compact given "by the people," but also "for the people."

As the plot progresses, Scotty frequently targets monolithic military thinking, commenting on the dubious prospect of intelligence in the military. When the thermite turns "a new civilization into a Fourth of July piece" (a conspicuously American reference), his dismay derides the thoughtlessness of "standard operating procedure." When word comes through from General Fogerty authorizing the thermite after the fact, Scott disdainfully gloats, "That's what I like about the army. Smart. All the way to the top." Hendry, whom he calls a "human clam," naturally becomes the verbal target of his frustrations. The captain, Fogerty, Air

Force Headquarters, even President Truman stand as obstacles to the truth in his mind. Scotty's animated frustration isn't purely motivated by principle, of course. He clearly worries someone will scoop his story and envisions his editor "climbing all over his office yelling, stamping his feet. He'll probably shoot himself by midnight." But for him, this story is really The Story, a sacred truth he has an opportunity to reveal like Moses on Mt. Sinai.

This brings us to Scotty's subtle representation of the American Christian heritage and its cosmology in crisis in 1951. Scotty's early description of the crash as "the biggest story to hit since the parting of the Red Sea" is the first of several indications he symbolizes that consciousness. But it is a troubled one. To this day, the uneasy relationship between religion and science creates social and political tension. The Biblical creation story posits a divine, omnipotent external maker and moral judge demanding philosophical fealty. However, science, especially evolution, opposes this view and backs it up with both scientific method and the resulting technology.

Additionally, the Bible never mentions extraterrestrial life, presenting another cosmological problem. We see this play out when Carrington and his team analyze the Thing's severed arm with its thorny fingers and plant tissue using an evolutionary framework. Scott and Carrington occupy center screen through most of the scene with Scott standing in for the American public, questioning this new reality and finding commonsense no longer applies. He assumes the Thing must be dead out in the cold and missing an arm, but Carrington tells him, "I doubt very much if it can die, as we understand dying." That's a weighty spiritual proposition. Theologically speaking, Christ lives specifically to die and be reborn as proof of Christian cosmology and inspiration for redemption through faith, but a creature that cannot die throws that out the window. There is no indication this consciously registers with Scott or the others, but it may register unconsciously as his demeanor grows consistently agitated with the discussion of evolution. In any case, the exobiology motivates the scene into the territory of spiritual crisis.

Upon hearing this, Scott exclaims "Holy cats!" (an expression he uses frequently). As the scientists divulge the creature's vegetable nature, he says "Oh for Pete's sake!" to express disbelief, frustration, and dismay. "Holy Cats" has a debatable origin but "For Pete's sake" refers to the torments of Saint Peter, the Christian martyr crucified upside down for his faith. Such oaths have their origin in medieval protective magic wherein evoking a powerful name supposedly warded off a spiritual attack. The name of Christ would be the most powerful, but that violates the third commandment to "not take thy Lord's name in vain," so phrases like this became acceptable substitutes. These phrases politely sidestep religious profanity, a good indication of Scott's upbringing and philosophical underpinnings. At least metaphorically, the information he absorbs gets treated like a spiritual threat.

Scott's reaction intensifies as Carrington describes the type of evolution that would produce an "intellectual carrot." Spencer's delivery expresses disbelief, moral offense and even anger. The very subject of evolution triggers an aggressive tone and language. He cocks his head disapprovingly as Carrington connects humanity to early Pliocene evolution and tries to cut off Carrington saying, "Look, doctor..." in a manner suggesting evolution is just too farfetched to accept. This culminates, of course, when Scott admits Carrington's accomplishments make it hard to say he's "stuffed absolutely clean full of wild blueberry muffins," but he is openly hostile as the scientists begin to describe earthbound vegetation that can "think." Scotty's objections stop cold when the creature's hand revives by absorbing blood right before his eyes. From there, MacPherson walks in with an axe to confront the Thing, and in true Hawks style, the plot advances before its philosophical issues can slow it down.

In all of this, Scott exemplifies huge numbers of average Americans rejecting evolution theologically and culturally at the time. "The leading biology textbooks in the 1950s had scarcely changed since the early 1900s. Noticeably absent were discussions of evolution and other topics such as human reproduction. One could not even find the world *evolution* in high school biology textbooks" (Bybee 309-310). Narratively, Scotty's questions, resistance and hostility to the evidence mirror what would be expected in much (if not most) of the audience. It adds to the plot's plausibility and echoes the national problem of dependency on science for survival and growth in a country simultaneously inclined to reject evolution.

Ned Scott could have easily been reduced to a comical character. He's emotional, awkwardly lanky, forever missing the shot or forgetting his camera. He even passes out after the big climax. But he connects the elements of the film to the audience as its representative, especially in the final lines:

North Pole, November 3rd. Ned Scott reporting.

One of the world's greatest battles was fought and won today by the human race. Here at the top of the world, a handful of American soldiers and civilians met the first invasion from another planet. A man by the name of Noah once saved our world with an ark of wood. Here are the North Pole a few men performed a similar service with an arc of electricity. A flying saucer which landed here and its pilot have been destroyed, but not without casualties among our own meager forces. I would like to bring to the microphone some of the men responsible for our success but as senior Air Force officer Captain Hendry is attending to demands over and above the call of duty, Dr. Carrington, the leader of the scientific expedition is recovering from wounds received in the battle.

And now before giving you the details of the battle, I bring you a warning. Every one of you listening to my voice, tell the world, tell this to everybody wherever they are: Watch the skies, everywhere. Keep looking. Keep watching the skies.

The potency of the final call to "keep watching the skies" gets much deserved attention but Scotty's comments also tie religion, science and the military in a heroic bond. He honors the soldiers in general, Captain Hendry (whom he needles through most of the film) in particular, and even Dr. Carrington in a way we might expect from Ernie Pyle. And in the end, he finally gets to speak to and for the American people. Thus, not surprisingly, the phrase "Keep watching the skies" slipped into pop culture, especially among UFO enthusiasts.

A GROUP OF INDIVIDUALS

With regard to the characters as a whole, the fluid, natural interaction of the minor characters arguably cements the film as a great work of the silver screen. The Thing from Another World does what most impactful films do--supply audiences with "real people" as characters. Ironically, this comes from sketching them out with just enough detail to make them recognizable but broadly enough to adapt to the individual viewer's experience. Relatability is (or at least it should be) a minimum requirement for main characters but an ensemble of believable people, each with intuitively imaginable backstories, embeds an audience in the narrative emotionally, intellectually and experientially.

Hawks' decision to cast relative unknowns reflects this understanding. Moreover, the film provides a microcosm of society in its characters—with figures representing human traits ranging from humor to fear, supreme intellect to practical wisdom. This kind of panoply serves as a foundation for several of Hawks' pictures such as *Rio Bravo* (1959). As Robin Wood expresses it, "What makes the characters live is the values they embody. The affection of the characters for each other reflects that which Hawks feels for them: an affection warm but unidealizing, dignified by respect" (109).

Anyone who has experienced long term group dynamics recognizes the characters in *The Thing from Another World* as personality types representing human responses to stress and crisis. It works because one can easily imagine these characters at a backyard barbecue. MacPherson constantly wisecracks, Dykes assesses the women, Barnes predicts a rain-out, Tex makes an appearance and slips out unnoticed, while Bob fixes the grill's gas line and sets up the keg.

This social dynamic resides just beneath the military/scientific/civilian microcosm ostensibly structuring the film. One might read this as a kind of "idealized democracy" (as Wood read Hawks' *Air Force*) or perhaps "something more relevant to an idealized Marxism" (Williams 58) where each person's individuality contributes to the good of the group. In either case, individuals cooperate seamlessly in the face of danger (an idealized situation indeed) and "implies the importance of a community or group acting collectively" (58). This, again, reflects America's post-war concept of itself as a unified world savior with room for individuality but not dissent in a crisis (which explains Carrington's expulsion from the group under duress and re-absorption when the threat has ended).

PRODUCTION

Even without big names, *The Thing from Another World* still had a big budget due to its technical requirements. In an Associated Press release in early November 1950, Hawks revealed that the film merited over a million dollars budget with a 51 day shooting schedule, assuring readers he would not "gamble that kind of money on a phony" ("Howard Hawks"). That general figure popped up in the press lines consistently (though reported shooting days were inconsistent) and in the end, the grand total was $1,257,237 (Turner).

Getting the military to provide equipment necessary to sell the story on screen became impossible. Hawks sought cooperation from the Air Force, and he'd done enough war pictures to have credibility with the Pentagon, but the contemporary UFO craze changed the equation. The official rejection letter, reprinted in George Turner's discussion of the film in *Cinefantastique* Vol. 12, demonstrates how seriously the Air Force viewed the power of science-fiction:

> The script of Winchester Pictures' proposed production The Thing has been reviewed, and it is regretted that we will not be able to extend cooperation as the story revolves around flying saucers and their possible contents.
>
> The Air Force has maintained the position for some time that there are no such objects as flying saucers and does not wish to be identified with any project that could be interpreted as perpetuating the myth of the flying saucer. Also, the Air Force seriously objects to any mention of Air Force personnel and equipment, or pictorial sequences representing Air Force personnel or equipment, being included in the film.
>
> Providing your company plans to proceed on the production without Air Force cooperation, we request every consideration be given to the Air Force objection in the interest of maintaining goodwill and relations.
>
> The Air Force has dispatched a wire to the Commander-in-Chief, Alaska Theater stating their objections.
>
> Sincerely,
> DONALD E. BARUCH
> Chief, Motion Picture Sect. Pictorial Branch (81-82)

In addition to the written refusal, co-producer Edward Lasker apparently had an audience with Air Force brass at some point before production began wherein he was personally rebuffed. "USAF officers explained that they had just spent half-a-million-dollars proving that flying saucers did not exist and asked, 'Why should we help you make a picture about one?'" (Graham).

The film takes a sideways swipe back at the Air Force with a discussion in the cockpit as the crew returns with the Thing in tow. Reading from a training bulletin, MacPherson snidely repeats the official position: "The Air Force has discontinued investigating and evaluating reported flying saucers on the basis that there is no evidence." Scotty follows with his own jab directed at Hendry but clearly critiquing the military line. "They'll probably make you a general for destroying evidence that they're wrong." This might be a mere insert for a laugh if it were not for the release date referenced in MacPherson's set up: December 27, 1949... the very day Project Grudge officially released its findings referred to in the rejection letter.

Without Air Force cooperation, Hawks and Lasker had to make do. Uniforms were no issue, of course. Hollywood costume departments were flush with WWII era service garb. Providing the Hendry's plane turned out relatively simple as well. The Air Force used Douglas C-47 Skytrains as primary personnel and cargo transport throughout the war and well beyond, with some in service into the 21st Century. But they were essentially converted DC-3 commercial aircraft which existed in abundance across the country, and indeed, across the globe. Johnson Flying Service from Missoula provided and converted the aircraft (Hampton).

LOCATION, LOCATION, LOCATION

Filming on location proved more difficult. The crew assembled in December 1950 in Cut Bank, Montana, where locals excitedly welcomed them with hospitality and plenty of food. Located about 30 miles south of the Canadian border, the site offered flat plains and a history of heavy snow. It also had a decommissioned army airbase, now a private airport, that became the North Pole installation for the film. By mid-November, a month before Hawks came, $15,000 worth of set construction was already underway ("Hollywood Studio" 14).

Unfortunately, just as the cast and crew arrived, the weather took an unseasonable warm turn. While the actors rehearsed in the local Elks Hall, crop dusters whitewashed the runways ("Cut Bank, Praying" 4). According to Robert Cornthwaite, the cast basically sat around chatting with the locals. When he told a woman they'd need 8-10 inches of virgin snow before shooting, she replied with concern: "'Don't they *know* that snow doesn't *stay* on the ground here?'" (Weaver, "Friend," 61). Unfortunately, no one realized that while the northern elevation offered lots of the white stuff, the plateau winds blew it away almost as fast as it fell. When Cornthwaite told writer Edward Lasker, he apparently went a little batty. "It *disturbed* him—he couldn't deal with it" (62). (Another version of the story holds that Lasker heard it from an airport employee, but the psychological result did not differ).

Apparently they tried to truck in snow from Glacier National Park and simulated a snowstorm using airplane propellers (Hampton), but the scene never quite looked right and the crew began searching for another location for the flying saucer recovery scene. One article claims Hawks himself flew about 26,000 miles over the northern plains, Canada and Alaska before settling on an area outside Lewistown, Montana ("'The Thing' May" 1). Given that the circumference of the Earth stretches about 25,000 miles, take that with a grain of salt.

In mid-December, with no snow in sight, 38 actors and technicians went back to Los Angeles to spend Christmas with their families (and cut expenses). Nyby stayed, however, and brought his family out to Montana to spend the holidays there. During that time, he did what he could to get aerial shots of the base and crash site with the help of Johnson Air Service using the converted DC-3 and Severton Air Activities (which had supplied a crop duster for painting the runways white) helped film the DC-3 in flight (Hampton).

Nyby also employed local actors during this period in the Lewistown area to pose as a dog sled team and various crew stand ins, but this too didn't go well. The *Great Falls Tribune* reported on January 14 that the hometown "stars" had trouble on skis and snowshoes and ended up "strewn all over the slopes near the local airport as they tried in vain to keep up with the hustling huskies" ("Sunshine" 4). Any hope of stardom for the 14 actors and 11 sled dogs vanished in the cutting room.

Hawks was also apparently in the area long enough to be "adopted into the Blackfeet tribe" with several of the actors and crew ("Producer Gets Colorful Welcome" 3). Hawks would likely have been happier with a white winter blanket covering his location, but gestures like these demonstrate just how excited the rural residents were to have a major Hollywood production in their backyard.

An early January snow brought crews back, but high winds kept blowing the surrogate Arctic bare in spots, bringing more frustration. Stand-ins filmed the flying saucer scenes in brutal conditions, but the rushes proved unsatisfactory. At that point, the fickle weather and delays were too much and Hawks decided to shoot the recovery scene in Encino, California.

At the beginning of March, with just weeks to go, the critical scene was finally filmed. Now, instead of enduring the freezing, windswept snow, the actors assembled in full winter gear on a hot, sandy outdoor set. Fake snow (a combination of shaved ice and Styrofoam) blown by wind machines got in Robert Cornthwaite's eyes, blinding him for 20 minutes and causing minor but permanent damage to his eyeball (Weaver, "Pal," 62). It caused problems for the sled dogs as well. In Cut Bank, the production had acquired real sled dogs acclimated for the cold weather. However, in California, the "stunt dogs" (as William Self called them) balked a bit. "We would be sweating and the dogs wouldn't want to perform on the artificial snow" (Self, 277-278).

The crew used a massive and rather convincing curved painted canvas called a cyclorama to produce the horizon. To create the circle of ice encasing the saucer, technicians partially buried a tail-fin and poured uncounted gallons of sodium thiosulfate, a photographic solution, over the sand to give it a glassy, crystalline appearance (Davidson 40). It yielded a stunning effect.

Incidentally, aerial shots taken in Montana by Nyby's crew late December crew revealing the crash site did make it into the film, though they are less than perfect. Visible lines where a tractor has pushed away snow mark the perimeter and cut across the icy circle in two places and the tractor itself rests at the end of the bottleneck formation, apparent for a second before the cut. Remarkably, however, most people never notice, a testament to the film's pacing and its generally entrancing quality.

Despite all the tribulations in getting this sequence, it critically initiates the shifting tensions between Carrington, Hendry, and Scotty (and thus all they represent). And it manages to carry significant weight:

> For all the strength and resilience of the characters, with their characteristic warmth, their admirable resourcefulness, the scene where the men spread themselves out on the ice to discover the shape of the space-ship and find themselves forming a perfect circle chillingly conveys a sense of man's smallness and helplessness in a vast and mysterious universe" (Wood 108).

Lesser filmmakers would have settled for an exposition of the discovery under these conditions, but Hawks and Nyby thankfully understood the visual power of a "flying saucer"… even if the audience never actually sees it.

A Fourth of July Piece

Blowing up the saucer with thermite created drama on screen and off. The script calls for a massive explosion as a plot point, and it had to be convincing in one take, so the film's pyrotechnic crew put in more than needed to ensure the onscreen effect. By all accounts, the resulting blast shocked everyone, including the residents of nearby Encino. The explosion knocked the actors to the ground and according to some, broke windows in nearby buildings. Kenneth Tobey remembered an accidental ad lib associated with the explosion. "When that blast went off, we were really ducking," he told Tom Weaver. "When I yelled, 'Hit the deck!' it wasn't a written line, I wanted everyone to get down!" (Attack 344).

Getting Chilly

As the action heats up in the film, the set cools down when the Thing cuts the oil supply to the facility to freeze his foes. For this effect, Hawks shot the frigid scenes (before heading to Montana) in the California Consumers Corporation Ice House, which had been working with various studios for more than a decade to produce icy temperatures in sunny L.A. for the screen. As early as 1937, they were the go-to sub-zero sound stage and had their own self-designed snow sprayers in 1941 ("Four Years" 11, 26). By the time Hawks arrived there, this sort of thing was old hat.

According to William Self, the Ice House was actually quite comfortable most of the time. Most of the film did not require cold temperatures and the compound built within the structure remained room temperature until the cold air scenes began. Still, filming in an ice house, even a professionally prepared one, had its problems. Apparently, at one point Hawks shouted out an order for two dozen heating pads causing his frosty cast and crew to cheer. However, he wanted them hooked up to protect the cameras. Kenneth Tobey asked Hawks, "Which is more important, a camera or an actor?" The look in Hawk's eye must have told the story because he retracted the question on the spot ("Heating Pads" 53).

In another incident involving Tobey, Hawks put him on ice, more or less literally. Dissatisfied with how warm Tobey looked when entering the compound (after supposedly enduring -40 degree temperatures), Hawks and Nyby sent him to sit in a refrigeration unit for 20 minutes. His discomforted look came genuinely ("Howard Hawks Gives" 6-D).

COOKING THE CARROT

One of the most dramatic moments comes when the Thing comes into the barracks area and the soldiers ignite it with kerosene and a flare pistol. As mentioned above, the approach of the Thing comes immediately on the heels of Nikki's solution to cook it. With more time to think, the characters might not throw buckets of fuel around the room, but emergent conditions propel hasty solutions, creating not only a remarkable scene but genuinely dangerous one as well.

By the 1960s, the burning man became an action movie trope, but it was relatively uncharted territory in 1951. The effect required several days of planning and had to be done with limited takes due not only to the heat and flames but also the short time stunt men could stay in the specially designed suits. According to John Johnson, make up man Lee Greenway used special fireproof material from Sinclair Paint and applied several layers and a heavy mask (204-205). To carry all this out required "eight stuntmen, four cameramen, five electricians, two grips, two prop men, a cable man, six special effects men, one painter, two firemen, and a doctor" (Turner, "Howard," 83-84). The stunt actors had about one minute of oxygen coming from a concealed tank so when the suit was sealed, they had to shoot quickly, with the second stuntman ready to step in as time expired. Consequently, the scene required precise planning and execution, no small task when tossing liquid fuel in an enclosed space.

To make matters more intense, a special flammable paste was painted on the suits to increase the brightness of the flames. One of the stunt men, Tom Steele, remembered that cinematographer Linwood Dunn wanted additional paste applied right before shooting but fortunately that order never got carried out (J. Johnson 204-205).

AND ANOTHER THING...

A unique problem came out of left field just as Hawks began to promote the film under its original title, *The Thing*. A novelty song called "The Thing" from band leader Phil Harris hit the Billboard charts in mid-November of 1950. Harris, who had a long and varied show business career (including voice acting for Disney animated features in the 1960s and '70s), had his own radio program for NBC, so much of the nation heard the goofy but popular tune. Consequently, it spent 14 weeks on the charts and peaked at number one, making it a national sensation ("The Thing"). In fact, Danny Kaye and Arthur Godfrey made quick recordings as well in December, capitalizing on its popularity and compounding the confusion to come. Even Adam West, TV's Batman, would eventually cover the tune.

Seemingly, since the song has nothing to do with space aliens, it should have posed no problem for Hawks. It recounts a fellow who finds a strange object in a box on the beach that's never identified and referenced only with three strokes on a bass drum. Everywhere the singer tries to show it, he's told "Get out of here with that bump-ba-bump" in exasperation. Listeners could thus mentally insert any phrase they liked, from the vulgar to the banal. Amazingly, however, interviews and news items show people really seemed to care about the identity of the "thing" in Harris's nonsense song and of course, he had no answer for them.

Unfortunately, Hawks was playing the same game with his new monster but aiming for the opposite effect—and Harris had beaten him to the punch with a joke. Pre-production press releases worked hard to build the menace of *The Thing* by stressing the unknown nature of the monster so audiences would take it seriously. A sober and mysterious invader anchored his entire publicity campaign which was already underway. Now, suddenly, Hawks had to worry people would expect a lighthearted farce because of the song—a concern amplified by the proposed alien-themed romantic comedy, *Morning Star*, he'd publicly teased out a year before as a career launcher for Margaret Sheridan.

So, when the song topped the charts in the first week of December 1950, the decision was tentatively made to change film's name to *The Thing from Another World*. Aline Mosby reported on December 7 that Harris's refusal (or inability) to identify his "thing" had people wondering if it might be from outer space. She wrote that the success of the cryptic tune "brought a big film factory to its knees" ("Phil Harris" 7), referencing Howard Hughes and RKO by name. She told readers to expect the longer title, *The Thing from Another World*, in advertisements going forward. "'We want to avoid changing the title,' a harried studio spokesman explained. 'We may have to depending on what Phil Harris says The Thing is'" (7).

The stunning title sequence reflects the quandary the song created for Hawks. "From Another World" was clearly added on after the original burning reveal of "The Thing" blazes across the screen under the weight of some surging music. Filming of the chilling opening titles, therefore, must have taken place before any other filming since the song emerged in November and the crew did not start on location until December. The effect uses a glass plate with the title painted on in white. Initially, it is covered by a thin black sheaf which slowly melts way under applied heat. Light projects beneath the slightly angled glass illuminating a fog seemingly blown through a cut-out mirroring the lettering.

Strangely enough, fate seems to have set the two Things on a collision course weeks before. On November 15, Erskine Johnson's "Exclusively Yours" column for *The Daily News* in Los Angeles paired Harris and Hawks "Things" side by side. She announced Winchester Pictures' new "hush-hush scientific-adventure story" (19) just above Phil Harris appointment as honorary mayor of Encino, California (ironically, the very city Hawks would eventually default to for the creature recovery scenes). Harris may simply have been having a water crest year, but the mention also strategically put his name in the papers two days before the song released. Interestingly enough, adjacent to Johnson's tidbits, Ezra Goodman's "Behind the Camera" featured an effusive Hawks launching his "what is it?" advanced publicity campaign. Ostensibly, no one involved realized how tangled the Hawks and Harris would become due to their identically titled guessing games.

But is that true? Writer and researcher Phil Hore, author of *The Thing: The History of a Monster Franchise*, thinks it was no accident. In an email interview conducted for this book, he said the timing got under his skin and he "uncovered a clear pattern" of quick capitalization by the song's writer. "Charles Randolph Grean had a habit of writing, recording and releasing songs based on a current fad within a week to cash in," Hore wrote. "To me it's clear Grean saw the potential of the name thanks to RKO's wave of publicity around the upcoming movie and jumped on the bandwagon." Given that Grean would lose a plagiarism case in 1958 and exploited the popularity of *Dark Shadows* and Leonard Nimoy later in his career, it is certainly plausible that his biggest hit was no accident at all.

MUSIC

Howard Hawks drew on another *Red River* contributor for the musical score, Dimitri Tiomkin, a Russian-born, classically trained composer. Tiomkin came to New York after the Tsar and his aristocracy fell to the Bolsheviks. When the Great Depression hit, he left for Hollywood and slowly built one of the most impressive and prolific careers of any screen composer. His credits include *Mr. Smith Goes to Washington* (1939),

D.O.A. (1950), *High Noon* (1952), *Giant* (1956), *Gunfight at the O. K. Corral* (1957), *The Old Man and the Sea* (1958) and *The Guns of Navarone* (1961). He worked frequently with Alfred Hitchcock, scoring *Shadow of a Doubt* (1943), *Strangers on a Train* (1951) and *Dial M for Murder* (1954). He wrote for television as well, creating the memorable *Rawhide* theme. Tiomkin was nominated for 21 Oscars (winning three) and several Golden Globes.

Tiomkin worked with Hawks on six films including *Big Sky* in 1952, *Land of the Pharaohs* in 1955 and *Rio Bravo* in 1959. Hawks slated him for *Hatari* in 1961 as well but fired Tiomkin on the spot for using a violin in the first drafts. According to Hawks, he told Tiomkin he didn't want a hint of classical instrumentation in the film. "I don't want one violin. I don't want one cello. I don't want any woodwinds" (McBride 126). Apparently when Tiomkin called the next day to ask if Hawks was kidding, he said, "You're fired, Dimi. . . Anybody who doesn't want to do what I tell them to, I don't want" (126). Kathryn Kalinak, however, remarks that "It seems unlikely that Tiomkin's mild insubordination was the determining factor here, but rather Hawk's desire for a more contemporary sound" (159). In any case, Hawks held Tiomkin in high esteem even after the severance, not just for his skill but also his humility.

Writer Thomas Hischak wrote, "The only characteristic of Tiomkin's music that is easy to pinpoint is his felicitous talent for melody" (582). However, he also notes that in the score for *The Thing from Another World*, "Virtually abandoning melody, Tiomkin wrote a series of chords and percussive phrases using an odd assortment of instruments" (582). This included various harps, organs, pianos, percussion (including a flexatone, a double-malleted, handheld metal instrument that distorts sound as it's striking surface bends). Tiomkin also had a wind machine in the orchestra room (Hall) and employed a Novachord in the score, "an early multi-voice synthesizer that was slow to change color, so most composers used a 'string' or 'organ' setting and played chords (also true in this score)" (Russ). George Turner states that the voices of four women were used as well to make the eerie tones ("Howard" 84).

The soundtrack did not, however, include a Theremin, despite the popular misconception and frequent repetition of this 'fact.' Instead, the eerie music cues symbolizing the monster came from the Ondes Martenot, an instrument utilizing a keyboard, or alternatively, a metal ring pulled along a wire, creating electronic oscillations in vacuum tubes or transistors. Invented in 1928 by Maurice Martenot, a cellist and WWI radio operator, the device evolved quickly to feature three "diffuseurs" (speakers) producing different and potentially haunting tones.

An interview by Christopher Palmer with conductor Charles Gerhardt (recounted by Roger Hall in "Dimitri Tiomkin's Golden Decade") notes that the Ondes Martenot "replaced" the Theremin in the orchestra. Internationally acclaimed symphonic orchestrator and music arranger, Patrick Russ, confirms Gerhardt's account of the Ondes Martenot. "In fact, there are three of them in the soundtrack (they only play when the alien is represented, so not at the beginning of the score)... Because the Ondes can only play one note at a time on its keyboard, the three individual instruments could play together in chords." Furthermore, he pointed out that film score lacks a traditional string section (using only basses instead) and notes, "The quarter-tone bends in the woodwinds and brass are a wonderful unsettling effect and are used throughout the film" (Russ).

Tiomkin's process included time on location and he had access to the dailies and rough cut. However, delays put the film in a crunch and music could not be completed until the shots were done and assembled. With time running out with the first screenings only a few weeks away, the flying saucer scene was still not complete. To get everything in on time, the actors assembled a rehearsal of the flying saucer scene before it was shot so Tiomkin could time and compose it (Weaver, "Pal," 62). In the end, the soundtrack wrapped in time to get the film in theaters by early April as planned.

RELEASE AND RECEPTION

The Thing from Another World opens with the familiar RKO spinning globe, flashing radio tower and Morse Code beeps, but technically speaking, Hawks' Winchester Pictures produced the film independently with RKO contracted as the distributor. However, Hawks maintained strong professional ties with RKO and pulled from its resources and talent by arrangement. For him, it meant he did not have to worry much about studio brass meddling and could make decisions without having to justify them. For RKO, the bulk of the financial risk was contained, a boon for the slowly crumbling giant.

The film hit theaters in the first week of April. Trade showings across the country took place on April 3, 1951 ("RKO" 19) with the first traceable public screening on April 4 in Kansas City at the RKO Missouri Theater ("Two New Pictures" F-1). The next day, Ohio theaters screened the thriller, including the RKO Keith's Theater in Dayton, the epicenter of the movie's first ambitious ballyhoo campaign. On April 7, a press release circulated widely in the United States and Canada announcing the film's arrival and again reminding readers it had nothing to do with the Phil Harris song. By the end of the week, it was in theaters across the continent.

The Thing continued to perform admirably more than a year after its release drawing American audiences to drive-ins and double feature spinechiller shows for most of the decade before finding new audiences on television. It also did well overseas and cracked the Australian market in May 1952 where it remained popular throughout the summer. The film opened in London on August 1, and *Variety International* reported success for a solid month: "strong for the holdover class is 'The Thing from Another World' with $5900 in fourth week at London Pavilion" ("London Pix").

As with most movies, reviews were mixed with a few surprising results. Syndicated "In Hollywood" reviewer, Jimmy Fidler, found *The Thing* "fair... a pseudo-scientific horror drama interesting in its conception, but too slow paced to pack a great punch," (Fidler 16). It makes one wonder what Fidler would require from a film, especially since he called the largely forgotten musical comedy *Tales of Hoffman* a "must see" in the same column.

Photoplay's Sara Hamilton had a hard time getting beyond the "vegetable" nature of the antagonist, but said "it is nevertheless so well directed, produced, written and acted, one becomes completely lost in the vampirish goings-on" (27). She also noted that the cast "are such a likable, natural bunch of kids, they lend a certain credence to the tale" (28). Similarly, *Harrison Reports* called it "an effective and imaginative thriller that should more than satisfy those who enjoy weird, horror-like tales" (54), warning further that some scenes might be too much for children.

A surprisingly glowing review came from the Catholic Film Institute's *Focus: A Film Review*—a British magazine--in the September 1952 issue. The mission of the publication is "to further the cause of Christian culture by means of the cinema" (192), and thus, it might well have been influenced by Ned Scott's religious dialog as noted above, since the subject of alien life extends beyond the Bible's scope and horror and science-fiction do not get an easy pass. The review begins where *Harrison* left off, appealing to parents: "You cannot very well take the children to see this film. If you do they will keep you out of bed for several nights on end"

(J. C. 203). However, the reviewing priest praises the film's quality and performances, remarking, "Suspense is a difficult atmosphere to maintain and the producer has managed it." The writer did not find the ending particularly convincing and called for more atmospheric shots of the Arctic to satisfy the eye (perhaps missing that the claustrophobic tones maintain the suspense).

Conclusions

The Thing from Another World resonates to this day for several reasons. The quality of the writing, acting and production is primary but other deeper factors make the biggest difference. First, it cultivates a type of horror that simply could not exist just 10 years prior. Nuclear warfare and the Cold War suddenly made worldwide destruction—literally the end of human society and perhaps existence itself—not just imaginable but a real possibility. Prior to "the bomb," such a concept only existed in abstract Biblical terms. An angry god (from the sky, incidentally) might wipe us out, but even in Western religious apocalypse scenarios there could be salvation. And since few people continue to connect hurricanes and earthquakes with divine retribution, the power of that concept was, practically speaking, limited. But nuclear war meant mass destruction no longer needed deific agency—humans were now fully capable of self-annihilation.

Millions of people across the world saw *The Thing from Another World* within a year of its release and it set the tone for much film art to come. With its radioactive monster poised to wipe out humanity, *The Thing* reigns as the first widespread and impactful symbolic representation of total nuclear annihilation in cinema. It establishes the most common alien motif in film, the invader, and scientists, soldiers and civilians must band together to stop a new menace. The audience rides along in the process of figuring out the unknown and determining its weak spot. These are all common place in film now, but the science fiction monster film as we know it originates in the Arctic in 1951.

Works Cited

"32 Top Budget Films Brighten RKO '51 Horizon." *Film Bulletin*, 18 Dec. 1950, p. 26.

Barton, Bill. "Thing Arrives; Winner Selected." *Dayton Daily News*, 6 April 1952, p. A-7.

"Branches Cincinnati." *Exhibitor*. 18 April 1951, p. NT-1.

Campbell, John W. *Who Goes There?* (eBook Online). Golden Age of Sci-Fi. http://www.goldenageofscifi.info/ebook/Who_Goes_There.pdf

"Cut Bank, Praying for Snowstorm, Reverses Usual Montana Stand of Waiting for Chinook." *Great Falls Tribune*, 13 Dec. 1950, p. 4.

Davidson, Jim. "The Thing about Filmmaker Christian Nyby." *Filmfax*. August/September 1992, p. 36-46.

"Erie." *Exhibitor*. 13 June 1951, p. NT-4.

Fidler, Jimmy. "In Hollywood." *Quad-City Times*, Davenport, IA, 17 April 1951, p. 16.

"Five Unknowns Named to Head Big Movie Cast." *Vancouver News-Herald*, 6 Jan. 1951. p. 12.

"Four Years in an Ice House." *International Photographer*. Vol. XII, No. 12. Jan. 1941, p. 11, 26.

Fuhrmann, Henry. "A 'Thing' to His Credit." *Los Angeles Times*, https://www.latimes.com/archives/la-xpm-1997-05-25-ca-62224-story.html, 25 May 1997.

Gentry, Ric. "*Red River*: An Interview with Christian Nyby." *The Criterion Collection*. https://www.criterion.com/current/posts/3186-red-river-an-interview-with-christian-nyby

Gould, Brandon R., and Stanley A Horowitz. *The Eleventh Quadrennial Review of Military Compensation*. "Chapter 6: History of Combat Pay." Institute for Defense Analyses, 2011.

Hamilton, Sara. "The Thing." *Photoplay*, July 1951, p. 27-28.

Hampton, Kate. "Hollywood Invades the Prairie." Montana History Revealed, https://mthistoryrevealed.blogspot.com/2013/10/hollywood-invades-prairie.html

Harrison, P. S., ed. "'The Thing' with Margaret Sheridan, Kenneth Tobey and Robert Cornthwaite." *Harrison Reports*, 7 April 1951, p. 54.

"Heating Pads Needed to Safeguard Camera." *Charlotte Observer*, 24 Dec. 1950, p. 53.

"Her life can be counted in seconds" (Advertisement). *Motion Picture Daily*, 22 Mar. 1951, p. 5.

Hischak, Thomas. "Dimetri Tiomkin." *The Encyclopedia of Composers*. Rowman & Littlefield, 2015.

"Hollywood Studio May Make Movie Scenes in Harve Area." *Great Falls Tribune*, 15 Nov. 1950, p. 14.

Hopper, Hedda. "Big Plans for Clift." *Kansas City Star*, 4 March 1949, p. 28.

———. "Hollywood." *Daily News*. New York, NY. 15 July 1949, p. 55.

Hore, Phil. "Thing Book Quotation." Email correspondence with Sean Kotz. May 21, 2022.

"Howard Hawks Gives Actor the 'Deep Freeze.'" *Charlotte Observer*, 11 February 1951, p. 6-D.

"Howard Hawks' 'The Thing' has Hollywoodites Guessing." *Fort Worth Star-Telegram*, 5 Nov. 1950, Section 2, p. 13.

Lederer, Charles. *The Thing from Another World* (8/29/50 Draft). *Leon Scripts*, https://leonscripts.tripod.com/scripts/THING51. htm

"London Pix Biz Brisk; 'Scaramouche Sock $19,000, Dreamboat Fast 8 1/2 G, 'Just for You,' 'Affair' Start Solid." *Variety International*, 10 September 1952,

Lovell, Glenn. "Elusive James Arness sets record straight." *Sarasota Herald-Tribune*, 9 Sept. 2005. https://www.heraldtribune.com/article/LK/20050909/News/605236986/SH

J. C. "The Thing." *Focus: A Film Review*, Vol. V, No. 9, September 1952, p. 203.

Jewell, Richard B. *RKO Radio Pictures: A Titan is Born*. University of California Press, 2012.

Johnson, Erskine. "Exclusively Yours." *The Daily News*. Los Angeles, California, 15 Nov 1950.

Johnson, John J. *Cheap Tricks and Class Acts: Special Effects, Makeup and Stunts from the Films of the Fantastic Fifties.* McFarland & Company, Inc. Publishers. Jefferson, NC. 1996.

Klaes, Larry. "'An Intellectual Carrot – The Mind Boggles!'" Dissecting *The Thing from Another World." Centauri Dreams,* 3 May 2019. https://www.centauri-dreams.org/2019/05/03/an-intellectual-carrot-the-mind-boggles-dissecting-the-thing-from-another-world/

Kalinak, Kathryn. "Scoring the West: Dimitri Tiomkin and Howard Hawks." *Howard Hawks: New Perspectives* edited by Ian Brookes. BFI/Pelgrave, 2015, p. 158.

Lovecraft: Fear of the Unknown. Directed by Frank H. Woodward. Wyrd Studios, 2008. Amazon.com

McCarthy, Todd. *Howard Hawks: The Gray Fox of Hollywood.* Grove Press, 1997.

McBride, Joseph. *Hawks on Hawks.* University of California Press, 1982.

Mosby, Aline. "Phil Harris is Swamped with Questions But Won't Say What 'The Thing' Is." The Courier-Journal, Louisville, Ky., 7 Dec. 1950.

Naked Monster, The. Directed by Ted Newsom and Wayne Berwick, Performances by Kenneth Tobey, Robert Cornthwaite, Robert Clarke, Brinke Stevens. Heidelberg Films, 2005.

"Newspaper Fact Sheet." *Pew Research Center.* https://www.journalism.org/fact-sheet/newspapers/

"Newark." *Exhibitor.* 20 June 1951, p. NT-4.

"Odd Movie Produced in Secrecy." *The Charlotte Observer,* 11 Feb. 1951. p. 66.

Othman, Frederick C. "Hollywood Rocked by Theaters' Blast of Ace Film Stars." Courier-Post, Camden NJ. 4 May 1938, p. 6.

Poole, W. Scott. *Wasteland: The Great War and the Origins of Horror.* Counterpoint. Kindle Edition. 2018.

"Producer Gets Colorful Welcome." *Great Falls Tribune,* 15 Nov. 1950. p. 3.

"Richmond." *Exhibitor.* 23 May 1951, p. NT-4.

"RKO Pictures Inc. Trade Showings of Winchester Pictures Corp. Presentation of Howard Hawks' 'The Thing from Another World.'" Motion Picture Daily, Wednesday 28 March 1951, p. 19.

Quigg, Jack. "'The Thing' Puzzling Hollywood." *Oakland Tribune,* 17 Nov. 1950. p. 4-B.

"Ritz" (advertisement). *The Progressive Age,* Scottsboro, AL., 16 August 1951. p.1.

Russ, Patrick. "Regarding Tiomkin's score for The Thing from Another World." Email correspondence with Sean Kotz. July 10, 2021.

Sheridan, Margaret. "I Found Romance in the Mountains." *Modern Screen,* May 1951. p. 36, 114-5.

"Shocking!" (advertisement). *Kokomo Tribune,* 26 June 1951. p. 5

"Sunshine Adds to Troubles of Snow-Seeking Film Crew." *Great Falls Tribune,* 14 Jan. 1951. p. 4.

"The Thing." *National Museum of American History.* https://americanhistory.si.edu/collections/search/object/nmah_670845

The Thing from Another World. Directed by Christian Nyby, produced by Howard Hawks, performances by James Arness, Robert Cornthwaite, Kenneth Tobey, and Margaret Sheridan. Winchester Pictures/RKO, 1951.

"The Thing is Inside" [photo]. *Exhibitor.* 16 May 1951, p. NT-2.

"The Thing May Be Shot Friday." *The Daily Inter Lake* (Kalispell, Montana), Thursday, Jan. 11, 1951, p. 1.

"'The Thing from Another World' is Shocker at the Goldman." *Philadelphia Inquirer,* 26 April 1951, p. 32.

"Third Pal of Trio Lands Film Role." *Fort Worth Star-Telegram,* 22 April 1951, Section 1, p. 9.

Thomas, Bob. "Hollywood." *Opelika Daily News.* Opelika, AL. 7 April 1951. p. 2.

Tobey, Kenneth. Interview with Tom Weaver. Attack of the Monster Movie Makers. McFarland & Co. Inc., 1994, pp. 340-355.

"Two New Pictures North Pole Terror and a Familiar Family." *Kansas City Star*, April 1, 1951, p. F-1.

Turner, George E. "Howard Hawks' Thing from Another World." *Cinefantastique*, vol. 12, no. 5 & 6, July/August, 1982.

Turner, George E. "The Thing from Another World." *American Cinematographer*, 9 April 2020. https://ascmag.com/

Weaver, Tom. "The Thing's Pal." *Starlog Magazine*, Issue 178, May 1992, p. 61-69.

William Self. Interview with Tom Weaver. *Eye on Science Fiction*. McFarland & Company, p. 269-301.

Williams, Tony. "Encountering the Thing from Another World." *CineAction,* vol 84, Spring 2011, p. 56-62.

Wood, Robin. *Howard Hawks*. Doubleday & Company, 1968.

Zeitlin, Ida. "A Tobey and a Peck." *Photoplay*, vol 41, no. 4, April 1952, p. 58-60.

Photos

4

Maj. Jesse Marcel poses with weather balloon debris a day after Western U.S. newspapers reported the U. S. military recovered a flying disc near Roswell, New Mexico in 1947. The "Roswell Incident" was quickly dismissed and forgotten for decades but according to Col. Philip J. Corso in his book *The Day After Roswell*, the weather balloon story was staged and a saucer and occupants were recovered. Corso claimed his agency influenced The Man from Planet X. Credit: Fort Worth Star-Telegram Collection, University of Texas at Arlington Libraries. Major Jesse A. Marcel of Houma, Louisiana. 1947. UTA Libraries Digital Gallery, https://library.uta.edu/digitalgallery/img/10000258. Accessed 21 Dec 2021.

Rotwang, played by Rudolph Klein-Rogge, hovers over the unconscious Maria, Brigitte Helm, in Fritz Lang's groundbreaking science fiction film from 1927, *Metropolis*. He represents the cinematic archetypical "mad scientist," a trope that surged through science fiction film until the 1950s.

The GIGANTIC SERIAL SPECTACLE! 13 CHAPTERS of STRANGE WORLD ADVENTURES!

CARL LAEMMLE presents

FLASH GORDON

BUSTER CRABBE as FLASH GORDON
JEAN ROGERS as DALE ARDEN

CHAPTER 6 "FLAMING TORTURE"

A UNIVERSAL PICTURE

Flash Gordon was a popular character in books and comics even before the movie serials of the 1930s. However, these stories had little if anything to do with science and brought absurd aliens wearing costumes better suited for German opera than serious science fiction.

Before aliens came to us, our films took us to outer space, a more comfortable notion. 1950's *Destination Moon* was a big budget movie striving for realism, as demonstrated by the astronaut's space suits in this lobby card. With the less realistic *Rocketship XM*, the Earth was primed for alien invasion films.

This ad for *The Thing from Another World* exemplifies Howard Hawk's strategy for selling the film—mysteries and enigmas. This one, published on page 20 of *The Film Bulletin*'s April 9 issue, targeted theater owners and promoters, promising in fine print a national circulation of 185,761,000. Interestingly, this suggests a creature closer to that in the source material, John Campbell's *Who Goes There*?

This ad appeared on page 17 of the Kokomo Tribune on June 28, 1951, and utilized press materials supplied to theaters. This time a child in a highchair has just seconds to live if The Thing gets loose. Note the midnight showing and the promise of Danny Kaye, Spike Jones and Frankenstein. Kaye had recorded the Phil Harris novelty song that gave Hawks such fits as production began.

This lobby card for *The Thing* played up offered a Hawksian love story on the left and a classic hero and damsel in distress on the right. However, liked Hawks strong heroines and never once in the film does Nikki (Margaret Sheridan) cower or need such protection nor is any clothing torn from her in the film.

This widely distributed publicity still used in ads and posters for the film emphasizes the "team" approach to facing down danger. Hawks scholar Robin Wood saw Hawks' tendency to create "idealized democracy" in his films. With the soldiers grasping weapons, Dr. Carrington (Robert Cornthwaite), true to character, shines a flashlight.

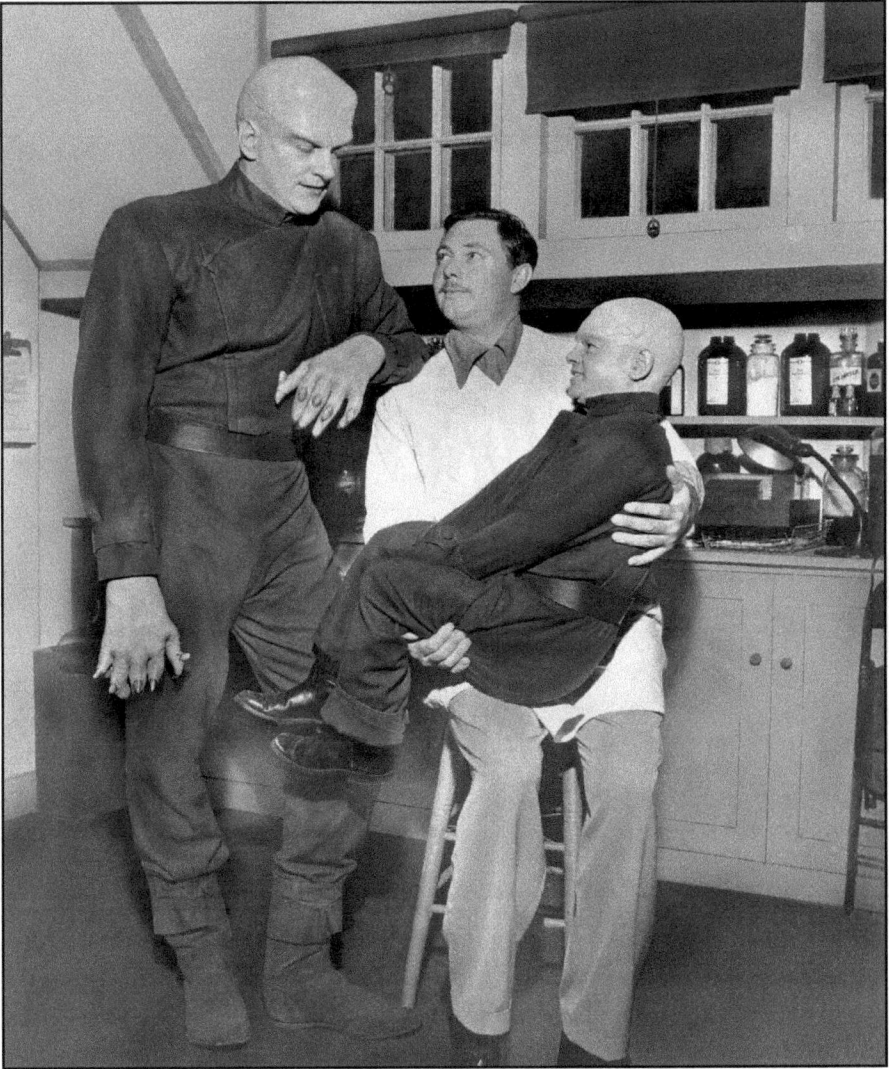

This picture taken before shooting the dramatic climax of *The Thing* features James Arness in full costume, makeup artist Lee Greenway and 4-foot 2-inch actor Billy Curtis. As the electrical arc essentially melts the title character, Curtis appears near the end of the sequence before being replaced by a 12-inch model. It demonstrates not just the process but the care taken by the special effects team.

A photo of the enigmatic "Thing" truck that toured the country stopping at various theaters to promote *The Thing from Another World*. Curious potential customers would walk into the pitch black trailer and get a sudden look at some "thing" in a flash of green light, leaving with a tale to tell. The Messmore and Damon creation is seen here in New Jersey with the managers of the Fabian and the Montauk theaters in the far right. Source: *The Exhibitor*, May 29, 1951, N-4.

Unlike the publicity materials for *The Thing*, the poster *The Day the Earth Stood Still* not only showed its outer space menace, it did so in a fashion worthy of the pulp magazines that inspired it. Supposedly producer Julian Blaustein developed an interest in sci-fi stories a few years before proposing the film.

Page one of a four-page ad spread in the Sept. 11, 1951, issue of *Motion Picture Daily* (and several other magazines) touting the prizes available for the ballyhoo contest sponsored by the studio.

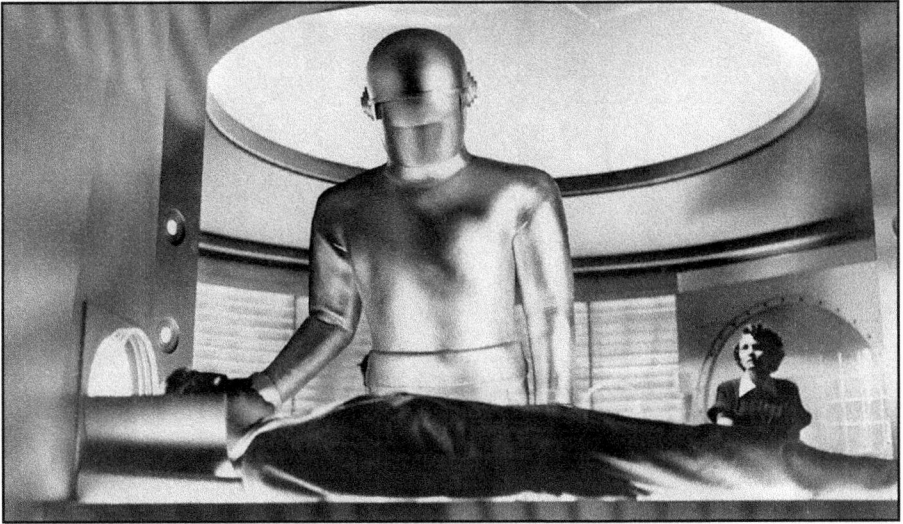

This publicity still was used for lobby cards and other promotions but the scene itself was almost cut as pressure came down from the Breen Office where the Production Code was adjudicated. Klaatu's resurrection by Gort was considered blasphemous and a line had to be added about the power of life and death being reserved for the "Almighty spirit."

Michael Rennie meets with the "real Professor Barnhardt," UCLA's eminent astrophysicist, Dr. Samuel Herrick. Herrick devised a real-world problem for the blackboard seen in the film. Credit: Samuel Herrick Papers, (Ms-1978-002), Special Collections and University Archives, University Libraries, Virginia Polytechnic and State University.

71.

137 (cont.)

Part of blackboard material:

Two body helioentric ellipse

Transitional orbit

Two body geocentric hyperbola

          KLAATU
       (with respect)
I can see that you were breaking down a barrier...
evidnetly you were beginning to wonder why mathematics
mathematicians maxx should be seeking only a
perfect solution to an ideal but unrealistic
problem... without much thought of practical uses...

          BARNHARDT
       (smiling, but with mounting enthusiasm)
Yes... the three-body problem has been almost
like the weather... everybody talking...
nobody doing... It occurred to me that even if we
had a solution, it would be only a somewhat better
approximation than a two-body solution because of the
other perturbations... planetary... equatorial
bulge... lunar... Why not,then, seek any approximation that is better than a two-body solution, even
if only for a limited time and a particular problem,
       (pointing to the blackboard)
such as this transitional orbit for a rocket approaching the earth.

          KLAATU
       (with equal excitement)
And use its constants in place of two-body constants
with a variation of parameters technique...

          BARNHARDT
Exactly...
       (then thoughtfully, as he gestures toward
       the blackboard)
but those darned integrals...

          KLAATU
Clumsy, aren't they... but when you expand them
into series everything below the ninth-order
terms drops out.

          BARNHARDT
       (turning toward the blackboard)
But this... I was working on it as you came in...

          KLAATU
Just keep on differentiating, and then resubstitute
these...
       (forgetting himself)
and then you'll see how good an approximation it
was. It worked fine...

Script page from the drafting process showing Dr. Herrick's notes and dialog suggestions to add validity to the discussion. In the end, much of this was simplified and rearranged. Credit: Samuel Herrick Papers, (Ms-1978-002), Special Collections and University Archives, University Libraries, Virginia Polytechnic and State University.

This ad ran as the back page of the May 2, 1951 issue of *Motion Picture Daily*. The producers make no secret about its exploitation potential.

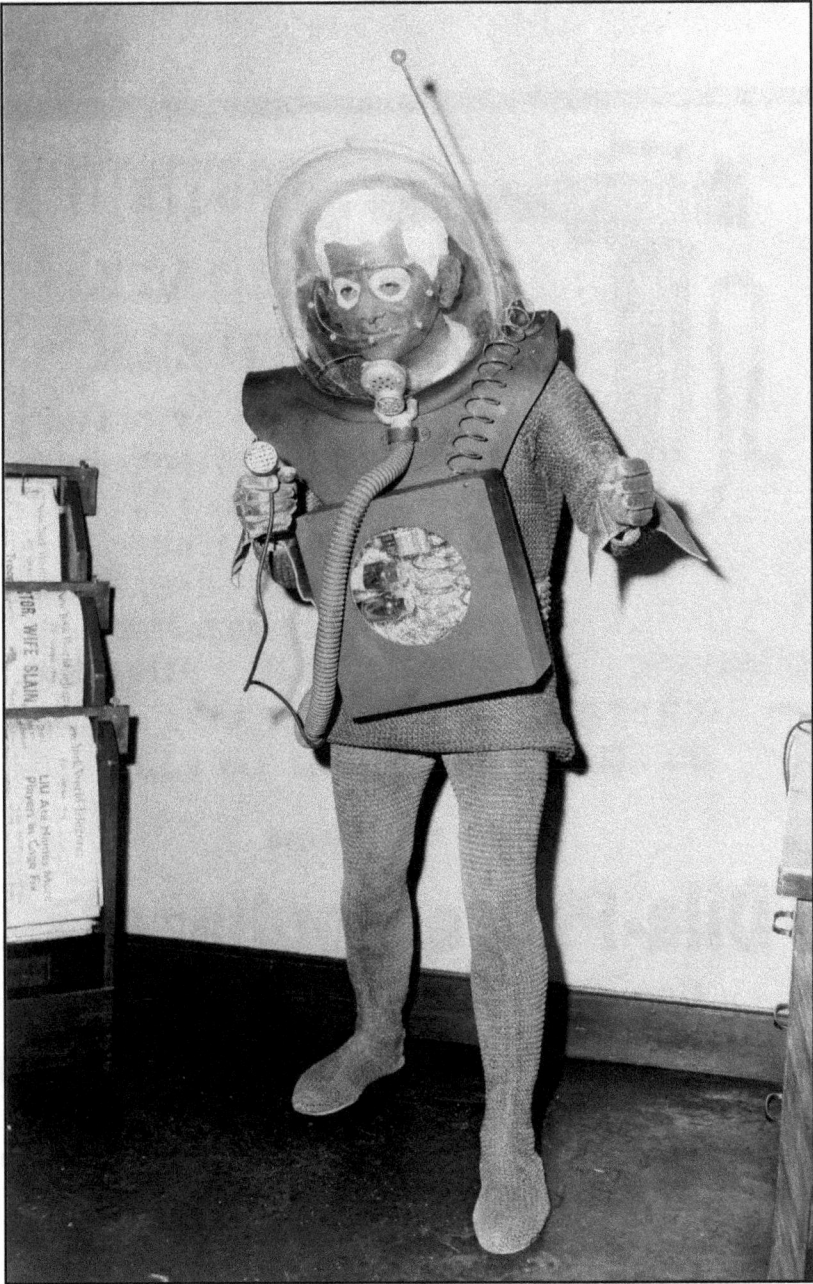

World Telegram photographer Dick DeMarsico took this shot of an actor or perhaps an employee of the Mayfair Theater posing as the X man to drum up ticket sales.

The "Dila-Therm" was a bogus prostate relief device the Federal Trade Commission clamped down on in 1950. In a few months, it made an appearance as the X man's ray gun.

The Day the Earth Stood Still

5

On January 1, 1951, syndicated writer Robert C. Ruark began his column with an odd hope for the coming year. "If I had just one wish to make for the infant year of '51 it would be that the flying saucer business turns out to be true and that some spaceship would land in every major capital of the world." With sentiments that President Ronald Reagan, a product of 1950s Hollywood, would echo before the United Nations decades later, Ruark thought that such an event might just unite a fractured planet. "It seems to me that mankind is ripe for a big scare—the sudden threat of extinction for everybody, before we fritter away the nice place the world has been, is and could be" (12). He'd get his wish symbolically on the silver screen nine months later when 20th Century Fox would finally give birth to *The Day the Earth Stood Still*.

In contrast to *The Thing from Another World*, which charts out the most common "Us vs. Them" theme of alien invasion cinema, *The Day the Earth Stood Still* offers a different kind of terror—the recognition that the problem is not "Them" at all. The problem is "Us." And while it can be classed as a nuclear war parable, it drills down to the root causes. As writer Sydney Perkowitz puts it, "Although some films use the sheer, unthinking violence of a nuclear bomb, *The Day the Earth Stood Still* (1951) is different, presenting moral issues instead of explosions" (96-97). That difference elevates the film to a superior thematic position compared to its two main competitors in 1951 and most before and after it.

Such a philosophically rooted film always comes with box office risks. *The Thing*'s good guy/bad guy story simply works more universally, echoing human fear of difference lodged so deeply in our psyches that it goes unquestioned. In other words, it's an easy sell. The straightforward conflict keeps people both engaged and entertained, and while there might be bad guys along the way, the finger doesn't point back to humanity itself. However, to ask the audience to see itself as fearful, primitive, self-destructive agents of our own woes requires more from both the film makers and the viewers in terms of subtly and honesty. Where *The Thing* creates a novel monster symbolizing the new potentiality of total planetary annihilation, it still works in a well-established format. *Day*, in contrast, embodies the painful reality that containing the monster of annihilation falls on the shoulders of squabbling, irresponsible children willfully creating it. Which, one may ask, is more frightening?

FAREWELL TO THE MASTER

Like *The Thing from Another World*, *The Day the Earth Stood Still* originated from a story first printed in a pulp publication. "Farewell to the Master" by Harry Bates appeared in *Astounding Science Fiction* magazine's October 1940 issue, a publication Bates edited in its first years (1930-33) before publisher William Clayton succumbed to bankruptcy and sold it to Street and Smith. Unfortunately for Bates, he never made any real money on the movie and this "left him embittered and unwilling to discuss the film" (Taylor and Finch 72). Producer Julian Blaustein initiated a search for potential science fiction source material and thought it would make a good film. He convinced 20th Century Fox to exchange the paltry sum of $1000 to Street and Smith, the official owners, for the rights. Bates apparently got just half that and never saw another penny on it even though Marvel Comics produced a version of the story in 1973 for their *Worlds Unknown* series.

Bates' tale differs radically from the film and according to screenwriter Edmund North they really just wanted the rights to the most basic elements. "The story had an interesting opening: it had the idea of a spaceship landing in Washington, on the Mall, and out of the spaceship came a man-like figure and a robot," North told Joel Gardener in 1980 for the UCLA archives. "What they bought it for was the idea of the spaceship landing in Washington," according to North, but a few other elements saw expression in the film as well.

"Farewell to the Master" follows a photographer/reporter, Cliff Sutherland, who comes each day to an "exhibit" memorializing a tragic event. In the story, humanity has attained limited space flight and colonized other places in the Solar System, but not made alien contact. We learn that a beautiful humanoid space traveler named Klaatu and a giant robot called Gnut in Bate's tale have come to make peaceful contact only for Klaatu to get assassinated by a religious fanatic who claims "the devil had come to kill everyone on earth" (Bates 4). Gnut freezes in place almost immediately and when doctors cannot revive Klaatu, the people construct a mausoleum nearby, memorializing his only words on Earth with a brief recording: "I am Klaatu and this is Gnut" (4). The spaceship, Gnut, and Klaatu's tomb all become (in Washington D.C. fashion) an enclosed museum.

Sutherland, obsessed with the whole thing, believes he has noticed slight position changes in Gnut over time, indicating that when the exhibit is closed, the robot moves about. He hides to solve the mystery but Gnut discovers him. Sutherland expects to get pummeled by the robot, an 8-foot-tall giant made of a flexible green metal with blazing red eyes. Instead, it goes into the ship, seemingly to continue its clandestine work. Two animals come out of the ship, a mockingbird and a fearsome gorilla (which turn out to be part of an experiment). The gorilla smashes up six government installed robotic museum attendants before it finally dies in a confrontation with Gnut, who shows an expression of sadness on metal his face.

Cliff returns the following day, after the destruction has been discovered, not revealing to other reporters he's witnessed the chaos. He returns the next night and witnesses the death of a man, Stillwell, an actor who narrates the official recorded story played for visitors to the exhibit. Sutherland is caught, arrested and interrogated, and conscripted to stay a third night and report on whatever events take place for billions of viewers. Meanwhile, Gnut gets encased in "glasstex" (Bates 23) but melts his way out late at night to continue his mysterious task.

Sutherland ends up inside the ship and learns Gnut has cloned Klaatu from the recording made just before he's slain. Klaatu does not last long, but before he expires, he tells Sutherland that, "unlike us, Gnut has great powers" (Bates 26). Apparently, Gnut can analyze the sound waves to make a reproduction, but an imperfect recording yields an imperfect (and doomed) clone. When Gnut learns the original recording apparatus could be obtained, he speaks for the first time, aggressively: "Give me that apparatus!" (27).

Sutherland stays with the second Klaatu until he dies and Gnut hands his body to the regretful reporter. Speaking to Gnut, he says, "'Listen carefully. I want you to tell your master—the master yet to come—that what happened to the first Klaatu was an accident, for which all Earth is immeasurably sorry. Will you do that?'" (Bates 27). Gnut's reply comes as a twist ending in an age before such things were common: "'You misunderstand,' the mighty robot had said. 'I am the master'" (28).

The original story has its merits, but cinematically, would not make much of a splash and would likely have come over as absurd. The material might have worked in a 25 minute *Twilight Zone* episode, but it offers no characters or relationships to develop for a feature length film. Additionally, "Farewell to the Master" was written before the menace of nuclear war and in the time of production, that reigned as the number one international issue. The story has its die-hard defenders, but by comparison, the film exceeds its mark in every way.

ROBERT WISE: THE NON-AUTEUR AUTEUR

It doesn't take long for a someone dipping a toe into the waters of film study to hear the term "Auteur Theory." The concept developed in the pages of the French post-WWII film journal *Cahiers du Cinéma*, where writers André Bazin, Alexandre Astruc and (later) director François Truffaut, stressed the role of the individual director as the primary "author" (i.e., *le auteur*). They suggested the best directors developed a personal style that allowed for individually nuanced expression, holding a highly cultivated uniqueness in the highest aesthetic esteem. The concept got an American translation in Andrew Sarris' short but influential essay, "Notes on Auteur Theory" in 1962, which offered it as the basis for rewarding critical film study. Thus, directors like John Ford, Alfred Hitchcock and Howard Hawks with distinctive methods and identifiable qualities garner much attention in this context.

However, that approach, which took hold just as most academic film studies programs developed in the United States, leaves a director like Robert Wise out of the discussion. Wise was the most versatile director of his generation with an extreme gift for adapting his methods to the story material. Where *The Thing from Another World* is so distinctively "Hawksian" that most fans and critics dismiss the role of director Christian Nyby, *The Day the Earth Stood Still* does not bespeak a specific established directorial style. Instead, it creates a form to be copied (generally poorly) by others with Wise himself in the background. As Richard Keenan puts it, "Wise lacks the ego and temperament of the artist—but his painstaking craftsmanship has created such truly great films as the film noir classic *The Set Up* (1949) and *West Side Story* (1961), which Bosley Crowther of the *New York Times* described as 'nothing short of a cinematic masterpiece" (vii). A brief list of Wise's filmography reveals how many great films he directed across the spectrum of genres including *Somebody Up There Likes Me* (1956), *Run Silent, Run Deep* (1958), *Odds Against Tomorrow* (1959), *The Haunting* (1963), and *The Sound of Music* (1965).

Wise dropped out of Franklin College in Indiana at the height of the Great Depression in 1933 and headed west to join his brother David, an accountant, at RKO for some work... any work... at the studio. He became a film porter in the editing department, running prints back and forth for RKO's technical staff to directors and executives. There he learned not just the techniques but how to apply them to different formats and how editing could make or break a movie. Wise parlayed that into a shot at editing in 1939 with *Bachelor Mother* and *The Hunchback of Notre Dame* with Charles Laughton before moving on to work with Orson Welles on *Citizen Kane* (1942) and *The Magnificent Ambersons* (1942).

Welles, whose Golden Boy status at RKO was rapidly turning to dust, began splitting his time between *Ambersons* and work for the state department to produce a Good Neighbor film for Brazil as part of the early war propaganda push. He also simultaneously rushed *Journey Into Fear* (1942) into production to finalize his commitment to the studio. Early cuts of *The Magnificent Ambersons* yielded laughter and walk-outs with test audiences, requiring cuts and new scenes on the fly, at least one of which fell to Wise as his first true directing opportunity (Leeman 57-59).

Wise's premiere feature film as a director, *Curse of the Cat People* (1944), picked up where the source film, the Jacques Tournuer/Val Lewton masterpiece *The Cat People* (1942) left off, this time as a ghost story. After the success of Universal's horror classics, RKO producer Val Lewton was charged with producing six horror films with just three stipulations—the budget could not exceed $150,000, the films must not exceed 75 minutes and they must be based on titles (typically sensationalized) supplied by the RKO execs. These conditions forced Lewton to eschew special effects in favor of psychological horror, inventing in the process a new direction for the genre. Wise's offering, *Curse of the Cat People*, rounded out the original six films brilliantly. "Despite its lurid title (assigned by the studio), *The Curse of the Cat People* is a dreamy and poetic tale about Amy, an imaginative young child played by [Amy] Carter, who is punished for the beauty, delicacy, and poignancy of her melancholy reveries" (Nemerov).

Wise's opportunity came, like so many others, when the original selection for director got canned in favor of a younger, hungrier and faster talent. Wise was editing the film instead when Lewton and B-unit executive Sid Rogell called him for a lunch and offered him the director's chair. They wanted him to take over on Monday, but Wise had to return to the set that Saturday to work with the oblivious director Gunter von Fritch, making Wise uneasy. Rogell told him Fritch would be out on Monday no matter what and someone would be there, whether that was Wise or not:

> I knew it was the chance I had been waiting for and simply said, "I'll be there." Fortunately, I'd been on the set and knew the people I was going to work with. I only had a little problem with the production manager. I guess he was disappointed that he wasn't given the opportunity to take over. So much so that, at the end of the second day, I had to turn on him and tell him that if he didn't like it he could leave the picture. From then on he was fine. (Leeman 65)

Between *Curse of the Cat People* and *The Day the Earth Stood Still*, Wise helmed 11 features including the atmospheric thrillers, *The Body Snatcher* (1945) with Boris Karloff and Bela Lugosi, and *The House on Telegraph Hill* (1951). In 1950, he directed Patricia Neal (later to become Helen Benson in *Day)* in *Three Secrets* for Warner Bros. in a standalone deal. A decidedly heavy drama originally titled *The Rock Bottom,* it was the first of three pictures he'd do with Neal, who was cast before a director was chosen. Wise, familiar with Neal's work, saw it as an opportunity to work with an actress he admired (Leeman 94).

The studio announced that Wise would direct *The Day the Earth Stood Still* in a press release that hit the papers on March 19. The film came between *The House on Telegraph Hill* (1951) and *The Captive City* (1952) in the dead center of a six film contract he had with 20th Century Fox. But Wise knew this one had potential for cultural impact as a so called "message film." "'Interestingly enough, I made seven or eight pictures for 20th Century Fox between 1950 and 1957,'" Wise told Allan Asherman, "and without question, *The Day the Earth Stood Still* is the one I was most keenly interested in doing'" (72).

As a director, Wise seems to have garnered nearly unanimous re-spect and love. His reputation as a willing collaborator and an approach-able leader interested in maintaining goodwill on the set trademarks his career. "I have really great memories of him," Bill Gray (Bobby Benson) recalled, noting that Wise made several kind remarks about his acting over the years. "With no real effort on his part, he was just a really sweet guy" (Gray).

MICHAEL RENNIE

As Richard Keenan wrote, "A number of factors come together to make *The Day the Earth Stood Still* a memorable film, not the least of which is the polished and urbane performance of Michael Rennie" (74). Rennie graduated from Leys College, a Cambridge boarding school, at 18 and worked in his family wool mill, eventually becoming manager. He took a job working at a rope plant his uncle managed but wanted to become an actor, a path his uncle might have aided as a chair of a theater chain but offered Rennie no connections. He tried selling automobiles for a while but was forced to work for his uncle until he finally found his way to act-ing through his own perseverance (Asherman 75-76).

Rennie was 29 years old when World War II broke out. He enlisted in the Royal Air Force but was deemed too old to fly initially. The age limit lifted as the crisis surged but Rennie had to wait six months before train-ing could begin. He used the time to make British war pictures, *Danger-ous Moonlight* (1940), *The Big Blockade*, *Pimpernel Smith*, and *Ships with Wings* (all 1941). None of these were starring roles, but he did play the heroic and romantic lead in the 1941 film, *Tower of Terror*, an espionage flick Rennie considered his worst film. Eventually he'd complete his flight training but found himself state-side for the duration of the war as a flight instructor for the US Army Air Force, a fate that seems symbolic of his ca-reer. Capable, prepared and willing, he'd spend much of his acting career just behind the front, so to speak.

Rennie had no trouble finding work in general, however. He ap-peared in several films between the end of the war and *The Day the Earth Stood Still*, but did not translate as a lead very frequently, perhaps due to his palpable English control and reserve, or perhaps because he was, once again, just a little too old. Instead, Rennie's bearing enabled him better for roles of authority like the Centurion in *Caesar and Cleopa-*

tra (1945), King Edward in *The Black Rose* (1950), and the tragic Major George Templeton in *Trio* (1950), who finds love only to die a short time later. This quality would keep in him in film and television work throughout his life, playing a number of political and military leaders including British icon, General Bernard "Monty" Montgomery in *The Battle of El Alamein* (1969).

Rennie's arrival at Fox seems almost like a destiny. Reportedly, Tyrone Power first recommended Rennie for a contract to Darryl Zanuck, 20th Century Fox's head, but it was screen tests from *Trio* sent by London talent executive Ben Lyons that inspired Zanuck (Asherman 77). However, he seems to have been on Zanuck's radar well before that, as Louella Parsons reported in September of 1946 that "20th Century is trying to borrow actor Michael Rennie, British actor for 'Forever Amber'... After Zanuck saw Rennie in 'Root of All Evil' with Phyllis Calvert, and in another movie with Margaret Lockwood, he cabled Rennie's agent" (9). Variations on this story exist, but Zanuck definitely wanted Rennie who was happy to leave the struggling British film industry behind. He began his contract by working on *I'll Never Forget You* (1951) for Fox prior to being cast as Klaatu. The role essentially defined his type and he fulfilled it so completely that he would play Klaatu again for the Lux Radio Hour on January 4, 1954.

Just as production began, a syndicated article came out by Harold Heffernan about the tendency for producers and directors to choose relative unknowns for science fiction roles to increase believability. His appraisal of Rennie's casting seems spot on: "the six-foot-four leading man was chosen because of the photogenic dignity of his features, his high cheekbones, angular jaw and lack of resemblance to any established star" (15). For Americans, he was a newcomer and his British polish and reserve seems simultaneously comforting and alien. In his interview with Tom Weaver, Robert Wise recalled Rennie as a consummate professional who believed in the anti-war message of the film and was "very good to work with, a warm and easy going guy" (345). Bill Gray remembers Rennie as a "super-professional actor," who maintained his carriage of dignity on and off screen and leveraged his cultured English charm. Gray recalled, "He was very solicitous of my mother, who was a very good looking woman. Attentive in the extreme, making sure she always had a chair and things like that."

I am Klaatu

Michael Rennie's best remembered role almost went to someone else. Apparently, Zanuck first suggested Spencer Tracy, but Blaustein argued that if a movie star of his caliber stepped off the spaceship, people would not take it seriously (Rubin 22). "Claude Rains had been [Wise's] first choice for the part, largely based on his previous performances in similar roles, particularly as a supernatural emissary in Alexander Hall's *Here Comes Mr. Jordan* (1941) and Archie Mayo's *Angel on My* Shoulder (1946)" (Keenan 72). Rains had also brought his talents to *The Invisible Man* (1933) and *The Wolf Man* (1941), making him a familiar face for genre fans. He also had a distinct and commanding voice appropriate for the role, but he was tied up with a play in New York and instead it went to Rennie. Robert Wise said on several occasions that casting Rennie instead was a stroke of good fortune and credited Zanuck for stepping in to cast him. "So that's one of those lucky breaks that happened, so much better for us than having a known actor like Claude Rains" (Wise, Kreisler Interview).

Ultimately, as Wise suggests, this was probably a good thing not just for Rennie but the film as well. His slender six-foot four-inch frame (Rains was 5' 7") has a distancing, otherworldly quality, and he naturally looks down on everyone in the film (except, of course, for Gort). From the outset, Klaatu's moral superiority finds visual reinforcement as he towers over the "shoot first and ask questions later" humans and he embodies a Spartan, almost ascetic manner. Despite his sincere interest in Bobby and respect for Helen, Klaatu never cultivates anything akin to a family relationship and his physical detachment from the norm helps form the character into a believable representative of an advanced society.

In North's February 21 script draft, we can see he has this enlightened detachment in mind for Klaatu. When Klaatu first arrives, North tells us: "Klaatu is above all an impressive man—a man of tremendous dignity and presence. He has the tolerant superiority that comes with absolute knowledge." Later, when Harley comes to visit Klaatu in the hospital, the dignity never waivers. "Even sitting up in bed, with his shoulder strapped in bandages, he is a figure of great authority. His face reflects inner dignity and assurance." In the final scenes, "he is a figure of intense dignity in his impressive otherworld tunic. He stares with even defiance at the armed soldiers, as though holding them off by sheer weight of his personality."

The film develops Klaatu's character with a sense of mystery to enhance all this. We don't know what planet he comes from (though Mars is a good guess based on the 250 million miles he claims to travel). We never know exactly how he escapes the hospital or acquires L. M. Carpenter's dry cleaning. When he and Bobby arrive at Barnhardt's house, the door is definitely locked, but Klaatu seems to open it with ease, implying he has some degree of power he transfers through his hands to the tumblers. And ultimately, his resurrection is a byproduct of science but its mechanics lies beyond our understanding, reminding one of Arthur C. Clarke's famous observation: "Any sufficiently advanced technology is indistinguishable from magic."

The enlightened power envisioned in the character helps develop Klaatu's symbolic connection to Christ, a link so hard to miss it seems almost cliché to mention it. He arrives on Earth from the heavens with a mission to save humanity that demands we consciously change our moral course. If Christ's new commandment is for mankind to love one another unconditionally (John 13:34-35), then there would be no greater expression than to follow Klaatu's commandment to discontinue our self-interested and violent ways. We can see the basic elements of the Christian story in Klaatu's adopted name, Carpenter, Tom's betrayal of Klaatu for money, and Klaatu's persecution, death and resurrection. He even emerges as the saucer wall slides away from his surrogate tomb to address humanity one last time before ascending, quite literally, to the sky. Supposedly, 20th Century Fox head Darryl Zanuck saw the connection in the script and told Claude Rains he'd be playing a "'modern Christ'" (Wise, Weaver Interview, 346).

Oddly enough, Robert Wise claimed no conscious effort to create this symbolism but understood how people would see it in the film, in no small part because of Rennie, whom he called a "tall, thin, ascetic, almost unreal visitor from the heavens" (Taylor and Finch 73). Rather than reject that reading, Wise saw it as "another valid interpretation of a multi-layered, carefully conceived work" (73). "Once we had it pointed out to us, we felt like, 'Of course!' and we didn't know why we had not seen it! I had the book too close to my face, I think" (Wise, Weaver Interview, 346).

However, for writer Edmund North, the allegory was not only there, but something of a "private little joke" (Rubin 18) that he never discussed with the producer or director. He wanted the audience to receive it subliminally rather than as a Sunday school lesson and claimed nobody ever mentioned it until it started appearing on network television 10 years later. The allegory "gave the film a kind of form and was there for anyone who wanted to see it," he told Steve Rubin, "but I don't think it was part of the fabric," adding that if no one had ever acknowledged the Klaatu-Christ parallels it would not have bothered him (22).

However, the allegory did not escape the Breen Office, Hollywood's moral clearinghouse that enforced the Production Code. "[T]he censors were particularly sensitive to the possibility that the Klaatu-Christ parallel was verging on blasphemy" (Keenen 72) and blatant efforts to sidestep this show in the final cut. One of the most obvious comes after Gort revives Klaatu temporarily and Helen asks if Gort "has the power over life and death." "No," the alien replies with a slight smile, "that is a power reserved to the Almighty Spirit." Naturally, this confirms the reigning Christian cosmology and allows one to believe Klaatu is simply closer to its source. Edmund North called this a "foolish compromise" to placate the censors. "It was a really nasty confrontation that had us all boiling over. The Breen office certainly made life difficult for us" (Rubin 22).

Wise's concentration on the surface level anti-war message seems to have been a blessing. The Christ symbolism could easily have come over as heavy-handed with the wrong director, but instead, concentrating on the primary message lends power to the symbolic one in Klaatu's final statement: "Your choice is simple. Join us and live in peace or pursue your present path and face obliteration. We will be waiting for your answer. The decision rests with you." For what it is worth, consider this same speech without all the Judeo-Christian symbolism to simultaneously anchor and mystify it… it might well have been considered "Red" propaganda.

PATRICIA NEAL

The Day the Earth Stood Still benefits greatly from the talented Patricia Neal who portrays the grounded and subtly world-weary secretary, Helen Benson. Neal was only 25 years old when she took the part of a war widow with a pre-teen son, though her bearing in the film carries her character beyond such youth. Physically, the five-foot eight actress projected maturity, and while she was once Northwestern University's 1946 "Syllabus Queen," Neal's broad, strong face, jutting chin and raspy voice gave her significant presence and gravity on screen not found in Hollywood's pin-up girls.

Unlike Margaret Sheridan, Neal had studied acting extensively in high school and college and spent significant time on stage before her film career. She honed her craft on Broadway, capturing a Tony in 1947 (the first year of the award) for her performance as Regina Hubbard in Lillian Hellman's play, *Another Part of the Forest*. She and Hellman would remain close friends and it was Hellman who ultimately introduced her to her future husband, Roald Dahl, the famed British writer.

Patricia Neal's life played out like a character in a Greek tragedy, complete with triumphs and tumbles, irony and pathos. On one hand, her talent and good fortune abounded, and she garnered instant respect with her ability to play drama with compelling realism. She parlayed her rapid stage success into a film contract with Warner Bros. and starred opposite of Ronald Reagan in 1949's *John Loves Mary*. Her second role, as Dominique Francon, deposited her with Gary Cooper in *The Fountainhead* (1949), igniting an off-screen romance that resulted in an aborted pregnancy in early 1951 while she was filming *Operation Pacific* with John Wayne.

In her autobiography, *As I Am*, Neal speaks candidly about her affair with Cooper, who had something of an open marriage, though it still required discretion. She recalled that initially both wanted to keep the child but "the next morning my joy, my strength drained out of me as rational terrors whipped my brain. Career. Family. Oh God—my Mother! She would kill herself if I had a baby out of wedlock!" (133).

At the same time, Warner Bros. did not renew her contract and she wound up at 20th Century Fox soon after to take her first assignment there, *The Day the Earth Stood Still*. She was not eager to take the part as a sci-fi movie seemed a step down in 1951, but she "did not want to begin my career at Fox by going on suspension" (Neal 136). The film reunited her with an old friend, Hugh Marlowe, who starred with her in a touring company version of *Turtle* years before. It also introduced her to Michael Rennie, another lifelong friend.

Neal has little say of her most famous film in her autobiography, though she considered it the best science fiction movie ever made. Instead, the social pressure of the moment dominated her life. Gary Cooper's marriage publicly dissolved while she filmed T*he Day the Earth Stood Still* and Neal was hounded as the catalyst while trying to concentrate on the role. She had lost her status as the "young darling of Hollywood" and was instead a juicy target for gossip and sensationalism, "the unsympathetic side of a triangle" (Neal 136). The situation became so bad that eventually Michael Rennie suggested that each time the press asked her about her role in the breakup, she should reply with a line from the film: "*Klattu barada nikto*" (136). (Ironically, she reported struggling with the line in the film, having to bite her lip to keep from laughing in rehearsals until Rennie finally asked if she planned to do it that way on screen.)

"The press was relentless now," she wrote. "They followed me everywhere, even onto the set, but I would not speak to them" (136). Instead, Fox's publicity people made up responses for her as quotations that ranged from innocent to "haughty," but the results did little to stem the needling. Louella Parsons wrote in her column for the August 1951 issue of *Modern Screen* that the public should not entirely blame Cooper for the breakup, suggesting Rocky's (his wife) social demands were partly to blame... before setting her sights on Neal:

> Two days before Gary's return (from Florida), Patricia Neal popped off in the newspapers that she had "nothing to do" with the Cooper's parting and was very "upset" that her name was being gossiped into the case.
>
> Why Pat felt she had to say anything, I'll never know. No one has officially mentioned her in the case, certainly not Mrs. Cooper, and her outburst drew a lot of attention her way she might have escaped (19).

Ironically, of course, Neal was silent and Parson's chiding of the "outburst" should have been addressed to 20th Century Fox's PR department. And in another twist, two issues later Parsons would describe Patricia Neal as Cooper's "new heart" in the same column for the same publication without additional comment (7). This would have hit the newsstands just weeks before the film came out.

Patricia Neal's life would continue to provide significant peaks and valleys. She would go on to win an Oscar for her performance in *Hud* (1963) and a Golden Globe for her role as Olivia Walton in *The Homecoming: A Christmas Story*, the film that would give birth to the long running CBS drama, *The Waltons*. (Neal's uncertain health led to Michael Learned getting the television role, for which she won three Emmys.) Her marriage to Roald Dahl in 1953 produced five children before it came to an end after his 11 year affair with Felicity Crosland was too much to bear. In 1960, her four-month-old son's baby carriage was hit by a taxi cab, causing the child significant brain damage. Two years later, her first child, Olivia, who was never vaccinated for measles, died at the age of seven from encephalitis in 1962. And then in 1965, while pregnant with her youngest daughter Lucy, she suffered three cerebral aneurysms and fell into a coma for three weeks. She had to relearn basic motor skills and how to speak before returning to acting.

THIS IS MRS. BENSON

Despite the stress and angst in her personal life—and perhaps in some degree because of it—Neal's performance has great depth and believably. As Richard Keenan puts it, "Patricia Neal's portrayal of the strong but emotionally vulnerable young war-widow offers, in proper balance, a sense of mystification and hesitant trust" (74). He also notes "Neal had begun to establish a screen personality as a woman whose wit and charm were inextricably tied to a certain formidability and strength of character" (59). These qualities require a careful balance, especially in the 1950s, when independent women were neither common nor encouraged much in cinema. "Wilting flowers" populated female roles in genre films from horrors to Westerns by default, and a woman's primary power came either from her desirability before marriage or her maternal suitability afterward.

This makes Helen's dilemma in *The Day the Earth Stood Still* more poignant. As a war widow, her status as a single mother had instant acceptability, validity and sympathy in 1951 (as opposed to a divorcee or unmarried woman). She works as a secretary for an unnamed government agency in the nation's capital, but this would pay her very little, explaining why she must raise her son in a boarding house. Social and financial pressures to marry a stable man for the sake of her child and future welfare would register with the film's first audiences and they'd see the practicality of hitching her wagon to Tom Stevens (Hugh Marlowe) even if she was not really in love with the horse that pulled it.

Helen functions as a second protagonist in the film, one of Klaatu's few allies, and the key to completing his mission. Klaatu confides in her as she rides with him in the cab meant to take him to Barnhardt where he can address representatives of various nations. While in the taxi, Klaatu tells her he's concerned about what Gort might do if the soldiers capture or kill him. "There's no limit to what he could do. He could destroy the Earth. If anything should happen to me, you must go to Gort. You must say these words: Klaatu barada nikto." As noted above, Neal struggled to keep a straight face during rehearsals of the cab scene, but the line, which she ultimately delivers with grave seriousness, became iconic in science fiction. The phrase is not merely a directive to resurrect Klaatu; rather it reflects his wish to give humanity one last chance, in no small measure because of what he sees in Helen.

As Helen arrives at the spaceship, Gort is in the process of disintegrating the block of "KL 93," a clear plastic substance "stronger than steel" supposed to immobilize him. He's just vaporized two guards when she walks up. Gort glows as the KL 93 melts away and she stops in fearful apprehension. She now knows better than anyone on the planet just how dangerous Gort can be and must conquer her fear to deliver the message that will save the world, at least temporarily. Gort approaches her. Her lips quiver and she swallows hard as she draws deep breaths. She backs against a wall and falls with a fearful scream. Gort stops and his visor rises. Here she calms herself and delivers the message: "Klaatu barada nikto" emphatically as the camera pulls her into a full close up.

While the scream might lead one to dismiss Helen's character as just another helpless woman in a sea of sci-fi heroines, she's just the opposite both before and after this moment. She's dignified and thoughtful, and takes time with her decisions, showing no impulse toward rashness. Her moment of primal fear makes sense based on what she knows and has witnessed, and without it, the film might lose some of its tension. Moreover, this scene gives Patricia Neal the single most important line in the film, something rarely entrusted to women in this period, especially in a genre film. If the filmmakers had wanted to reinforce stereotypes, a man would have delivered that line, most likely Professor Barnhardt. But we know and appreciate Helen's struggles, her values and independent decisions. She's the kind of person who justifies hope for the world and the best possible choice to carry the message to Gort.

BILLY GRAY

By the time Bill Gray got the role of Bobby Benson, he'd already appeared in dozens of films, typically without screen credit. The California native began acting professionally after an incident in a playhouse where his older brother was performing. "I was running around in the audience, making a pest of myself, at about five or six years old. A lady asked me to take her to my mother. It turned out that, totally by coincidence, that lady was my mother's agent," Gray told Michael Stein in *Filmfax* 96 (57). His mother, Beatrice Gray, was a veteran of '40s and '50s Westerns. Much of her work went without screen credit as well, but she had a few starring roles and knew how to make a living in Hollywood. She only appeared in a movie with her son once (in separate scenes), in *Abbot and Costello meet Boris Karloff, the Killer* (1949), but she was there on set whenever Billy had work.

Gray's roles increased and improved in 1949 and '50 with two higher profile film appearances right before playing Bobby Benson. He played the title character of Jim *Thorpe—All American* (1951) as a child and the troublesome little brother to Doris Day in *On Moonlight Bay* (1951). "I seemed to get every interview I went on," Gray said. "And I loved it. I was a smart-assed kid and I loved the whole thing" (Gray). Still, Gray had to audition for the part against other competition but never questioned whether he'd get it, especially since he'd been running hot for a few years.

Ultimately, Gray would go on to have one of the best careers of any child star in the 1950s, doing both movies and TV, including his most famous role, James "Bud" Anderson, Jr., the son on *Father Knows Best* (1954-1960) where he earned an Emmy nomination. Gray displayed a genius for physical comedy and became the first on screen kid to spend most of his time in blue jeans. Just after the show ended, a possession of marijuana arrest clipped his entertainment career significantly, but he became a successful Class A motorcycle racer on the California circuit. (He'd actually started while working on *Father Knows Best* but when the producers found out, they clamped down... though he still rode a bike to work each day, which he said was much more dangerous.) Gray, a lifelong tinkerer, has several inventions and innovations to his credit including a back massager, guitar accessories and a marine hose clip.

CAN I HELP YOU LOOK FOR THE SPACEMAN?

In general, kids don't appear too frequently in science fiction films, especially in the 1950s, and when they do, often kids constitute the target audience. Given the overwhelming atomic paranoia themes of the time, if kids do find their way to these pictures, they tend to appear as catalysts for the plot. For example, Pepe from *20 Million Miles to Earth* (1957) discovers the Ymir egg and causes some trouble along the way, but he's more or less forgotten after he's served his purpose. Exceptions to the draw-play-discard rule regarding children in sci-fi like Jimmy Hunt's David from *Invaders from Mars* (1953) and several 30 year old "teenagers" fighting space blobs and giant spiders exist, of course. However, Bobby

Benson constitutes a critical element of the film, a fully conceived character whose actions affect both the plot and its message.

We meet Bobby and his mother when Mr. Carpenter first comes to the boarding house looking for a room. The boarders are arranged in a semi-circle, backs to the camera, facing Drew Pearson's television broadcast. He's just made the tension-inducing observation that Klaatu might be "our bitter enemy, he could be also a newfound friend." In a carefully choreographed moment, Bobby turns to his mother to ask a question and his eye catches Klaatu who has entered the house unnoticed. Just as Pearson remarks that no existing photographs show his face, the camera reverses direction to reveal Klaatu's backlit, shadowy figure standing as motionless as Gort. The low angle shot subtly replicates Bobby's point of view from the floor. He steps deeper into the shadows and it's important to remember that a first time audience would still have no clear idea of his intentions, a quandary reinforced by Pearson saying in the otherwise silent room, "We may be up against powers beyond our control."

While most of the group project nervous apprehension toward Klaatu, Helen smiles warmly and Bobby runs with the hope that he might be an FBI man needing help looking for the spaceman, who has "a big square head and three great big eyes!" It is an introduction to both characters, but with Bobby, this scene establishes his basic personality traits—exuberance, curiosity, friendliness and imagination. So far, Klaatu has seen little to recommend our species—he's experienced prejudice, ignorance, self-interest and violence firsthand—but Bobby is the first person to offer him more laudable qualities. Charmed by the boy, he smiles for the first time in the film in a way that doesn't suggest superiority and as the plot ultimately unravels, there is reason to believe that Bobby offers the species some redemption, so to speak, in Klaatu's eyes.

The following day Bobby leads Klaatu on a tour of the city, starting with Arlington National Cemetery, where Bobby's father rests, a victim of the brutal battle at Anzio where allied troops got bogged down in the marshes and suffered relentless shelling. Klaatu is initially speechless and reveals to Bobby that where he comes from, war does not exist. Bobby's innocent reply, "Gee, that's a good idea," garners another smile. It's an interesting moment as Bobby, a child made fatherless by war, represents Earth's future and demonstrates some hope that his generation might conceive of a peaceful future. And for what it is worth, given Klaatu's mission and the various Biblical elements of the story, one might intuitively recall Isaiah 11:6 which promises a living peace on Earth once the

Messiah is acknowledged: "The wolf also shall dwell with the lamb, and the leopard shall lie down with the kid; and the calf and the young lion and the fatling together; and a little child shall lead them."

Symbolically, Bobby represents the line between innocence and acculturation. In other words, he takes the world as he sees it, the way a kid does, but he's not far from adulthood with its more rigid social rules, economic pressures and conformist expectations. He is the potential future who naturally leans toward Klaatu's idealized world but, simply because he's human, he carries our history of death and destruction whether he likes it or not.

THE SMARTEST MAN IN THE WORLD

Sam Jaffe, through his role as Professor Barnhardt, unmistakably stands in for Albert Einstein, whom writer Edmund North mentions by name in the earliest outlines (Rubin 12). Einstein remains to this day the single most visually recognizable scientist in history and posters of him still sell in college bookstores across America. His shock of wild hair, bushy eyebrows and distinctive facial features visually engendered the mid-century atomic scientist trope, and his reputation for professional concentration plays into it as well. He made the cover of *Time Magazine* twice before *The Day the Earth Stood Still* (and twice after), including the July 1, 1946, issue displaying his famous $E=mc^2$ equation floating in a mushroom cloud. Einstein's name thus equates directly with intellect. In 1950, if you asked an American to name an important scientist, chances are, Einstein would be the first (and likely only) name mentioned.

Barnhardt's Einstein connection can be seen in both his physical appearance on screen and his portrayal of the kind of deeply devoted and somewhat ethereal scientist the public imagined in Einstein. His bushy, unparted hair rises up and lays back over his scalp and his emotive dark eyes look very much like the scientist's. His heavy tweed suit mirrors those worn by Einstein in popular photographs as well.

In characterization, "Sam Jaffe is, as always, the master of wide-eyed wonder. He fills the bill as the woolgathering mathematician, suggestive of Albert Einstein, taking his own brilliance-cum-humility and his awe of Klaatu in stride" (Keenen 74). The pair first meet after Klaatu has left his mathematical calling card on Barnhardt's blackboard. When Barnhardt asks if the man before him has tested this theory, Klaatu says, "I find it works well enough to get me from one planet to another." Jaffe's facial expression might be fear or awe, we don't know initially, but when presented with the opportunity to turn in Klaatu, he does just the opposite and with a smile invites Klaatu to sit down for "several thousand questions." In Barnhardt's willingness to help, Klaatu sees a third person meriting faith in humanity.

The scene also resonates as the origin of the most significant plot point and the film's title, Klaatu's dramatic but non-violent solution to getting humanity's attention effectively. Klaatu never does sit down, but Barnhardt does, allowing for camera angles to look down on the professor and up to Klaatu, positioning the audience in Barnhardt's seat symbolically, clarifying both the master and the pupil. Klaatu then lays out his mission: to give Earth a chance to wake up and join the other planets in peace or be eradicated before we spread our violence outward.

This causes Barnhardt to rise from his chair (he will go up and down a few times and pace the room, adding visual interest and tension to a scenario that lesser films will replicate statically). He approaches Klaatu, pulling Barnhardt closer to his level as he senses the importance of the coming moments. Klaatu reveals he's losing patience and threatens "violent action since that seems to be the only thing your people understand," suggesting the complete destruction of New York City or the Rock of Gibraltar. This exemplifies Klaatu's horrifyingly pragmatic, utilitarian ethics: the salvational benefits of sacrificing two highly visible places outweigh the lives of unsuspecting humans. And it might register well with the film's mid-century audiences. This seemingly cold moral mathematics echoes the American rationale for dropping atomic weapons over Hiroshima and Nagasaki—two acts of utter destruction to prevent millions of additional casualties in an invasion. And now, ironically, those very weapons have created a new problem that might require a similar solution.

In contrast, Barnhardt approaches the situation from a humanitarian point of view and asks if Klaatu will speak to a group of scientists he's calling together. He also realizes scientists often go unheeded and plans to expand the group to "leaders of every field, the finest minds in the world." With this suggestion, Klaatu eases his frustration and sees some hope in Barnhardt and people like him. The professor asks about alternatives if Klaatu's appeal fails, mortified by the answer: Earth would be "eliminated." The concept staggers Barnhardt, who sits back down and the exchange between he and Klaatu has genuine potency. Barnhardt rises again and requests a demonstration before the meeting to emphasize the grave reality. "I wouldn't want you to harm anybody or destroy anything," he says, which Klaatu seems to admire as "quite an interesting problem." In the last few seconds of the scene, Barnhardt sits back down a final time, slowly, appreciatively and carrying the anxiety that comes with knowing just how closely destruction looms.

This plan recalls a similarly dramatic request Einstein made of international scientists for precisely the same reason. In 1946, he formed the Emergency Committee of Atomic Scientists with physicist Leo Szilárd. After meeting, they concluded that once unleashed, an international nuclear war would be unstoppable with no possible defense and carry globally crippling consequences. On May 25, the *New York Times* published a now famous appeal for $200,000 "for a nation-wide campaign to let people know that a new type of thinking is essential if mankind is to survive and move toward higher levels" (Emrg). Though hard to assess in a world that has thus far avoided an international nuclear exchange, these early efforts to unify scientists and raise reasonable alarms may have influenced later events in a way that would satisfy Klaatu.

Additionally, it is worth noting that Einstein's co-founder, Leo Szilárd, appealed to President Harry Truman on behalf of the Manhattan Project scientists to not deploy the A-bomb as it potentially normalized nuclear warfare and perhaps made it inevitable. The so-called Szilárd Petition, dated July 25, 1945 (just weeks before the Hiroshima and Nagasaki attacks), accepted a need for a swift conclusion to the war but said with Germany's nuclear potential nullified, the urgency was over. It called for a "public announcement" of the technology and a set of terms clarified for Japan to avoid setting the precedent for nuclear warfare (Szilárd). Additionally, Farrington Daniels, who worked in Chicago on the project, polled 150 fellow scientists involved in the production of A-bomb technology. 83% polled favored some sort of demonstration of the weapon rather than a combat use (Szilárd). Barnhardt's request for a peaceful demonstration of Klaatu's power follows this very line of thought. In both scenarios, a "demonstration of power" offers a chance to change the course of behavior to a peaceful future.

Barnhardt also fits into the Christian messaging of the film. As Jerome Shapiro notes in *Atomic Bomb Cinema*, Barnhardt "receives a revelation he cannot understand... in the form of a scientific problem that Barnhardt is working on but cannot solve (81). Where this would traditionally emerge as a dream or vision in myth and religion, in the age of science, the elusive and mystical key to the universe resides in mathematics. Klaatu's "calling card" for Barnhardt is his correction and near completion of the problem, opening the door for their creative solution to bypass official leadership. The scientist and philosophers will become "charged with warning the heretical" of our impending doom and damnation, very similar to the long tradition of prophets charged with spreading the word of God. However, there is a new twist here: "it is not until the 1950s that these wise old men were expected to understand astrophysics" (81).

We see Professor Barnhardt twice more in the film. During the standstill, Barnhardt appreciates the shutdown while his housekeeper frets, noting with pleasure, "What a brilliant idea. I never would have thought of it." He calmly asks if everyone has arrived for the meeting later that night and checks on "Mr. Carpenter's" scheduled appearance as she bustles around in the office. "Tell me, Hilda," he asks, "does all this frighten you? Does it make you feel insecure?" When she replies, "Yes sir, it certainly does," he smiles. "That's good Hilda. I'm glad." At first glance, this might just seem like a bit of filler, but it gives us an insight on exactly why this would be effective. If we imagine our own reactions when things shut down, fear and insecurity describe the response well. These emotions tend to lead toward action, of course, and set the stage for Klaatu's final appeal.

Barnhardt also appears at the climax of the picture. He's told to leave by the Army because "the robot's on the loose now." He's speaking to the crowd when Klaatu and Helen emerge from the spaceship and steps aside rather amazed. He will not speak again in the film, but he stands next to Helen as Klaatu delivers his ultimatum. They are the last two people he will gaze upon, which he does with a warm smile. As we've seen, Helen and Barnhardt represent our capacity to be our better selves and have the courage to think freely and accept change.

As a final note, Jaffe was Wise's choice from the start, but there were complications. He'd been pegged as a communist sympathizer and put on the so-called blacklist. "I heard a story about that," Billy Gray said. "When the casting department got the word that they wanted to see him [Jaffe] in the part, they said, 'No, you can't use him. He's on the blacklist.' And [Darryl] Zanuck pretty much gave them the finger and pretty much said, 'fuck off. I'm using him. Sue me'" (Gray). Zanuck, the head of 20th Century Fox at the time, had served in the Army Signal Corps and helmed much of the Hollywood propaganda efforts during World War II, so no one questioned his loyalty, and he had the clout and independence to defy the edicts as he saw fit.

HUGH MARLOWE

Hugh Herbert Hipple. One can understand how the actor who played Tom Stevens, Helen Benson's ill-suited love interest, would want to change it to Hugh Marlowe for professional reasons. In fact, his earliest two film credits, both from 1936, *Brilliant Marriage* and *It Couldn't Have Happened (But It Did)*, list him as John Marlowe—even though he used Hugh for his stage work at the same time.

Born in Philadelphia in 1911, Marlowe began acting in Chicago as a youngster before honing his craft at the Pasadena Playhouse in the early 1930s. He stayed busy in the '30s and '40s on both the screen and the stage and spent a significant amount of time in touring companies. In fact, he and Patricia Neal became friends in a Chicago production of *Turtle* when she stepped in for Vivian Vance (of *I Love Lucy* fame) in 1945 (Neal 65). He also played detective Ellery Queen on the radio and later on television for many years. Marlowe's extensive career included radio, stage, film and especially television roles but like Rennie, rarely had major film leads. One noteworthy exception is his performance as Dr. Russell Marvin in *Earth vs. The Flying Saucers* (1956), the only other science fiction picture he did until 1966's schlocky *Castle of Evil*. For many people, he was best known as Jim Mathews in the soap opera *Another World*. He played the role in nearly 2000 episodes between 1964 and 1982, when he died of a heart attack at age 71. He was one of four actors to play Matthews but when he died, the character did too.

I DON'T CARE ABOUT THE REST OF THE WORLD

We first meet Tom when he comes to pick up Helen for a picnic. They embrace and kiss deeply as soon as he says "Good morning," and look happy to see one another. This establishes the stage and intensity of the relationship for the audience quickly. When Helen reveals she has no one to stay with Bobby, Tom's disinterest in bringing him along registers in his tone and facial expression. He's very quick to accept Klaatu's offer to spend the day with Bobby and the scene ends there. From this short exchange, we know Tom's drive to monopolize Helen motivates his quick approval despite her visible unease at leaving her child with a man she really does not know. In other words, Tom demonstrates an instinct toward selfishness the first time we see him.

We next see him as the pair pull up in front of Helen's home and once again they kiss passionately. Before she leaves, he says, "You still haven't answered my question," referring to an off-screen marriage proposal. She wants time to think about it, to which he replies, "A good insurance salesman wouldn't give you time to think about it." Of all the professions he might be, an insurance salesman relates most symbolically to Helen's situation. He's offering her security, a type of life insurance, in exchange for her hand in marriage. It also tells us a little about Tom's capacity for manipulation. We have no trouble imagining him pressuring people to get them to sign on the dotted line.

At this point, Tom Stevens clearly starts falling into the trope of "the unfit suitor," a flawed character competing for another's romantic attention, typically with the intention of marriage. (Most of the time, it's a male pursuing a female, but not exclusively.) The unfit suitor tends to be in place first and have some outwardly desirable qualities, especially good looks or social status, but lacks some moral or personality quality that would seal the deal. Normally, jealousy and possessiveness rise up when a newcomer arrives, offering a foil to the romantic lead (even though Klaatu has no intentions for Helen). This emerges the next time we see Tom. He comes to pick up Helen for a date and when she mentions Mr. Carpenter, Tom snipes, "Well I hope Mr. Carpenter won't think I'm intruding" within earshot of Klaatu as he comes through the adjacent room. He admits, "I don't like the way he's attached himself to you and Bobby. After all, what do you know about him?" The line washes a look over Helen's face as though she's seeing this side of him for the first time. Tom accepts Mr. Carpenter without question when it benefits him but the moment he suspects an attachment, he casts suspicion on the newcomer. And to contrast all this, upstairs Helen finds Klaatu helping Bobby with his homework, a paternal task he seems to accept without hesitation.

When Tom and Helen return from the movies, she finds Bobby awake and agitated, having followed Klaatu to the spaceship where he witnesses Gort dispatch a pair of soldiers before Klaatu enters the ship to arrange the shutdown of electricity. When Klaatu does not answer a knock on his door, Tom enters and finds a stray diamond. A few moments later, Tom tells Helen, "I think the guy's a crook. I never did trust him!" (contradicting their first meeting). We see him next in Bleeker's Jewelry where he discovers the unique nature of the diamond. Simultaneously, Klaatu reveals his mission and its importance to Helen, who now realizes the significance of the electrical shutdown and pledges to help Klaatu avoid capture before reaching the spaceship.

The next time we see Tom, he tells Helen he's going to report Klaatu to the authorities despite her urging. In essence, she's asking him to trust her judgment, which he dismisses. While waiting on the phone for General Cutler to report Klaatu, he says, "You realize, of course, what this would mean to us? I could write my own ticket. I'd be the biggest man in the country." She's repelled by his self-interest and pleads, "It isn't just you and Mr. Carpenter. The rest of the world is involved." He replies in an unguarded moment, "I don't care about the rest of the world." The script reads:

> It is as though he had slapped her across the face. Suddenly he has revealed himself, naked and distasteful. Feeling guilty as he sees the contempt and revulsion in her eyes, he tries the old charm, holding his hand over the phone.

> TOM: You'll feel different when you see my picture in the papers.

> HELEN: (staring at him starkly) I feel different right now.

> TOM: (uneasily) You wait and see. You're going to marry a big hero!

> HELEN: I'm not going to marry anybody.

This is the last time we will see Tom on screen and it packs one of the best punches in the film. For one thing, it makes a commentary about standing on ethical grounds in the context of Tom's marriage proposal. On the surface, Tom looks like a good catch. Affable and successful, he puts on a good show. But underneath, he's shallow and driven by ego desires. His interaction shows signs of dismissing Helen as a person, an indication of the type of marriage he actually offers her, so her decision to stand on her own bears some consideration. She's better off struggling alone than succumbing to social pressures to marry an indifferent man with such questionable ethics.

More importantly, Tom exemplifies exactly what makes humans so dangerous to one another (and in the context of the film, the rest of the galaxy). He masks his self-interest with false virtues and vague patriotism and when the moment comes, he willingly risks world destruction on the chance that he'd be personally served by taking a risk. In short, a world full of people like Tom Stevens should expect destruction eventually.

GORT

In a film packed with memorable moments, the appearance of the robot, Gort, reigns supreme for many fans of *The Day the Earth Stood Still*. While "mechanical men" populated literary fiction at least as far back as Edward Ellis' *The Steam Man of the Prairie* (1868), robots rarely appeared in cinema before 1951 in any serious way. The first screen robot was likely in the Vitagraph one-reeler, *The Mechanical Statue and the Ingenious Servant* (1907), an obscure piece of silly entertainment. Comic robots appeared here and there over the next decade or so until 1921 when an Italian film, *L'Uomo Meccanico* (a.k.a. *The Mechanical Man*), featured the first evil robot, a menace ultimately destroyed by an antithesis mechanical man created just for that purpose. American audiences might have remembered the false Maria from the landmark German film, *Metropolis* (1927), but would have been more familiar with the hapless Tin Man from *The Wizard of Oz* (1939) or goofy mechanical minions from serials like *Flash Gordon* (1936), *The Undersea Kingdom* (1936) and *The Phantom Creeps* (1938). None of these entries would have inspired much awe or terror, even for the audiences of their day.

With Gort, however, the destructive potential comes just moments after the spaceship has landed when a trigger-happy soldier shoots the communication instrument from Klaatu's hands, dropping him to the ground. Gort emerges from the craft announced by powerful, threatening music and begins vaporizing weapons with a laser beam shot from its cycloptic eye. The first truly menacing robot of the silver screen, Gort symbolizes annihilation due to human failings. Thus, Gort, ultimately, gives the film its potency.

Gort is perhaps the ultimate 1950s robot image, a single, seamless entity over eight feet tall, polished silver with an anthropomorphic head concealing a single, deadly laser eye beneath a visor. However, in Edmund North's February 21, 1951, draft, Gort still closely resembles Gnut from Bates' "Farewell to the Master." North's script says:

> The robot is ten feet tall, is made in the almost-perfect image of a man. He is to be played by an actor and his flesh appears to be made of a greenish metal. His eyes flash as though lighted internally. His perfectly fashioned, muscular body is covered only with a loincloth. This is GORT.

North stresses that Gort's face never shows change or expression. Additionally, he describes Gort's destruction of the military weapons differently from the way it occurs in the film: "From inside him there comes an ominous crackling sound, as though power were being generated within him. His eyes flash toward the tank from which Klaatu was shot." Collapsing tanks and artillery clatter and crunch in the draft as though Gort's power crushes, rather than disintegrates, them. And importantly, he's provided with human features, including eyes. (One wonders why he needs a loin cloth, of course, as the creation of something to cover would also imply something of use.)

In January, apparently Victor Mature was considered for the role. Hollywood columnist Sidney Skolsky wrote, "one of the leads will be played by a robot that looks like Vic Mature. 'This,' said Vic, ' will be Mature's greatest performance'" (15). However, somewhere along the line, someone realized a human in metallic green grease paint would not work out, but it is hard to know who. Addison Hehr and Lyle Wheeler, the art directors, designed the final version and Melborne A. Arnold constructed the robot, but it probably came based on decisions made by Wise, Blaustein and North, who had final say on all the design elements as collaborators (Taylor and Finch 74-75). Carrying off a metallic green robot (especially in a black and white film) portrayed by a human in grease paint probably would not have had much impact. And a stop motion robot would have been difficult to integrate successfully with the many of the scenes, especially near the end of the film (apologies to Ray Harryhausen's Talos, of course, which sounds very much like North's original conception). But the revised Gort design, without distinct human facial features, probably aids in selling the character who serves his purpose without pity or empathy.

Ironically, Gort, seemingly an invincible physical force in the film, was portrayed by a rather frail man. Unlike James Arness, who was both big and strong, Joseph Lockard Martin (or Lock Martin as most knew him) had very little physical strength despite his towering height. The seven-foot seven-inch gentleman had a growth hormone disorder that extended his bones and features but did not equate to body power. However, in Hollywood, he managed to make a minor career out of his remarkable height despite his disability. He made promotional appearances for clients even before he broke into the movies, attracting commercially exploitable attention, and spent most of his career using his height as a walking attraction. Martin had bit roles in three movies between 1944 and 45, but landed his best remembered part when, as director Robert Wise put it, "someone remembered that the Grauman's Chinese Theater in those days had a terribly tall doorman" (Leeman 105).

"One of the challenges was the Gort character himself," Robert Wise recalled. "He was not a very strong man and that suit was heavy" (Leeman 105). Thus, managing the role took ingenuity and engineering. For example, when Gort carries Helen Benson from the pavilion it required some engineering. Backing away from Gort, who has just disintegrated a pair of soldiers, Helen she falls down over a group of clattering chairs and delivers her most famous (and lifesaving) line, "Klaatu barada nikto." Wise directed Martin to pass before a partition as he approaches her. The audience would visually perceive this to shield the actress's last position on screen. Wise stopped the camera after Gort passes by and turns it back on when he reverses direction, this time with Benson in his arms. Patricia Neal was elevated into position with the help of a crane and supported by wires and thus Martin never had to actually support her weight. The sharp-eyed can detect the cables and even see the profile of the threading on the suit, but remarkably, the power of the scene immerses most viewers too much to see or care.

Similarly, for the reverse angle shots going into the spaceship, Gort carries lightweight dummies representing Helen Benson first, then Klaatu's dead body, retrieved from a prison cell (Leeman 105). The nighttime setting, the distance of the shots and the angle make this very convincing. However, once in the spaceship, Michael Rennie's face must show, so his body is supported by a rolling dolly out of camera view. After a moment, Wise cuts to Helen Benson's reaction of wonder and anxiety before turning back to Klaatu, now positioned on a table with Gort pulling his arms away.

Additionally, Martin could not stay in the suit for very long and Wise said he thought about a half hour was all he could comfortably stand (Leeman 105). That became a serious problem when they filmed the final scene. According to J. J. Johnson, Martin struggled to maintain himself and nearly passed out in the hot and ponderous suit (257). Steve Rubin paints a more dire picture based on conversations with the actor and famous prop collector, Bob Burns, who befriended Martin. To complete the scene, which took about five hours, Martin needed to stand still on the incline of the ramp in the stifling suit. "'He began to shake and if you look hard enough you can see his hands shaking up there. Between the heat and the order to stand perfectly still, and the danger of falling over, it was one of his most terrifying moments'" (19).

In "Farewell to the Master," Gnut is a freethinking robot, the true master, capable of great destruction but also empathy and evaluative thinking. Gort, however, is more of a classic robot with two tasks, aiding Klaatu and maintaining interplanetary peace through extreme force. Once activated, Gort dispenses judicial enforcement dispassionately and therein lies the potential for fear in the audience. It does not speak, gesture or even seem to relate to humans in any way. Its head is featureless except for a visor that lifts to unleash a weapon of unimaginable power. Gort has no mind of its own, no ability to evaluate or scale transgressions, no love or pity for humankind. Instead, Gort reigns as an unassailable, indifferent adjudicator and police force in one. One cannot reason with Gort and if you find yourself with cause to do so, it is already too late.

The most important difference between the Thing and Gort reflects this. Where the Thing symbolizes planetary annihilation through an external cause (i.e., invasion or perhaps symbolically, nuclear war), it thus acts as a pestilence. Gort symbolizes human annihilation as well, but through an internal cause—our own moral failings. In the former example, humans have no choice. There is no sense that we have done something to deserve our destruction. Captain Hendry's crusade for world preservation comes over as noble and his use of violence is sanctioned by circumstance. But in *The Day the Earth Stood Still*, that very tendency toward violence as a means for problem-solving promotes our doom at the hands of Gort, the cosmic enforcer. Our human propensity for selfishness, paranoia, immaturity and delusion—all avoidable by taking responsibility for our actions—seem to guarantee Gort will wipe us out one day. In *The Day the Earth Stood Still*, we are the pestilence, one which cannot be allowed to leave the earth to infect the galaxy.

Interestingly enough, where we might argue *The Thing*'s monster breaks new ground, Gort represents a very old world, or more accurately, an Old Testament, concept. As outlined above, Klaatu makes a neat and tidy Christ symbol and, like Jesus, offers salvation, not destruction, stressing his message of peace. However, the Old Testament stresses divine law and punishment, with no shortage of catastrophic consequences for disobedience to the higher force. In Western theology, the whole of human history stems from disobedience in the Garden of Eden. Subsequently, the various acts of divine destruction foisted upon families, nations and even the earth itself in the case of the Great Flood, consistently reflect human transgressions rooted in arrogance, willfulness, obstinance in the face of divine law.

Gort, and presumably other robots like him, enforce interplanetary law much the same way, indifferently and absolutely. As Klaatu explains in his closing speech: "In matters of aggression, we have given them absolute power over us. This power cannot be revoked. At the first sign of violence, they act automatically against the aggressor. The penalty for provoking their action is too terrible to risk." With this warning, Klaatu identifies Gort as an instrument of enforcement, clarifying that, if humanity continues on its path of violence against the interplanetary law, Earth "will be reduced to a burned-out cinder." The ecclesiastically minded, no doubt, will see the connection to II Peter 3:10 (KJV): "But the heavens and the earth which now exist are kept in store by the same word, reserved for fire until the day of judgment and perdition of ungodly men." If Klaatu symbolizes the Second Coming of Christ to deliver the word of God as a final warning, the Gort becomes the hand of a displeased and angry God, ready to eradicate humanity as the "ungodly" elements of the interstellar community.

Gort's laser beam "eye" bears mention in this context too. Symbolically, the eye relates to divine omniscience and power. As J. C. Cooper notes, the eye has historical symbolic associations across cultures with "enlightenment; knowledge; the mind; vigilance; protection; stability; fixity of purpose," all of which relate to Gort directly or indirectly (62). The tradition of the eye as an instrument of divine judgment goes at least as far back as ancient Egypt, where "'the All-Seeing Eye' once belonged to the Goddess of truth and judgment, Maat" before becoming associated with Horus, who judged souls before entering the afterlife (Walker 294).

Gort's laser eye also embodies the symbol of fire, a destroyer, transformer and purifier (Cooper 66-69), which again relates to Gort's task of policing the galaxy. Gort's fiery eye is the first on screen, but Celtic mythology offers at least one predecessor in the horrible giant, Balor. Known variously as Balor of the Flashing Eye, the Balor of the Evil Eye, and Boleros the Flashing One, the monstrous warrior ruled as a tyrant. "A god of death and the most formidable of the Fomorii… he had one eye whose gaze was so malevolent that it destroyed whatever it gazed upon" (Ellis 39). The eye remained shut until Balor entered the battlefield, where he could unleash its blinding flash (with the aid of four men to lift the lid) and slay whole armies. The eye was sometimes described as poisonous and, combined with the searing heat and blinding flash, sounds very much like radiation. Naturally, the Celts would have no concept of nuclear warfare and it is unlikely that director Robert Wise or screenwriter Edmund North had Balor in mind consciously. However, the myth does lay a groundwork for a figure like Balor to be reborn for a modern audience with the same capacity for fearful annihilation.

THE AMERICAN PEOPLE

The film positions us to consider the American populace as a composite character at many points. "In order for its political message to be taken seriously," Bradley Schauer notes in *Escape Velocity*, "*The Day the Earth Stood Still* had to be set squarely in a plausible facsimile of 1951 America, from its political structure to the limits of its scientific knowledge" (Schauer 47). Predictably, the America brought into focus here mirrors the same image Hollywood constructed on a regular basis in the 1950s— a post-war world of clean streets and well-dressed conformist citizens, dutiful and patriotic under the leadership of an unquestionably straight, white and Christian patriarchy. We never see the President, for example, but when referenced in the film, some facsimile of Truman or perhaps Eisenhower comes to mind largely because no other option would have been fathomable in 1951. This predictably homogenized construct of national cohesiveness reflects the way the United States projected itself to the world through virtually all media—orderly, self-controlled, unified and dominantly white.

However, *The Day the Earth Stood Still*'s power comes from revealing the dirty underbelly of that projection. "The film depicts America as xenophobic, bellicose, and paranoid, as the visiting alien Klaatu is met with hostility at nearly every turn" (Schauer 58). Klaatu exits the ship in "peace and goodwill," only to be shot by a soldier who can't imagine the alien could hold anything but a weapon in his hand too. Klaatu immediately gets locked away in Walter Reed Hospital and denied his request to address the whole world. As he walks the streets, he hears radio reports describing him as a monster, and suspicion and fear seem to bubble up everywhere when the veneer of control rubs away. As the scenes with Secretary Harley (Frank Conroy) demonstrate, selfishness and stupidity are not exclusively American traits, but the United States covets their visitor and behaves with no faith or enlightenment to signal a higher moral awareness.

Two scenes in particular put the less noble reality of America under the microscope. The day after Klaatu arrives at the boarding house posing as Mr. Carpenter, he sits down to breakfast with the other tenants. It's really his first chance to observe average people personally. As they pour over their papers, smoke cigarettes and sip the last drops of coffee, commentator Gabriel Heatter (one of several real news reporters and commentators in the film) asks questions he says plague the country on that Sunday morning:

> Where is this creature and what is he up to? If he can build a spaceship that can fly to Earth—and a robot that can destroy our tanks and guns—what other terrors can he unleash at will? Obviously, we must find this monster. We must track him down like a wild animal and destroy him.

As his tirade (which Heatter composed himself based on notes Blaustein supplied) continues, Carpenter's face shows mild signs of disgust and exasperation. Meanwhile, Mrs. Barley (Francis Bavier) looks at a sensational full page newspaper illustration with invading spacemen and Gort crashing through a crowd in full pulp-art exaggerated style. The title reads "How long are we for this world?" Agitated, she hounds him to turn off the radio. He then asks why the government does nothing (as the spaceman sits right in front of him) and follows at the first opportunity to malign democrats (whom he claims are "not people"). He also wants to know why the alien is "hiding." Tellingly, Carpenter remarks that someone from another planet might want to get to know the people and would find Washington, D. C. a strange place. Defensively, Mrs. Barley asserts, "There is nothing strange about Washington" before insinuating with self-satisfaction that the Russians lurk behind the mystery. Only Helen considers the possibility that Klaatu comes in peace. If he has mingled among the people to get an understanding of them, this does not speak well for Americans as rational creatures ready to accept his message.

Later the same day, Klaatu has another taste of American society when he and Bobby join the crowd surrounding the saucer. Bobby wonders about the speed of the craft and how it could land (which Klaatu, of course, knows firsthand). He begins to explain the problem of overcoming inertia only to realize he's attracted an audience. One man in the crowd, grinning from ear to ear, says, "Keep going mister. He was falling for it!" which draws approving laughter. Here we have a man too ignorant to understand the basis for the conversation, someone who assumes the point is to humiliate a gullible child, but simultaneously someone with more sway in that moment than Klaatu himself. In short, this average American, socially rewarded for ridiculing science and intellect, should not give Klaatu any reason to hope his mission will succeed.

Immediately after, a man-on-the-street reporter approaches Klaatu, assuming they are father and son. The reporter primes the interview with "I'm sure you're just as scared as the rest of us" in a cajoling tone, but Klaatu's response throws him: "In a different way, perhaps. I am fearful when I see people substituting fear for reason." Without finding fuel for the fire, the reporter quickly moves on, disappointed and essentially ostracizing Klaatu for his more enlightened view. Again, Klaatu sees the tendency in the people to indulge emotion and their disinterest in hearing what he has to say—even when they don't know he's the "spaceman." The scene, incidentally, was added after completion of the February 21 script, which tells us Wise wanted to point this quality out specifically. Further, we might consider the call letters displayed on the reporter's mic as a message: WEAN. Klaatu has come to wean humanity out of its childish tendencies, but the reporter doesn't really want to hear it, drawing back his mic and walking away.

Finally, in so far as the film makes commentary on the American people, it's worth mentioning the great irony in playing this out in one of America's most notoriously segregated cities. Segregation in Washington, D.C. glaringly exemplifies the contradictions in 1950s American society. As the Smithsonian Institution's American History website puts it:

> In the 1950s the city's government, including schools, was under the control of Congress. Its members proudly portrayed the city as the capital of the free world, where democracy and personal freedoms were defended against the threat of communist totalitarianism. Yet, most of the city's public facilities, schools, and housing were segregated by law or practice.

While Klaatu never says anything about this directly (in part because he likely sees humanity as an errant whole), one can't imagine he'd approve of segregation any more than he would of another form of injustice, inequality and exploitation. Admittedly, Klaatu exemplifies the "white savior" motif common in Western film and literature, an enlightened man of European descent come to elevate the "savages." However, Klaatu deviates from this at least somewhat since the savages this time are white as well. For Klaatu, racism and segregation would seem just as backwards as war. Obviously, no person of color would have been considered for Klaatu's role in 1951 but his whiteness does function as a passport into the racist society. He can travel unhampered and unnoticed and ultimately speak a palatable message to the white hierarchy (both in the film and in the nation) which it would never accept from an African American.

To Wise's credit, he includes African American women among the saucer spectators and two African American men, including a clergyman, among other black representatives attending the conference called by Professor Barnhardt. In fact, faces of various ethnicities receive carefully framed shots to remind us that humanity extends beyond an Anglo-American form. The February 21 script specifically calls for this:

> They are the cream of Earth's intellectuals—scientists, churchmen, educators, leaders of social and political thought. There are several women among them. There are turbaned Indians, Chinese, Japanese, several Negroes. All religions are represented. Every important world power is represented.

Today, that might look like mere tokenism, but by comparison, consider *When Worlds Collide*, also from 1951. To save humanity, Earth must desperately launch rockets full of passengers, also the "cream of Earth's intellectuals," to a new planet and the American effort does not include even one person of color. In other words, the George Pal production either did not have the imagination or the courage to include non-whites. In contrast, North, Blaustein and Wise's decisions reflect thematic goals and a significant cinematic moment of anti-racist sentiment. Wise said he wanted *The Day the Earth Stood Still* "to get a point over about our world and where we're going with it" as a "message film" (Taylor and Finch 71). Including these unnamed African American actors as Barnhardt's hand-chosen guests in the midst of legalized segregation may have been a bolder statement than it first appears.

WAIT A MINUTE LADIES AND GENTLEMEN...

Since the birth of science fiction cinema, the genre has struggled with "realism." Even so-called "hard sci-fi," which draws from real scientific principles, theories and technologies, tends to stretch into speculation occasionally to tell its story. Serious science fiction must somehow indulge fantasy enough to satisfy the audience's craving for wonderment but not drift into preposterous scenarios or pseudo-science and lose them. To suspend disbelief, establishing and maintaining a viable reality proper to the story matters more than anything else. *The Day the Earth Stood Still* solves this problem by using journalism as its initial narrative framework.

After the opening credits give way to American and British military surveillance units in Asia spotting the craft on radar, the film establishes the global reality with radio announcer cut-ins from India, France and England before turning to a familiar American voice, Elmer Davis. Davis had a nightly five-minute news update on the CBS radio network at the beginning of WWII before his appointment by President Roosevelt to run the newly formed Office of War Information in 1942. As he speaks, B-roll cuts to scenes across the country with Americans from various walks of life listening in rapt attention at work and at home as Davis tells them, "Whatever it is, it is something real."

The film briefly cuts in an anonymous voice-over tying in new information before turning to H. V. Kaltenborn, another veteran news reporter, interviewer and analyst working for NBC at the time. He reports that "Here in the nation's capital, there is cause for anxiety and concern, but no signs of panic." He asserts unaffected D.C. tourist crowds still visit the public monuments, a segue to the coming shots of the saucer approaching and landing on the Ellipse, settling between two baseball diamonds, effectively showing scale in the context of the All-American "national past time."

After a montage of quick response shots featuring police cars, ambulances and tanks speeding to the scene, reporter Drew Pearson takes over in a special "radio-television broadcast" from WMAL. (WMAL radio still broadcasts as of 2022, but the TV enterprise evolved into WJLA 7). Even in the first outlines, writer Edmund North called for a "name commentator" with Drew Pearson and Walter Winchell specifically mentioned (Rubin 10). His February 21, 1951, final draft reads: "A nationally known news commentator—for purposes of this script—let's say Drew Pearson—is seated before a radio mike [sic]. He is also being photographed by TV cameras." This expresses not only Pearson's reach and authority, but it also acknowledges the growing importance of television, giving it a modern edge in its day. Pearson brings us to the precipice of the story's action, urging levelheadedness and cataloging all the official precautions underway before saying, "the tension is just beginning… wait a minute ladies and gentlemen. I think something is happening." This neatly pulls the audience into the story, framing us to witness the emergence of Klaatu and Gort with anticipation in a unique "you are there" moment.

Radio and news continue to play a role when Klaatu, disguised as Mr. Carpenter, walks down a city street looking for a place to stay. We hear the voices of Davis and Kaltenborn again but a third, unidentified broadcaster stirs the pot of fear. No sooner has Kaltenborn said "he is not eight feet tall as reported, nor does he have tentacles" than the next announcer says, "there is no denying there is a monster at large." It is in this context that Klaatu walks into the boarding house to see the breathless tenants circled around the television watching Pearson who says that "though this man may be our bitter enemy, he could be a newfound friend." This back and forth between anxiety and rationality neatly models one of the film's main points, the human struggle to control and overcome our fears… made all the more difficult when powerful voices coax our base emotions. It also frames the emotional tension of the film, but does so in a realistic, grounded manner.

This strategy apparently came directly from the top of 20th Century Fox. Darryl F. Zanuck suggested the film establish its ground with a documentary style in the opening scenes (Schauer 47). It would feel comfortable and realistic to the audience of the day and it works with potency. A great number of 1950s science fiction films would copy the format in one way or another, though normally in a shorthand way. Some films would provide a journalist (sometimes as a main character) to distill the events for the viewers, but many more settled for opening narration to do the trick, especially as the decade wore on. Though the technique begins with *The Man from Planet X*, *The Day the Earth Stood Still* legitimized the practice with its heavy hitters from broadcast news.

PRODUCTION

Robert Wise tends to get credit for the quality and success of the now classic film, but without producer Julian Blaustein, *The Day the Earth Stood*

Still would not be what it is or even have gotten to the screen. In 1949 Blaustein started taking an interest in the rising market for sci-fi magazines targeting adults. He may have been interested in the content as well but at minimum he saw potential for the right story to cash in on the rising tide, giving him some leverage to present "an experiment" to Darryl Zanuck, who would have final say (Rubin 6).

Blaustein compiled a stack of figures demonstrating the financial viability sci-fi and showed them to Maurice Hanline, an assistant story editor working for him at 20th Century Fox and instructed him to search for a suitable story for development. Both men knew the importance of cost control. Expensive projects lay dormant due to falling ticket sales, so Blaustein stipulated that he wanted an "earthbound" alien story. That would minimize special effects, construction and location requirements, costuming and other financial concerns. Hanline brought him a copy of *Adventures in Time and Space*, an anthology published in 1946, where Blaustein found the story that fit the bill: "Farewell to the Master."

Zanuck was not particularly impressed with nor particularly resistant to the story when Blaustein approached him to purchase the rights. The producer had earned some confidence and Zanuck authorized the request on the premise it would pay off in development. They acquired it for $1000, a pittance, and Blaustein brought in writer Edmund North to restructure the story for a contemporary audience with Cold War realities in mind.

According to Steve Rubin, early on (in the first discussion, in fact) Blaustein had decided the "'Our theme is that peace is no longer a four-letter word'" (6). The rights were secured in Spring of 1950 and North composed a 35-page outline exploring the peace premise. Meanwhile, the international political situation was heating up. For months, saber-rattling stories on the Korean War stirred anxieties and suddenly the pair had concerns that Zanuck would shelve the project. In an interview with Joel Gardner, Edmund North recalled:

> Julian Blaustein and I were sick because we said, [Darryl] Zanuck will never make this picture now: peace message and all this, and here we are, at war, suddenly.' He just started through the script, his normal routine, and we had about a two or three hour talk about it; he said he loved it! Finally, Julian said to him, 'Darryl, what about this war thing?' 'Oh,'

he said, 'To hell with it.' He said, 'This is a good piece of entertainment, let's make it.' Which was great. He had courage, he
had a lot of courage; he was a gambler and a good one.

Even if Zanuck had hawkish tendencies, he must have realized that passing on this project meant passing on an industry trend, not something he
would likely do, in any case. And, interestingly enough, Blaustein said in
early May, "This is a plea for a stronger United Nations with an effective
police force" (Thomas 9). Whether that sentiment actually drove Blaustein remains debatable, but it certainly made selling the peace message
more palatable.

Generally speaking, the outline and the final film match up well, but
an early detail may help explain why Blaustein and North expected the
project to stop at Zanuck's desk. Originally, the story began with Klaatu's
flight through space to Earth with voice over narration from the pilot.
Klaatu describes Earth before turning his attention to a plot device ultimately excised from the finished film, a "highly fissionable" element—
still undiscovered by Earthlings—called "Korium" (Rubin 5). "Korium"
sounds very much like Korea, especially to the 1950 American ear. Korium supposedly lay in large deposits at the poles, areas of international
dispute. (Here, one might recall Capt. Hendry's line in *The Thing*: "Could
be Russians. They're all over the poles, like flies.") Further, Klaatu notes
the concentration of "crude fissionable materials," Uranium and Pluto-
nium in two specific areas (i.e., the United States and Soviet Union) (5-6).
Given that North intentionally laid in Christ references without telling
anyone, "Korium" was very likely meant to refer to the Korean conflict
and the nuclear dangers embedded in it.

The envisioned sequence got the ax from Zanuck himself, "insisting
that the opening be done through the point of view of people on the mall
[sic] in Washington" (Rubin 10), though vestiges remain in the titles. Cost
probably played into the decision more than political concerns, but whatever the reason, Zanuck's instincts produced a more powerful opening
that moves quickly and generates mystery and drama.

Other aspects of the outline were changed as well. The spaceship
is described as having a "nose" and devices resembling a periscope and
antenna come out of the top after it has landed. The robot, still called,
Gnut, exits the ship first and begins throwing soldiers out of his way as
he moves through them. Klaatu is shot, but in the outline, the soldiers
cannot reach him due to a type of force field. And rather than vaporize

tanks and weapons, Gnut demonstrates his power by destroying a tower at the nearby Smithsonian Institution, a detail referencing the original story.

Other interesting outline details cut from the film offer some insight on the early process. For example, Klaatu initially carries a pair of glasses enabling him to see through walls and later, when asking Bobby about Arlington Cemetery, he explains he's been away in Tibet. North also envisioned Klaatu getting a wider tour of American life with Bobby including a baseball game, an inspection of our "primitive" technology, and a chance to play with a yo-yo, which he finds fascinating (Rubin 12). As a side note, common folklore would have us believe the yo-yo originated as a Philippine weapon that later transmuted into a toy (Oliver). If North had this in mind, such a device would nicely symbolize turning nuclear science away from war and toward peace.

Additionally, in the outline, Bobby does not take Klaatu to see Professor Barnhardt; instead, Klaatu tracks him down alone. In that scene, he reveals much of his mission, material wisely redirected to the end of the final film. The elevator scene does not take place either, but instead Klaatu reveals himself to Helen in the boardinghouse. Klaatu sinks the Rock of Gibraltar in the outline to make his point, but this obviously gets changed to a suggested demonstration of power. Klaatu has no alien vocabulary yet, so the most famous lines, "Klaatu barada nikto," emerge in later drafts. Most interestingly, when Helen does speak to Gnut (aka Gort), he more or less smashes and blasts his way through the city to retrieve Klaatu, a sequence abandoned due to the required costs (Rubin 12-13). All in all, these differences indicate a more confrontational and violent Klaatu and Gnut/Gort in the early concept, but fortunately both characters transform into figures more consistent with the peace message.

The film was still in the outline stage when the first public announcement came on April 29, 1950 (nearly a year before production began) through Hedda Hopper's "Hollywood" column. Touting *Farewell to the Master* (the working title) as a "pseudo-scientific yarn" (terminology *du jour* applied to *The Thing* and *The Man from Planet X* as well), Hopper announced Anne Baxter as the female lead ("Anne Baxter" 13). Baxter was a prime commodity at the time. She boasted a Best Supporting Actress Oscar (*The Razor's Edge*, 1946) and 1950 Best Actress nomination for *All About Eve*. She would have given the picture more name recognition than Patricia Neal, but no industry announcements subsequently attached Baxter to the project and by June, no one repeated the claim. Most likely, Blaustein just wanted to connect 20th Century Fox's hottest heroine to his project to attract attention and she probably never expected to play in the film.

THE REAL PROFESSOR BARNHARDT

As we've seen, Howard Hawk's press releases and interviews regarding *The Thing* hammered home the realism of his exotic tale, claiming he had consulted with scientists to create a new type of terrifyingly realistic cinema. But if that's true, no record of whom he consulted exists. However, Wise and Blaustein definitely consulted with one of the world's foremost astrophysicists, UCLA's Samuel Herrick.

Strictly speaking, Herrick's cooperation did not break new ground. Consultants of all kinds, including scientists, visited Hollywood producer's offices, writers' rooms and backlots for many years before *The Day the Earth Stood Still*. For example, paleontologist Barnum Brown, discoverer of the Tyrannosaurus Rex, aided in Willis O'Brien's depiction of the dinosaur (thought accurate in its day) in *King Kong*. However, Dr. Samuel Herrick's assistance with Wise and Blaustein's invasion tale was the first time an astrophysicist aided a production with the goal of designing a viable spacecraft. Perhaps more importantly, it marked the first time a consultant demanded to be paid based on worth.

When 20th Century-Fox first approached him, the original offer did not meet his expectations. Herrick's papers (housed in the Newman Library's Special Collections archive at Virginia Tech) contain notes he made to address their "insufficient remuneration." He makes it clear that he "would like to work with Blaustein but only if appreciated." Herrick argued he was the only person "in the country" who could address all their concerns and consultation needs. He could advise on interplanetary travel, realistic spaceship design, the mathematics of celestial mechanics and proper scientific dialog and interaction. He offered more acceptable terms in his negotiation—$25 an hour (approximately $264 in 2021) or $75 per day ($791 in 2021) or, if they wanted him on retainer, $300 a week for a minimum of six weeks ($3165 in 2021). Blaustein agreed to his terms and Herrick ended up getting the day rate of $75. His services amounted to six and two-thirds days, yielding $499.50 by the letter of the contract. To put that in perspective, "commerce figures show the average new car price in 1950 was $2210 and the median family income was

$3319" annually (Leinart). Since shaky science could have rendered the peace message as just another "yarn," Blaustein saw the wisdom in meeting Herrick's terms.

By the time Herrick began working on the project in late January 1951, the film's title had been officially changed to *The Day the Earth Stood Still* from the less inspiring *Journey to the World*, a briefly adopted moniker Blaustein used once the outline got approval. Herrick spent a few hours on the 24th and 25th reading the first complete script draft before visiting the studio on the 26th. Herrick then prepared a detailed series of notes on February 1 and met with Edmond North the following day to discuss them. The notes, which contain both suggestions and critiques, fall into three categories. The first regards practical issues of space flight and the dynamics of entering the atmosphere and landing. Klaatu's space travel and arrival originally slated to open the film were present in the draft Herrick saw and he made technical notes on travel velocity, orbit and deceleration aimed at improving accuracy. It's hard to know if these concerns played into dropping the scenes, but the sequence disappears in the February 21 draft.

The international radar reports (which became the opening the film) caught Herrick's attention and he made notes for accuracy based on a speed of 4000 miles per hour in Earth's atmosphere, a detail first mentioned by the British radar unit. Incidentally, the speed of the craft became a Hollywood topic in Erskine Johnson's column on May 2, a tidbit almost certainly designed to keep the picture in the news:

> How fast a man can go is raising the ulcer hazard at Fox. Writers put a 6000 mile speed on the space ship in 'The Day the Earth Stood Still.' When technical advisers screamed, the speed was dropped to 1000 miles an hour. Then Uncle Sam announced plans for a jet speed of 2250 miles an hour. The movie's space ship has now been speeded up to 6000 miles an hour. ("Icebox" 20).

6000 mph may, in fact, have been in the draft Herrick saw, but his notes say 4000 mph without any indication that he felt like screaming. Cold war headlines touted the latest speed records and proposed craft routinely and while Herrick worked on the film, Douglas announced the X-3 which they expected to reach 2280 mph (Miles 1). Perhaps this caused some discussion, but the notion of Herrick getting upset seems like pure hyperbole. In any case, Klaatu tells Bobby, "Maybe four thousand miles an hour. And outside the Earth's atmosphere a good deal faster."

Herrick also felt Klaatu's home planet merited definition to render travel times and distances accurately in the dialog. He recommended restricting the choice to Mars or Venus since travel from another star system would take centuries, presumably based on speeds he thought possible. A curious note resides under the Mars/Venus suggestion: "These only habitable by Klaatu." Herrick probably did not believe these planets could produce and maintain a humanoid civilization but deduced these offered the only realistic possibility in context. But Herrick also wrote "OK not to use," suggesting he saw no reason to name Klaatu's planet for the audience. The best clue to their decision would be Klaatu's reference to traveling 250 million miles, the approximate distance between Earth and Mars when the planets lie in opposition.

Secondly, Herrick spent much of his critical energy on the portrayal of science and scientists, especially Professor Barnhardt. He made notes about the interaction between scientists and laymen, and between Klaatu and Barnhardt, which he noted ran long and inauthentically in places. Klaatu comes over as "supercilious" to Herrick, which he found (rightly) unnecessary and said the "Three-body problem not proper place for such gab." He felt Klaatu's attitude of superiority should only come out in frustration with human stupidity, and the pair should interact as colleagues, a quality that comes over in the film. Herrick also recommends that Barnhardt express the need for other types of intellectual leadership besides scientists and stress the possibility of education for everyone based on the study of the spaceship, not just individuals.

The equation on Barnhardt's blackboard is a practical application of the "three body problem" Herrick devised himself. In general, a three body problem calculates the interrelated orbital movement of three objects in space accounting for both the laws of motion and gravity using initial positions and speeds of those objects and projecting them forward in time. No singular "closed form" (i.e., universally applied) solution exists due to the number and condition of the variables. Regarding the equation, Herrick's notes say that "Barnhardt should be seeking solution to practical problem or application," suggesting a line: "Everybody talks about it but nobody does anything about it." He further suggests that Klaatu should see and approve of Barnhardt's method and "merely articulate the next step," executed in the film in a way that provides dignity for both characters. This equation required effort and the art crew had trouble getting it on the blackboard. Herrick put in nearly two full days of work (broken up over time) between March 29 and April 4 to ensure its accuracy. Given the fast and loose manner in which most cinema replicates science on screen, devotion to detail stands as an accomplishment, especially since only a handful of people would even recognize the effort.

Finally, Herrick made significant contributions to the design of the spaceship and other mechanical devices, such as his "telescope," the object smashed in Klaatu's arrival scene. Regarding the ship, it appears the draft Herrick first saw uses terms like "the rocket" and has what he calls "Blaustein's folding wings" which he identifies as important for landing but "immaterial in outer space." Herrick advises in general against "overestimation of gadgetry and electronics," and explains that weight would matter greatly in design, promoting a minimized and sleek interior. This may account for why the periscope and radar dish in the early outline was dropped.

Additionally, Herrick writes a column of notes called "Reasons for saucer, for & against" but does not clarify which notes apply to which category. However, its fairly certain he was ultimately in the "for saucer" camp. For instance, he lists "current hysteria" and "current misconceptions," but these things might well be reasons for a filmmaker adopt the saucer design rather than reject it. Ultimately, of course, the saucer won out and Herrick's influence seems to have mattered.

Further, on February 16, he sent a letter to Julian Blaustein, writing:

> A word more on my hope that you will consider bathing your flying saucer in light. From my point of view, it will have the effect of obscuring the mechanical features of the device, i.e., the external manifestations that might be taken as indicating a specific (and questionable) way in which the thrust is being applied.

The letter indicates Blaustein was considering a jet of light which Herrick thought opened the door for criticism. He rationalized that "the light might be dismissed as an external and incidental manifestation of atomic forces at work within the vehicle." He lobbies further for investing in the effect, asking Blaustein to consider the awe value of the pulsating glow on film. As we see from the final cut, Blaustein took his advice.

On February 2, the day after compiling his observations, Herrick meet with Edmund North to discuss the script. They spent a full day together and North asked Herrick if he'd rewrite some of the dialog between Klaatu and Barnhardt. Herrick's handwritten changes were typed up and he met with North again on the 5th to review and revise. Herrick's dialog ran for four relatively dense pages. Much of it gets restructured, condensed, relocated or eliminated in the final film but the tenor of the conversation between two colleagues remains, as well as Barnhardt's decision to call up non-scientists for the meeting. The final result comes over elegantly and efficiently in the film we know today.

A Two-Sided Love Triangle

The film, of course, develops no real romance between Klaatu and Helen, and he primarily serves as a model for mature male behavior, something lacking in Tom. However, Wise said in an interview a few weeks before the film hit the theaters that he'd gotten pressure to develop a love relationship between the characters. "'I didn't want a love story, but one of the men in the front office did'" he told Virginia MacPherson. But the filmmakers had a hard time conceiving of just how it would work out and kicked around various theories on love on another planets, if it even existed. "'We fooled around with the idea of getting our planet-man and Pat in the moonlight,'" Wise went on. "But we were not sure he'd know what to do. We weren't even sure they'd have moonlight on other planets'" (6). He further explains they considered theories based on a range of reading materials from comic books to scientific musings. Perhaps on Klaatu's planet, conception did not involve physical contact and love never developed. Push button or pill popping reproduction offered little promise and, in the end, they dropped the idea which would have cheapened the film and the message significantly. What we have instead is a kind of mental synergy and respect. As Klaatu leaves, Helen looks at him with an adoring expression and at other times the two share smiles generally reserved for on screen lovers of the time. Wise promised that viewers would "'get the love angle,'" (6) though it remains thankfully Platonic.

A Tale of Two Cities, One Army and Three National Guards

The stars never left the 20th Century Fox backlot, but work was done in Washington, D.C. by a second unit led by Bert Leeds. Wise went to Washington but only to line up the shots with Leeds. The crew then filmed various shots of D.C. streets and landmarks, with prominent work emerging in the finished film when Bobby and Carpenter visit the city. The scenes in Arlington National Cemetery and at the Lincoln Memorial were done with rear projection in a soundstage environment. The actors performed on a set while second unit footage rolled behind them on a giant screen (Gray). The second unit also shot high angle footage of South President's Park, better known as the Ellipse, near the White House for the dramatic landing shots at the beginning of the film.

Like Howard Hawks, Robert Wise asserted that he got no cooperation out of the Department of Defense. According to Wise, "They wouldn't give us an okay because they didn't like the theme" (Leeman 107). The director suggested to interviewer Harry Kreisler: "they didn't like our message of peace, I guess." The content of *Day* might also challenge their official position that flying saucers did not exist, or perhaps the fact that the military is helpless in the face of Gort made them uneasy, especially as war loomed on the Korean Peninsula.

Wise frequently said that he drew on National Guard resources instead, citing the D.C. Guard in some interviews (Leeman 107 and Weaver 347) and Virginia Guard in others (Kreisler Interview). In Wise's defense, these interviews came several years apart and, of course, Wise stayed in Hollywood while the D. C. shots took place. But regardless of where the men and tanks originated, the story remained otherwise consistent. He told interviewer Harry Kreisler in 1998:

> Fox had a very smart lobbyist in Washington at that time. He got a brilliant idea, he went over to Virginia and got the National Guard. And they didn't have any problem with the script so all the equipment and everything that we had, the tanks, all came from the National Guard of Virginia, not the War Department.

However, Fort Meade in Maryland, which fell under the Department of Defense, also seems to have played a role, allowing the crew to film tanks racing out of the gates of their motor pool to respond to the otherworldly threat. And the tank visible in Klaatu's entrance scene bears Fort Meade markings. According to Jay Graybeal, chief curator at the Army Heritage and Education Center in Maryland, shots from the film show the "Brave Rifles" insignia on a tank used by the 3rd Cavalry based at Ft. Meade

(Graybeal). Thus, the U. S. Army does seem to have provided men and equipment to the second unit for the shots on the Ellipse. Unfortunately, no official records are known to exist on this.

Shots during the arrival scene featuring Klaatu in frame with the tank using the Brave Rifles insignia (as well as machine guns and artillery) utilized a double in the nation's capital. Klaatu's helmet obscures his features and Rennie's voice could be added later if Wise or Leeds wanted to make use of the available tanks and equipment. Additionally, shots of Gort from behind as he blasts the weapons include the Fort Meade tank. Neither Martin nor the costume ever went to D.C. so they composited footage of Gort over the D.C. footage for those shots. However, military equipment appears in scenes shot in Los Angeles too when Klaatu is hunted and gunned down while trying to return to the saucer. In that sequence, B-roll featuring units racing through Washington D. C. gets intercut with shots of several Jeeps and troop trucks rolling on the backlot. Costumes would present little problem, but the vehicles were probably not studio property. In an interview for this book, Bill Gray referred to California National Guard units getting involved but could not recall where he'd heard that.

And then there is a strange story about Patricia Neal's stand in, Marilyn Speirs, to muddy the waters. Speirs, a working model and very convincing double for the lead, lived in Arlington, Virginia. Apparently, when her scenes wrapped, about 20 District National Guardsmen came up to her and elected her their official pin-up girl on the spot. Speirs, who would do additional extra work in films like *The Greatest Show on Earth* (1952) and *The Court Martial of Billy Mitchell* (1955) according to her 2015 obituary (Obituary), seems to have taken them at their word and called her publicity agent who began promoting it. This attracted the attention of a small D.C. newspaper, *The Evening Star*, looking for a human-interest story. In turn, at the behest of an editor, a photographer escorted Speirs to the D. C. National Guard Armory for a shoot. Her "official pin-up girl" status was apparently news to the base information officer who thought the paper merely planned to send pictures of Speirs to her admirers. She described the situation as "distressing" and told the Star she just wanted to know "'whose little pin-up I am'" ("Pin-up" B-1). At minimum, the item proves the D. C. National Guard cooperated in some way.

A full picture doesn't clearly take shape from these facts, but a theory is possible. Wise told Tom Weaver he went to D.C. with Leeds and lined up the shots personally (345). While there, Wise may have initially hit a brick wall from the Army, which would account for his statements. However, once Leeds began work on the film, the situation may have changed. Additionally, Hedda Hopper reported on April 18, 1951, that the movie had "cooperation of top brass in the Pentagon" but "the soldiers were called out for Gen. MacArthur's welcome and the buildings were draped in bunting" (70). This would explain why troops and equipment from Maryland, Virginia, and Washington all might be involved, especially since the second unit would have to shoot over the course of several days. In other words, they'd have to take what they could get when they could get it. Moreover, the D. C. Guard footage might not have been usable for one reason or another, which would allow for their participation in the shoots even if they didn't make the cut.

FLYING SAUCER

Set designer Lyle Wheeler understood the need for both aesthetics and scientific viability in the spaceship and the sleek, genuinely futuristic craft reflects this. "'Our problem was to devise something (a space ship) that nobody has ever seen—at least, close up—that would be acceptable to everybody,'" he said in a Los Angeles Times article discussing the film. "'We tried to be completely different and far more advanced than any earth ship, so we based every working part on the light-ray principle rather than the push button principle'" (Scheuer Part IV, p, 3). Thus, Klaatu controls many aspects of his ship with merely with gestures, passing his hand over panels and in front of doors, for example. It adds to the "weirdness" as well as the futurism of the film, but the technology comes over as plausible in a world becoming increasingly automated and streamlined in 1951. (Only a few years later, "electric eyes" will begin opening doors at supermarkets across the country, in fact.) Additionally, the minimalist structure reflects Klaatu's society which has exchanged war, aggression and greed for elegance and harmony.

To bring the saucer down to Earth, Wheeler's team used a pair of physical models "laid into the live action footage with multiple exposures and a traveling matte" (Johnson 294). (Johnson reports that they were two and three feet across; Rubin records them as two and seven feet wide.) The saucers were photographed against a black background and superimposed later on footage using an optical printer, a device that shoots one film over another to create a composite. Reportedly, Fred Sersen spent two months processing the composite shots for the film adding in both the pulsating illumination of the saucer and Gort's heat ray at that time. The effects work exceedingly well and in TCM's 2005 documentary, *Watch the Skies, Alien* director Ridley Scott says watching the scene was the first-time science fiction impacted him. "The effects of the ship coming across the city didn't have those funny old, jagged lines and it didn't move in a funny fashion. That's why I started to buy into it."

Another important element of the illusion, the sound of the spaceship, required some creative trial and error. On July 6, while the film was in post-production, Sidney Skolsky reported that "They conducted a score of experiments before they decided on one. The sound is that of a baby's rattle put in a high-frequency vibration chamber" (15).

For exterior shots of the landed saucer, Lyle Wheeler and Addison Hehr built a life-sized mockup with one quarter cut out in the rear for access and operations. It measured approximately 100 feet across and stood 24 feet high (Taylor and Finch 74). The structure, with the exception of the sliding ramp, was more or less hollow and made largely of plywood and plaster, smoothed over and painted silver. In fact, the lightweight structure nearly blew away in a windstorm and every available hand had to rush out to hold it down (Fidler 9-B). The ramp required more engineering to support the weight of actors as they played out their parts, which took some trial and error to pull it off. Wise remarked that "At first it seemed to work jerkily and not really look like something from outer space. So, time was spent getting the kinks out smoothly and silently" (74). Ultimately, stagehands manually operated the ramp, concealed by the spaceship, after Hehr perfected a device that allowed the structure to slide smoothly.

THE WRIGHT MAN FOR THE JOB?

When the saucer door is open, viewers get a glimpse into a modernist interior, later seen more fully when Klaatu initiates the global electrical shutdown and during his revival scene. According to the Hollywood legend, producer Julian Blaustein reached out to America's preeminent superstar architect, Frank Lloyd Wright, and he consulted with Thomas Little and Claude Carpenter on the design. The visual details inside certainly look as though Wright had a hand in the production. His visual style integrates geometry to serve form and function elegantly and is trademarked by horizontal planes, aesthetic grids and curvilinear forms. Wright's works include some of the most famous buildings in the United States including the Fallingwater house in Pennsylvania, the Guggenheim Museum in New York City and the Johnson Wax Headquarters in Wisconsin which supposedly influenced the design of Klaatu's ship.

Unfortunately, no traceable, concrete evidence exists to support the claim. It seems to rest mostly on statements made by Paul Laffoley, an ivy-league educated architect and visionary (i.e., spiritually inspired) artist, and a document he hand-wrote and first put on his website in 1996 known as "Disco Volante," the Italian phrase for "flying saucer." There, Laffoley writes the following:

> In a sense, the movie was the first piece of collaborative architecture ever done by Frank Lloyd Wright (1867-1959). He was contacted in 1949 by Robert Wise to work on the set design because Wise knew of Wright's interest in flying saucers from drawings in progress using the flying saucer form. Both The Annunciation Greek Orthodox Church (built 1956) and the Sports Club for Huntington Hartford (unbuilt 1947) are examples.
>
> Working with set designers for the movie, Thomas Little and Claude Carpenter, Wright came up with the classic flying saucer profile: the soliton wave or curve of normal distribution. The interior of the ship was "lifted" right out of The Johnson Wax Company Administrative Headquarters Wright had been working on since 1936. The horizontal translucent plastic tubing motif was a perfect foil for the Bauhaus-like control instruments.
>
> The metal that sheathes both Gort and the Thanaton was, as Wright said at the time, "...to imitate an experimental substance that I have heard about which acts like living tissue. If cut, the rift would appear to heal like a wound, leaving a continuous surface with no scar."

The statement certainly sounds like Wright, especially when you consider that he conceived the Guggenheim Museum, still in design in 1951, as "a living organism." Reportedly, while visiting the construction site in 1957, Wright commented, "'It is all one thing, all an integral, not part upon part. This is the principle I've always worked toward'" (Mendelsohn).

Unfortunately, if Wright did work on the saucer design, only Laffoley seems to know about it. Margo Stipe, Director of Collections at The Frank

Lloyd Wright Foundation could find no corroboration of the statement or even Wright's participation:

> I have not found any correspondence between Wright and these set designers, nor is the film on the list of films that were shown at Taliesin. And we have a list beginning in the late 1930s. And Wright doesn't mention it in his talks to the Fellowship, although he does talk about film. So, it seems really odd to me that he would have been so involved and not have said anything about it.

Laffoley provides no sources or documentation for Wright's line about the ship (which he calls the Thanaton) and Gort being made of a self-healing experimental substance for cross-checking the statements. Theoretically, Laffoley might have met Wright and discussed the topic, but Wright died in 1959, two years before Laffoley began training as an architect, making a professional discussion unlikely.

A number of problems crop up when putting Laffoley's assertions about Wright's involvement to the test. His "Disco Volante" timeline gets dates and other information wrong. For example, he claimed that Wise had the idea for a flying saucer movie and he contacted Wright who agreed to design the saucer on February 3, 1949. However, all records show Blaustein originated the idea at least six months after the February 3 date. His date for beginning production is exactly one year too early (a typo perhaps). And as students of the UFO phenomenon will instantly recognize, his description of Wright's material concept sounds very much like the material supposedly found at a New Mexico saucer crash site in 1947 according to Charles Berlitz and William L. Moore's 1980 best seller, *The Roswell Incident*.

At this point, we must consider Laffoley and his relationship to *The Day the Earth Stood Still*, which he said inspired him to become an architect so that he could "design flying saucers," and to UFOs in general ("Disco Valonte" Timeline). The most complete source of information on Laffoley is a 2005 documentary (which had his participation) by Jean-Pierre Larroque called *The Mad One*, based on the French root of his name, *la folle*. Using cranial X-rays to demonstrate, Laffoley discusses the discovery of an object in his skull his "Disco Volante" timeline refers to as "a miniature metallic 'implant'" which he believed was "a 'nanotechnological laboratory'" capable of accelerating or retarding my brain activity like a benign tumor and "the main motivation of my ideas and theories"

(Laffoley). He also holds that he had periodic contact with extraterrestrials. Laffoley's intellect is unquestionable and he speaks lucidly about his own thought process, realizing that his brain—his reality—differs from the norm. But it is also clear that his information may come from a source impossible to substantiate objectively.

ONE COLD GOLF COURSE

Once the flying saucer was built, shooting could begin. The scenes came together on the 20th Century Fox backlot known by the long-time employees as "the golf course," since a course had occupied the space before they converted it to city streets. Not realizing that the links were long gone, Michael Rennie brought his clubs to work one day hoping to get a few rounds in when he saw "the golf course" listed as the shooting location on the call sheet (Fidler 19).

Production began in early April. "I have a vivid memory of the backlot of 20th Century Fox, which turned into Century City," Bill Gray said. "In those days, it was kinda rolling hills and that's where they had the spaceship." The plywood and plaster creation served in day and night shots, including the scene when Gray's character, Bobby, follows Carpenter and witnesses him entering it after Gort has disabled the two guards. "It was cold as hell and everybody was all around 50-gallon drums they had fires going in." In between takes, the cast and crew would warm up as they could and the fires were kept going until the work was done.

Offering a convincingly unvanquishable robot offered another problem. To create the illusion, the effects team constructed two suits of foam rubber. They made a mold for the body suit and covered it with fiber-glass cloth, allowed that to harden and then applied liquid rubber over it until the form was completed. One suit laced up the back (for front shots) and the second laced up the front (for back shots) (Johnson 11). The hands, feet and head (separate parts) went on once Lock Martin donned the suit. The head was made with sheet metal and covered in the same way. Hehr also crafted an identical but larger head for close-ups of Gort when he uses his heat ray (Rubin 21).

Because of the heavy and uncomfortable nature of the suit, they also made a static and slightly larger fiberglass Gort for shots where the robot remains unnervingly motionless. Wise and the technical crew had concerns regarding the way the legs crease at the knees when Gort walks, but the foam rubber molded right back into shape, which could all be chalked up to the exotic extraterrestrial materials, (perhaps contributing to Laffoley's idea that Frank Lloyd Wright first envisioned the material). At one point, however, the suit did tear at the knees as Gort comes through the jail wall to retrieve Klaatu's body and Wise began yelling for repairs. Reportedly an electrician commented on all the fuss: "You'd think Betty Grable had torn a run in her stocking" (Johnson, Erskine 12).

Music

Bernard Herrmann, the composer who scored *The Day the Earth Stood Still*, was something of a child prodigy. Born in New York City in 1911, he gravitated toward music at an early age and studied composition at NYU and Julliard, conducting on Broadway while still a student. By 20, he was performing special concerts at the Library of Congress. In 1933, he went to work for CBS radio, composing pieces for broadcast, and in 1938, he composed, arranged and conducted music for *Mercury Theater on the Air*, the Orson Welles program that began its short run with a radio version of *Dracula* and infamously produced a documentary style interpretation of *War of the Worlds* that panicked late arriving listeners the night before Halloween.

But there was a price to pay for his genius, namely Herrmann's fiery temper and stubborn, willful personality. The relationship between director Robert Wise and the composer exemplified this. It began a decade before *The Day the Earth Stood Still* when Wise was working as an editor on Orson Welles' *Citizen Kane* (1941). Wise admired Herrmann's educated and encompassing intellect but found him opinionated and vocal. Soon after their first meeting, the two butted heads. According to Wise:

> He started to raise heck about something with me, and finally I just got fed up with it. I told him to go to hell and get out of the room. He said something about, if he didn't get it straight then he'd go back to New York, and I said, "Well the hell with you – go back to New York! Who needs you?!" Half an hour later, I went to the commissary to have lunch, and there was Bernie at a table, waving me over, just as friendly as he could be. Nothing thought of it. (Smith)

Fortunately, the dust up didn't impact Wise's ability to work with Herrmann as they would be paired for two more RKO projects, *The Magnificent Ambersons* (1942) and *All That Money Can Buy* (1941), a cinematic retelling of "The Devil and Daniel Webster" with a musical score that won Herrmann his sole Oscar.

In his 1996 interview with Steven C. Smith, Wise could not recall if he or the studio arranged for Herrmann to score the film, "but I had tremendous respect for his talent," the director recalled. "I felt it was the kind of film that would intrigue him, and he would do a really outstanding job… It was something that gave him an opportunity to do something special, something a little different than he had done, and he did just that."

Like Tiomkin assembling the exotic orchestra used in *The Thing*, Herrmann saw the value of unconventional instruments for the unconventional story. Since *The Thing* came out in theaters just as production began on *The Day the Earth Stood Still*, it is possible this influenced the shape of the score and orchestra, but no record of that exists and its more likely that "great minds think alike" in this case. In any case, as music analyst Bill Wrobel notes, Herrmann made additions to a traditional orchestra set up with two theremins, two Hammond organs, a pair of vibraphones, a tam tam (a gong with no definite pitch) and an "electric violin, electric cello, electric bass" (5).

Wrobel also notes that "20th Century Fox was a pioneer of a multi-track technique," in an age before stereo recording was possible and used a process of layering mono tracks. "If Herrmann wanted certain instruments featured or highlighted (such as the use of two theremins), then they might be separately miked and recorded into another optical track. Later the remix sound engineer would set a balance that would be best for all concerned" (2). Essentially, tracks could be composed over top of one another to achieve depth and thus each time you hear a theremin, it has been recorded on its own track and laid in over two orchestra tracks.

The creative use of electric instruments "produced an effect of rising tension by reiterating ominous chords and phrases, usually in the lower register of the orchestra" (Raksin) that pleased Wise in the final product. "I was thrilled," Wise later recalled. "I thought it was beyond anything I'd anticipated, in terms of the strange instruments… the theremins…" (Smith). For his part, Herrmann remarked in an article a month before the national release, "We've tried to convey the atmosphere of power and terror these visitors from space carry" (Best A-7). The reporter seems to have picked up on that, describing the music marking Gort's entrance as "a combination of a hurricane in barbed wire, history's worst traffic jam, 100,000 angry Dodgers fans, and a boiler factory rolling down hill" (A-7).

Herrmann would go on to compose and conduct for both television and film for another 24 years, working with some of the most recognizable talents in Hollywood and producing films scores for a wide variety of films, especially thrillers of one sort or another. His work can be heard on several Hitchcock films including *The Wrong Man* (1956), *Vertigo* (1958), *North by Northwest* (1959), *Psycho* (1960) and *The Birds* (1962). He also penned scores for the Ray Harryhausen stop-motion adventure tales *The 7th Voyage of Sinbad* (1958), *Mysterious Island* (1961) and *Jason and the Argonauts* (1963). His score for the strange horror film, *It's Alive* (1974), about a bloodthirsty baby who begins its killing spree straight from the womb, arguably elevates the movie out of pure schlock. Herrmann died on Christmas Eve after a long day of work on his final film, *Taxi Driver* (1976).

SELLING WORLD DESTRUCTION

On the successful heels of *The Thing* and *The Man from Planet X*, 20th Century Fox decided to go all-in on promotion of their first science-fiction film. Since the 1935 merger of Fox Film Corporation and Twentieth Century Pictures, the company focused on dramas and its prestige rose through World War II. Struggling RKO and upstart Mid-Century Films were the kinds of companies one would expect to take a stab at a risky new genre, but 20th Century Fox was far more conservative. However, from the outset, Wise, Blaustien and 20th Century committed themselves to the project, so it's not surprising that the studio encouraged lots of ballyhoo, especially in the wake of the preceding films.

To generate enthusiasm, 20th Century Fox took out a four-page ad promoting a coast-to-coast exploitation contest in the September issues of *Motion Picture Daily, Exhibitor,* and *Film Bulletin,* trade magazines covering current and upcoming pictures with news items, reviews and advertisements. The dramatic red, white and black ad touted a $15,000 "Showmanship Contest" open to managers of "any theater across the country" ("Showmanship" 9). Top prize, $1000 (payable in a savings bond), equated to around $10,000 in 2022. *Film Bulletin* noted "The picture is currently being heralded with a giant teaser campaign with an expected readership of 450,000,000" (Barn 14). That number, an example of ballyhoo math, was likely supplied by 20th Century's publicity department and either an exponentially empowered typo or they expected everyone in the country to see the promo at least three times.

And 20th Century was more than willing to provide significant support. It offered a free promotion kit which included a press book, radio ads, teaser trailers featuring the film's news reporters, a full trailer, and a free billboard sized 24 sheet poster. Die-cut cardboard stand-ups and Gort masks were available as well. They also provided a "Startling Tabloid Herald," a four-page mock newspaper designed to play into the documentary news style opening. Promoters could get it at cost with "initial printing runs to 1,000,000" ("National Pre-selling" 49). Its front page featured Gort standing before the armored might of Fort Meade's finest with the towering headline, "World Threatened with Destruction by Distant Planet." There was even a sound effects record to play in the lobby or pump out into the street.

The hard-sell 28-page press book laid it on thick with remarkable urgency, perhaps indicating a lack of faith that its cerebral sci-fi "yarn" would do as well as *The Thing* and *Planet X*. It advised promoters to take out the largest ads possible in boldface and capital letters. "**Steal the page!**" it demanded in boldface. "DOMINATE IT!" It further insisted that success was guaranteed but only with a relentless commitment from the theater. "This type of picture is successful in direct ratio to the pressure you keep putting on the public consciousness!"

One of the more interesting (and telling) promotions suggested was a tie-in between *Look Magazine*, McGregor Sports Wear and the film. Klaatu's space-faring costume was supposedly designed by *Look Magazine* men's wear editor, Perkins Bailey, who got a screen credit for the effort (Bernard Herrmann, incidentally, did not). However, the costume almost certainly came from 20th Century's design department with Bailey getting his one and only screen credit as a publicity stunt. The press book promoted an article featuring the suit appearing in the Oct. 23, 1951, edition of *Look*, but it was really a way to vaguely connect McGregor and their new sports jacket to the movie. Made from "truly out of this world materials" (nylon, orlon and milium) it was "inspired" by fashion from "5000 years ahead of our own time" (Press Book). Exhibitors were encouraged to write to McGregor rep Leonard Rich who would contact local retailers for "high powered local level merchandising promotions." It is unclear if anyone did this or even saw the connection.

Many theaters took 20th Century up on the promotional packet and several had ideas of their own. The film premiered on September 20, 1951, at the Mayfair Theater on 7th Avenue in Manhattan. Famous for its multi-story wrap around advertisements, the Mayfair sported a dramatic ad above the marquee with Gort carrying a hapless stock female from the poster (not Patricia Neal) with a hand grasping the Earth in the background. *Motion Picture Herald*, a trade magazine for theater owners and promoters, called it "The biggest sign on Broadway," noting the $15,000 contest ("Biggest" 12). Free tickets on opening day also played into the hoopla. When the Daily News announced the premiere on September 9, they added that "Hobbyists who have constructed spaceship models are promised free admission on opening day if their designs have been submitted to the 20th Century-Fox office" ("Science Fiction Thriller Coming, Section 2, p. 6).

For months after the film's release, the *Motion Picture Herald* followed the contest lauding Phil Chaiton in uptown New York who tried to commandeer the Westinghouse robot, Elektro, and failing that, created his own seven-foot six-inch robot out front and another in the theater ("Phil Chaiton" 52). The same page featured a picture of promoter Ivan Ackery, of the Orpheum Theater in Vancouver, working on his campaign from a hospital bed flanked by a nurse and doctor. He would ultimately take second place with over 300 "stunts" including a "find Gort" contest in the city ("Ackery" 53). The grand prize winner, out of 211 entries, was Jerry Baker of the RKO Keith's theater in Washington, D. C., a natural for the city at the center of the film.

Reception

Reception in one way or another was positive for all three films featured in this book, but *The Day the Earth Stood Still* carried the most weight intellectually and is still generally held in the highest esteem. The Oscars were not ready for science-fiction just yet, but Bernard Herrmann's score was nominated for a Golden Globe. More importantly, *The Day the Earth Stood Still* won their Best Film Promoting International Understanding award, a prize begun in 1946 after World War II. Incidentally, it was the second movie produced by Julian Blaustein to take home that award. *Broken Arrow* from 1950 did so as well.

A few weeks before the official release, the Science Fiction Writers of America awarded the film a Certificate of Merit, the first for any film, at their 9th annual convention, which screened the film in advance of a national release. This probably constitutes a well-crafted publicity stunt since the group supposedly voted to use the film to promote interest in science fiction clubs, yet the official pressbook already included a list of 21 sci-fi clubs across the country for that very purpose. Fox's *Movietone Newsreel* (Vol 34, No.74) captured the event, which 20th Century "exploitation representative" Alec Moss arranged. In fact, Moss provided Klaatu's costume for an unnamed alien (quite possibly Moss himself) to sport before the cameras ("New Orleans" NT-4). "Kla-a-tu," as narrator Joe King over-enunciates it, "learns a quaint earth custom. He receives a certificate of merit from the science fiction convention at New Orleans. It's presented by Chairman Moore for the faithfulness of the film to the best science fiction traditions." The whole thing gets only 22 seconds of attention, less than a fifth of the time devoted to "America Hails 1952 Queens of Beauty."

On the day it opened, September 19, 1951, Jimmy Fidler's column encouraged ticket sales with his appraisal. "Amazing in its conviction, and breathtaking in its suspense, it's sure to be a favorite with all audiences" (6). *The Film Bulletin* saw the movie as a big money maker but also a "meticulously produced" film. "'The Day the Earth Stood Still' is the best so far in the science fantasy cycle with an intriguing story about visitors from another planet" ("Day" 19). *Exhibitor* held a similar view: "One of the best, if not the best, of the science fiction pictures to date, this is fascinating throughout and suspensefully unfolded. Performances are good and the direction and production are in the better class" ("Too Late" 3155). *Variety* praised the film as well—in so far as the publication ever praised science fiction in those days. "'Day the Earth Stood Still', Fox's entry into the science-fiction sweepstakes, differs from its predecessors in that the fantasy and suspense are tinged with a sharply-pointed moral... only seldom does its moralistic wordiness get in the way." It also noted that the cast was "secondary to the story but works well." Rennie is "fine," Neal is "attractive and competent," and Hugh Marlowe is "sufficiently a boor." Sam Jaffe and Billy Gray earn slightly higher praise. (Stal 6).

Gene Handsaker showed more disdain for the film in his review. Lumping it with *When Worlds Collide* (still two months from release), he told readers to "brace yourselves for a couple of real weirdies" which he called "unconvincing." While he commended Rennie for keeping his British accent "from getting too broad" and accepts that Klaatu learned English from listening to radio broadcasts, he wonders how he learned to read or master a necktie. "Not even Drew Pearson, Gabriel Heatter, H. V. Kaltenborn, and Elmer Davis, at their microphones, giving the lowdown on the spaceman, will make you believe all this is really happening" (21). Famed *New York Times* critic, Bosley Crowther, known for his negative reviews ranging from caustic ire to dismissive mockery, penned his opinion in similar tones. He found Klaatu's politeness and sophistication inappropriate and ultimately dull: "But in a fable of such absurd assumptions as this one amusingly presents, cold chills might be more appropriate than lukewarm philosophy. One expects more—or less—than a preachment on political morality from a man from Mars" (Crowther).

Another interesting response to the film came from William H. Mooring in *The Tidings*, the official newspaper of the Catholic Archdiocese of Los Angeles. Writing about several films in an article entitled "Genuine Prayer, Religion Virtually Taboo in Films," he laments that filmmakers use God like a "Hollywood extra":

> General references to God in some motion pictures are simply evasive. In one new film, "The Day the Earth Stood Still," which is a highly entertaining even though deliberately fantastic tale about a man and a robot from another planet who make a sweet landing in Washington via a flying saucer, the one fleeting reference to God's supremacy refers to him as "The Almighty Spirit." This sounds like something out of a tale about Red Indian tribes. Why did they evade the use of the blessed name of God? (23)

Given that the response comes in a religious paper, Mooring's position that films should work to confirm his personal beliefs is not shocking. However, he seems to have missed the Christ/Klaatu connection altogether and one would think he'd express more consternation about the resurrection scene itself… the very thing the "Almighty Spirit" reference was designed to ameliorate (and apparently did). Had it gone out as North and Blaustein intended, one wonders what Mooring would have said then. As it is, he rated the film "Good" a week later in his film review column with the caution regarding Klaatu's threat to destroy Earth if humans don't discontinue their militaristic ways: "There's a catch in it somewhere, but as long as we see it strictly for laughs, it's quite entertaining" (21).

CONCLUSIONS

In the decades since those early reviews, the film has only increased in its general reputation despite its 1950s special effects and framework (which seems more alien to first time contemporary viewers than either Klaatu or Gort.) *The Day the Earth Stood Still* requires a bit more patience and intellectual engagement from an audience than *The Thing from Another World*, but in that regard, also provides more as a payoff. The nuclear war theme seemed prescient in its time but as the Cold War posturing gradually reduced itself to a few vulgar gestures here and there, the film might seem to lose its punch. But perhaps that misses the real point of the movie. Humanity is its own worst enemy and that underlying problem has not gotten any better.

Ultimately, *The Day the Earth Stood Still* offers a few completely new concepts to cinematic science-fiction. It establishes for the first time an extra-terrestrial community of planets and civilizations that reflects the budding hopes of the United Nations in 1951. More importantly, it endorses a kind of responsible futurism as a minimum requirement for advancing our society. In other words, we must abandon war and conflict if we want to leave our little rock. Evolution works toward refinement in this theme, and it requires a new type of thinking and behavior. In retrospect, the film's iconoclastic qualities certainly could have caused problems since it calls into question the "Us vs. Them" mentality that drives *The Thing from Another World*. Klaatu's ideal society is probably not materialistic, capitalistic, segregated or martial in any way, a true counterculture vision in the age of the Cold War.

Works Cited

20th Century Fox, *Movietone*. "Newsreel 1952-Japan Peace Treaty, and Klaatu." *YouTube*, uploaded by cdgr0820, 29 Mar. 2016, www.youtube.com/watch?v=Y7YpjnMhp9M&t=292s.

"Ackery Lists 300 Stunts." *Motion Picture Herald*, 12 April. 1952, p. 53.

Asherman, Allan. "The Man Who Was Klaatu… Michael Rennie." Filmfax, No. 17, November 1989, pp. 74-79.

Bates, Harry. "Farewell to the Master." http://www.digital-eel.com/blog/library/Farewell_to_the_Master.pdf

Best, William. "Sound Score from Movie of Future Shocks Listener." *Hanford Daily Sentinel*, 22 August 1951, p. A-7.

"Biggest Sign on Broadway." *Motion Picture Herald*, 6 Oct. 1951, p. 12.

Cooper, J. C. *An Illustrated Encyclopaedia of Traditional Symbols*. Thames and Hudson, Ltd., 1987.

Crowther, Bosley. "Emissary From Planet Visits Mayfair Theatre in 'Day the Earth Stood Still.'" https://www.nytimes.com/1951/09/19/archives/the-screen-in-review-emissary-from-planet-visits-mayfair-theatre-in.html. Originally published in *New York Times*, 19 September 1951.

Daniels, Farrington. "Poll Results of the Chicago Scientists | The Manhattan Project | Historical Documents | Atomicarchive.Com." *Atomicarchive.Com*, 1945, www.atomicarchive.com/resources/documents/manhattan-project/chicago-poll.html.

"*The Day the Earth Stood Still* (1951) Press Book." *From Zombos' Closet*, 1951, www.zomboscloset.com/zombos_closet_of_horror_b/2016/11/the-day-the-earth-stood-still-1951-press-book.html.

"'The Day the Earth Stood Still' Sock Science Fiction." *The Film Bulletin, Vol 19*, No. 20, 24 September 1951, p. 19.

Ellis, Peter Berresford. *A Dictionary of Irish Mythology*. ABC-CLIO, 1987.

Emrg. "Einstein Enigmatic Quote." *Icarus Falling*, 24 June 2009, icarus-falling.blogspot.com/2009/06/einstein-enigma.html. Accessed 25 Aug. 2021.

Fidler, Jimmy. "In Hollywood." *Monroe News Star*, 5 April 1951, p. 9-B.

———. "In Hollywood." *Quad City Times*, 22 May 1951, p. 19.

———. "In Hollywood." *Quad City Times*, 19 September 1951, p. 6

Gehring, Wes. D. *Robert Wise: Shadowlands*. Indianapolis, Indiana Historical Society, 2012.

Gray, Bill. Personal Interview with Sean Kotz. 2 September 2021.

Graybeal, Jay. Email to Sean Kotz. 16 Sept 2021.

Handsaker, Gene. "Hollywood Column." *The Morning Call*, 18 September 1951, p. 21.

Haspel, Paul. "Future Shock on the National Mall: Washington, DC, as Disputed Ideological Space in Robert Wise's *The Day the Earth Stood Still." Journal of Popular Film and Television*, vol. 34, no. 2, 2006, pp. 63–71. *Crossref*, doi:10.3200/jpft.34.2.63-71.

Heffernan, Harold. "Boon for New Actors." *Kansas City Star*, 13 April 1951, p. 15.

Hopper, Hedda. "Anne Baxter Gets Lead in Story of Space Ship Landing in Washington." Chicago Daily Tribune, 29 April 1950, Part 1, p. 16.

———. "Standstill." Daily News. 18 April 1951, p. 70.

Johnson, Edward. "Bernard Herrmann – A Biographical Sketch." *Bernardherrmann.Org*, bernardherrmann.org, 1977, www.bernardherrmann.org/articles/biographical-sketch.

Johnson, Erskine. "Crawford, Derek, Donna Reed Star in Tabloid Film Tale." Fresno Bee, 6 June 1951, p. 12.

Johnson, John J. *Cheap Tricks and Class Acts: Special Effects, Makeup and Stunts from the Films of the Fantastic Fifties.* McFarland & Company, Inc. Publishers. Jefferson, NC. 1996.

———. "Icebox in Oldtime Hollywood Home Now Servant's Bedroom." Marshfield News Herald, 2 May 1951, p. 20.

Johnson, John. J. *Cheap Tricks and Class Acts: Special Effects, Makeup and Stunts from the Films of the Fantastic Fifties.* McFarland & Company, Inc. Publishers. Jefferson, NC. 1996.

Kennan, Richard C. *The Films of Robert Wise.* Scarecrow Press, 2007. pp. 69-74.

Laffoley, Paul. "Disco Volante." http://www.cybercom.net/~gsullivan/bvc/disco_volante.html. Accessed 4 November 2021.

———. "Disco Volante" (Timeline). https://paullaffoley.net/writings-2/disco-volante/. Accessed 4 November 2021.

Leeman, Sergio. *Robert Wise on His Films.* Silman-James Press, 1995. pp 57-107.

Lienart, Paul. "The True Cost of Buying a Car." *The Chicago Tribune*, 16 June 1996, https://www.chicagotribune.com/news/ct-xpm-1996-06-16-9606160132-story.html. Accessed 29 October 2021.

MacPherson, Virginia. "Planet Love Has Director Worried Stiff." *Santa Maria Times*, 27 August 1951, p. 6.

The Mad One. Directed by Jean-Pierre Larroque. Featuring Paul Laffoley. Doublethink Productions, 2005.

Mendelsohn, Ashley. "Wright's Living Organism: The Evolution of the Guggenheim Museum." Guggenheim.org, https://www.guggenheim.org/blogs/checklist/wrights-living-organism-the-evolution-of-the-guggenheim-museum. 20 June 2017. Accessed 4 November 2021.

Miles, Marvin. "2000 M.P.H. Planes to Fly at 125,000 feet." *Los Angeles Times*, 31 March 1951, p. 1.

Mooring, William H. "Genuine Prayer, Religion Virtually Taboo in Films." *The Tidings*, 21 September 1951, p. 23.

———. "Film Reviews." *The Tidings*. 28 September 1951, p. 21.

———. "Reviews." *The Tidings*, 28 September 1951, p. 23.

"National Pre-selling." *Motion Picture Herald*, 20 Oct. 1951, p. 49.

Neal, Patricia, with Richard DeNuet. *As I Am*. Simon and Schuster, 1988. p. 101-107.

Nemerov, Alexander. "This Pretty World: The Films of Val Lewton." *The Criterion Collection*, 4 Oct. 2019, www.criterion.com/current/posts/6620-this-pretty-world-the-films-of-val-lewton.

"New Orleans." *Exhibitor*. 12 September 1951, p. NT-4.

North, Edmund. *The Day the Earth Stood Still (Revised Final Draft)*. 12 February 1951. http://www.dailyscript.com/scripts/the_day_the_earth_stood_still.html

———. "Interview of Edmund Hall North." Interviewed by Joel Gardener. Tape Number 2, Side 1. 14 January 1980.

Oliver, Valerie. "The History of the Yo-Yo." *Museum of Yo-Yo History*, reprinted from Spintastics Skill Toys, www.spintastics.com, http://www.yoyomuseum.com/museum_view.php?action=profiles&subaction=yoyo. Accessed 20 October 2021.

"Obituary of Marilyn Lurene Novak | Adams Green Funeral Home." *Adamsgreen.Com*, 2015, adamsgreen.com/tribute/details/3483/Marilyn-Novak/obituary.html.

Parsons, Luella. "Good News." *Modern Screen*. August 1951. p 19.

———. "Good News." *Modern Screen*. October 1951. p 7.

———. "Hollywood." *Bangor Daily News*. Bangor Maine, 30 September 1946.

Perkowitz, Sydney. *Hollywood Science: Movies, Science and the End of the World*. Columbia University Press, NYC, 2007.

"Phil Chaiton Heard From." *Motion Picture Herald*, 22 Dec. 1951, p. 52.

"'Pin-up Queen' Wonders If She Is One." *The Evening Star* [Washington, D. C.], 14 May 1951, p. B-1.

Raksin, David. "Camera Three: Bernard Herrmann (Transcript)." *Bernard-herrmann.Org*, CBS News, 1997, www.bernardherrmann.org/articles/transcript-camera_three Originally aired September 1976.

Ruark, Robert C. "If Flying Saucers Land on Earth Our Troubles with Reds May End." *Springfield Leader and Press*, 1 January 1951, p. 12.

Rubin, Steve. "Retrospective: The Day the Earth Stood Still." *Cinefantastique*, Vol. 4, No. 4. pp. 5-22.

"Science Fiction Thriller Coming." *Daily News*, 9 September 1951, Section 2, p. 6.

Scheuer, Philip K. "Flying Saucer Film Dishes Up Choices." Los Angeles Times, 20 May 1951, Part IV, p. 3.

Schuer, Bradley. *Escape Velocity: American Science Fiction Film 1950-1982*. Wesleyan University Press, 2017.

Shapiro, Jerome. *Atomic Bomb Cinema: The Apocalyptic Imagination on Film*. Routledge, 2002, p. 80-82.

"Showmanship Contest." *Film Bulletin*. Sept. 19, 1951. pp. 9-12.

Skolsky, Sidney. "Hollywood is My Beat." *Los Angeles Evening Citizen News*, 19 January 1951, p. 15.

Skolsky, Sidney. "Hollywood is My Beat." *Los Angeles Evening Citizen News*, 6 July 1951, p. 15.

Smith, Steven C. "For the Heart at Fire's Center – Robert Wise." *Bernardherrmann.Org*, 1996, www.bernardherrmann.org/articles/smith-wise.

Stal. "The Day the Earth Stood Still." Variety, 5 September 1951, p. 6.

Stipe, Margo. Email to Sean Kotz. 3 November 2021.

Stein, Michael. "Billy Gray: The Boy Who Saw the Earth Stand Still." *Filmfax* no. 96, *2003*, pp. 57-58.

Szilard, Leo. "Petition to the President of the United States, July 17, 1945." *Harry S. Truman Library and Museum*, www.trumanlibrary.gov/ library/research-files/petition-president-united-states. Accessed 25 Aug. 2021.

Taylor, Al and Doug Finch. "Director Robert Wise Remembers *The Day the Earth Stood Still*." *Filmfax*, no. 17, Oct. 1989, pp. 70–75.

Thomas, Bob. "In Movieland." *The Monroe News-Star*, 1 May 1951, p. 9.

"Too Late to Classify." *Exhibitor*. September 12, 1951. p. 3155.

Walker, Barbara. *The Women's Encyclopedia of Myths and Secrets*. Castle Books, 1996.

Watch the Skies: Science Fiction, the 1950s and Us. Directed by Richard Shickel, Performances by Mark Hamill, George Lucas, Steven Spielberg, Ridley Scott, Turner Classic Movies, 2005.

Wise, Robert. Interview by Harry Kreisler. "Wise Films: *The Day the Earth Stood Still*," Conversations with History; Institute of International Studies, UC Berkeley, Regents of the University of California, 1998, http://globetrotter.berkeley.edu/conversations/Wise/wise-con7.html. Accessed 26 October 2021.

Wise, Robert. Interview by Tom Weaver. "Robert Wise." *It Came from Horrorwood: Interviews with Moviemakers in the SF and Horror Tradition*. McFarland and Co., Inc. 1996. pp. 341-351.

Wrobel, Bill. "Bernard Herrmann's Day the Earth Stood Still Film Score Rundown." *Film Score Rundowns*, 15 Jan. 2021, www.filmscore-rundowns.net/herrmann/dess.pdf.

6

The Man From Planet X

OF THE THREE FILMS, *The Man from Planet X* was technically released first, on March 9, 1951, in an advanced screening at the Paramount Theater in San Francisco. However, in terms of analysis, it places better after *The Thing from Another World* and *The Day the Earth Stood Still* as it has one foot in each. In the former film, the alien constitutes an unmitigated danger—nothing less than an enemy capable of wiping out humanity. In *The Day the Earth Stood Still*, Klaatu, comes to Earth as a harbinger of destruction, laying the responsibility for Earth's impending doom upon human moral failings. But *The Man from Planet X* gives us the good, the bad and the ugly. On one hand, the principal heroes of the film, reporter John Lawrence (Robert Clarke) and Enid Elliot (Margaret Field), demonstrate basic virtues and are not inclined toward violence. In contrast, Dr. Mears (William Schallert) exemplifies the very qualities Klaatu admonishes—greed, self-interest, deception and aggression. As for the ugly, we have the title character, an ambiguously motivated, physically repulsive representative of a dying world. But the film doesn't tell us what to think about this character—that's left for us to decipher from the events. And the question may not have a resolution. As we hear in the final lines, the man from Planet X might have been "the greatest curse to befall the world or perhaps the greatest blessing."

At the time, all three of 1951's alien films (as well as George Pal's *When Worlds Collide* which arrived in November of that year) constituted "exploitation" flicks, capitalizing on the flying saucer craze and budding rocket race of the day. But unlike the others, *The Man from Planet X* was an exploitation of the exploitation. In other words, similar to the way Lippert had rushed *Rocketship XM* to capitalize on *Destination Moon*'s advanced publicity, the producers knew exactly what they were doing in pushing forward this hastily conceived movie. As the film's star, Robert Clarke wrote in *Starlog 219*:

> I had the feeling that we were racing to get *Planet X* "in the can" in order to capitalize on *The Thing*... My hunch was confirmed when someone, I can't remember who (not Pollexfen or Wisberg), actually told me, "This will be a small budget picture, but what they're trying to do is capture some of the momentum, the publicity stuff that has gone out about *The Thing*" (29).

The Thing from Another World and *The Day the Earth Stood Still* had big budgets and took more than a year from conception to completion. Their effects saw careful development and oversight, their stories got several revisions, and their publicity campaigns approached A level treatment. In contrast, *The Man from Planet X* was an independent movie written, produced, filmed, edited and set for distributorship in about two months, and against expenses, by far the most financially successful of the three.

AN ODDLY MATCHED COUPLE

The producers/writers of *The Man from Planet X* made an unlikely but generally successful pair. Aubrey Wisberg, an Englishman, and Jack Pollexfen, an American, had quirky personalities as unique as their names. "They were an oddly matched couple of guys," William Schallert (Dr. Mears in the film) told Tom Weaver for *Starlog #184*. "I don't know that Wisberg and Pollexfen ever had any original ideas but they were very good at grabbing on to ideas that had some merit" (58).

All indications suggest the pair had a successful professional relationship spawned by mutual interest in writing and producing pictures for profit, content to make low budget exploitation movies with rapid shooting schedules and maximized returns. However, the relationship dissolved sometime around 1955. *Return to Treasure Island* (1954) was the last both wrote and produced together; *Son of Sinbad* (1955) was the last crediting the pair as writers. No single event ostensibly blew up the partnership. Instead, it seems to have run its course, though Wisberg had a habit of creating conflicts (including one with director Edgar Ulmer while filming *The Man from Planet X*) that might make working with him difficult. "Wisberg got into feuds with an awful lot of people—that was probably the main reason I finally broke up with him," Jack Pollexfen once recounted. "He would be irritated if, say, a cameraman who'd worked for us once was not available on the next picture, and things of that nature. Very touchy" (277). This appraisal mirrors Tom Weaver's experience seeking an interview with Wisberg. In the audio commentary for the 2017 Blu-ray release of the film, Weaver revealed that Wisberg denied him access merely because the interviewer had already spoken to Pollexfen.

Wisberg arrived in America around the age of 12 and later attended NYU and Columbia. He had a wide range of writing credits including novels, screenplays and journalistic efforts, publishing as early as 1930 at the age of 20 when his crime story, "The Informer," appeared in the *Daily News* (New York), which would publish many of his early tales. His first film writing credits date to 1942 for *Submarine Raider*. Reasonably prolific, Wisberg's screenwriting resume boasted twenty credits before he began working with Jack Pollexfen in 1949 on *Treasure of Monte Cristo*. Clarke recalled that "Wisberg was the more outgoing of the two; he was a bit more of the spokesman, it seemed to me. Nice men both, but very different from each other" (78).

Aubrey Wisberg died of cancer on March 14, 1990, having made very few films after the breakup with Pollexfen. His final film, *Hercules in New York* (1970) was Arnold Schwarzenegger's first (crediting the German muscleman and future governor of California as Arnold Strong). The dubious comedy received harsh criticism, even as late as 1991, when the syndicated "Phantom of the Movies" column chided Wisberg by name, calling his last movie "not only atrocious on every level but, with its broad gags, awkward reaction shots and tin-eared remedial dialog, hopelessly dated and out-of-it to boot, even by 1970s standards" ("Arnie's first" 43). Wisberg, however, would maintain a writer's life after *Hercules in New York* and produce stage plays in the 1970s and '80s.

The other half of the team, Jack Pollexfen, entered the game later than Wisberg but in a similar way. Like Wisberg, Pollexfen began writing at a young age, with bylined articles appearing as early as 1934 in the *Los Angeles Evening Post Record* and in-house references to him in the same paper a year earlier. According to Louella Parsons, he wrote a film in 1942 slated for Myrna Loy and MGM called *The Sob Sister* about a murder and misery reporter (7), but it never seems to have gotten past the story's purchase. However, it opened a door to Hollywood and a year later

Pollexfen's screenplay co-written with Dorothy Bennett called *Mister Big* made it to the screen. Still, his career would not gain much traction until he teamed with Wisberg.

Like Wisberg, Pollexfen's film career also quickly sputtered after the breakup, producing just three more films. He wrote and ultimately directed *The Indestructible Man* (1956) starring Lon Chaney, a picture that fell into the public domain and sees lots of circulation as a result. He also wrote and produced *Daughter of Dr. Jekyll* directed by Edgar Ulmer and starring B movie perennials John Agar and Gloria Talbott the following year, but after that did very little film or television work with one notable exception. *Monstrosity* (1963) began as a Pollexfen script under the title "The Brain Snatchers" in 1958 when it was shot and ranked as Pollexfen's least favorite and self-admittedly worst movie. "It was the only picture I ever tried to make without a first rate, professional crew. That was a lesson to me," he said (Pollexfen 282). "*Monstrosity*. The name describes it" (283).

After *The Man from Planet X*, Pollexfen would go on to write, produce and occasionally direct a total of 18 films, all low budget affairs, through 1963. He seems to have had a more even-keeled personality than his partner but remained something of a natural outsider in the business. William Schallert recalled him as "a really strange looking guy" that the cast privately referred to as the real man from Planet X (57). Robert Clarke said, "Jack was a kind of shy and diffident individual—erudite in his background, someone you could imagine plowing through volumes and volumes of research material to get correct detail into his script" (78). In 1964, at the age of 55, he married Anna Lee Hecker and the pair seemingly went into real estate. He died in 2003 at the age of 95.

KING OF THE BS

If you can imagine Ed Wood with depth, genius, talent and something to say, you can imagine Edgar G. Ulmer. This is no slight against the director. Ulmer spent the bulk of his career making the most out of the least, saddled with pitiful budgets and clunky scripts, applying an artist's eye to problem solving and pulling solid performances out of his actors under difficult conditions. But for one important decision early in his American career, his name might have been as recognizable as Hawks and Wise.

Ulmer was born on September 17, 1904, to Jewish parents in Olomóc, an important city in Austria-Hungary (soon to become Czechoslovakia after World War I). He became an orphan when his father died in the war, ending up in Swedish foster care as a young teen before returning to the continent and finding his way into cinema as a set designer in Germany's post-war expressionist explosion. His early life mirrored his adult life in its constant instability and shifting conditions, but Ulmer adapted each time, perhaps preparing him for his future.

Ulmer lived in the United States from 1924-28 but returned to Europe for four years before coming to America for good in 1932, just before Nazism would drive much of Germany's art community west. He'd worked in New York with Max Reinhardt's stage production of *The Miracle* in 1924 and with F. W. Murnau on his masterful silent classic, *Sunrise* (1928). Ulmer returned to Germany to co-direct *Menschen am Sonntag* (*People on Sunday*) in 1930. He directed the camera work and visual elements while Robert Siodmak (the other director) worked with the actors—a commonplace arrangement in post-war Germany according to Ulmer. Billy Wilder wrote the film which depicts life in Berlin in an observational style before Hitler came to power. However, he did not aspire to occupy the director's chair in the silent era. "He would never have become a director if Murnau had not died," according to Ulmer's daughter, Arianne Ulmer Cipes. "He would have stayed as an art director. He would never have in any way left Murnau because he was part of a troupe" (Cipes).

Ulmer's creative versatility and willingness to take work, as well as his connection to German ex-pats in New York and Hollywood, primed him for success. His American directorial debut in "talkies" was a 1933 moralist film fraught with mixed messages, *Damaged Lives* (which he co-wrote as well). In it, the young male lead unknowingly contracts syphilis from a one-night stand right before he proposes and predictably passes it on to his bride. The horrors of syphilis get lots of hammy verbal tread, but the film resolves with a hopeful message about treatments and the heroine saying in a melodramatic fluttering gush, "Oh Donny! We're laughing again!" In other words, the film tells us—paradoxically--the terrifying and socially unforgivable disease is no big deal. It's the kind of film where a physician (Dr. Gordon Bates) gets a "Clinical Supervision" credit in the opening titles and gives a full screen acknowledgment of The American Hygiene Association. But more importantly, it was the first of several Ulmer films to send self-contradicting messages that still work together—something essential in *The Man from Planet X.*

Damaged Lives is far from high quality cinema. None-the-less, many critics found it sincere, despite performances ranging from awkward to sappy, and it did surprisingly well at the box office, supposedly taking $1.4 million (Isenberg 83) versus a budget of $18,000 (Schaefer 419). More importantly, as writer Noah Isenberg notes in *Edgar Ulmer: Filmmaker at the Margins*, it begins a pattern in Ulmer's work of "The Art of Outcasts" (82), a motif seen in *The Man from Planet X, Detour* (1945), and *The Strange Woman* (1946) among many others. If nothing else, Ulmer's first feature deftly walked the thematic borderlands of propriety and exile, showing his ability to use the camera to convey ideas through implication.

His next feature, the brooding and remarkably potent Universal horror classic, *The Black Cat* (1934), stands as a groundbreaking entry from the Gothic cinema era. Featuring Boris Karloff and Bela Lugosi as old rivals settling a score years after WWI, the film has an arresting aesthetic with no true parallel in its time. *The Black Cat* takes place in a modernist castle built on a mass grave. It's elegant lines and visionary design hide a dungeon where black magic, necrophilia and symbolic incest play out below. The film has no titular monster or even many black cats--in fact, its primary connection to the Edgar Allan Poe story that "inspired" it is the title. Yet, *The Black Cat* ranks among the best of the 1930s thrillers, and for many, reigns as Ulmer's masterpiece.

Ulmer came to the director's chair for this major production through a friendship with Carl Laemmle, Jr., the young general manager of Universal Studios. In fact, Ulmer claimed bringing Lugosi and Karloff together was his idea and he was given "free rein to write a horror picture in the style we had started in Europe with *Caligari*" (Ulmer, Edgar 575). But Carl Sr., the true head of Universal Studios, found horror films generally unsavory (despite their popularity) so the film moved forward while he toured Europe. Senior argued against releasing *The Black Cat* even after its completion on the flimsy basis that it had too much classical music in it and supposedly nobody liked classical music (Ulmer, Shirley 232). But Junior likely saved Universal with his pet projects *Dracula* and *Frankenstein* in 1931 and Ulmer's American Expressionist horror film became another success.

Unlike his robust father, Junior (his semi-derogatory nickname) was a "skirt-chasing" hypochondriac with "a deep distaste for reading scripts and a weakness for the track" (Isenberg 54). In an extensive interview with Tom Weaver, Shirley Ulmer (Edgar's wife) pegged Junior as "a very psycho, mixed up young man and Edgar was playing psychiatrist for him or something" (232). Edgar's loyalty and attention landed him the job di-

recting *The Black Cat* with nearly total freedom regarding script and production. The initial budget of $91,125 (which he over ran by about $4000)
was the largest Ulmer would ever work with, but still just a fraction of
Dracula and *Frankenstein*.

The final product earns significant praise today from film historians
for its thematic courage and visual execution. Ulmer's power of suggestion reaches its height in the climactic scene where Dr. Vitus Werdegast
(Bela Lugosi) flays Hjalmar Poelzig (Boris Karloff) alive as punishment for
stealing his wife, killing his daughter and betraying him in the war. Shot in
silhouette, the scene avoids the gore forbidden by the Production Code but
manages to evoke true horror in the screams and shadows it presents. One
can almost feel Lugosi smile maniacally. Ultimately, the nearly secondary
young married couple escape with their lives as the house is blown to bits,
setting the blueprint for the finale of *The Bride of Frankenstein* a year later.

Given his genius and the quality of this film, Ulmer's star should have
soared but a love scandal derailed his career from the outset. Around the
time of filming *The Black Cat*, Ulmer began an affair with the script supervisor, 20-year-old Shirley Alexander, nee Kassler, who would ultimately
become his wife. "She met dad when one night he came over to work
on a script," Arianne Ulmer Cipes explained. "They went out that night
because her husband, Max, wanted to go to bed early. Mother was young
liked to talk about her writing. So, dad took her out—Max sent them out
actually and said 'keep Shirley busy'—and of course that was how they
got involved" (Cipes). Unfortunately, her husband, Max Alexander, was a
producer and nephew to studio head Carl Laemmle, Sr. According to the
story, outraged and humiliated, Laemmle had the pair effectively black-
listed in Hollywood after their marriage in 1936 and Edgar Ulmer never
had a chance to work on a major production again. Ironically, however,
the Ulmers would work with Alexander again during their years at Producers Releasing Corporation (Kalat 143).

The marriage lasted until his death in 1972. Shirley fell for Edgar and
his continental intellect, as their daughter recalled:

> My mother was just a very simple, middle-class Jewish girl
> from a banking family in New York. And Dad was, of course,
> a European, an Austrian-Czech, and very cultured and Dad
> had already worked for 10 years as an art director. He was
> highly sophisticated compared to her.

Shirley liked to recount her re-education. Edgar "locked her literally for a month in the apartment they had in Hollywood and educated her on musicians and composers and writers and that kind of thing because she didn't have that kind of background," Arianne Ulmer Cipes explained. "My mother was absolutely fascinated, and she was fascinated with him."

The pair worked together over the following decades on a variety of small productions including European and Yiddish language films. They made a good team, especially since Shirley bridged the language barrier. Edgar never lost his thick accent and struggled with English. According to their daughter, Edgar would commonly stay up most of the night working in his own room on storyboards, script changes and dialog and in the morning, Shirley would sort them out into functional English, especially with the PRC films (Cipes). *The Man from Planet X* differed from this pattern, however, because Wisberg and Pollexfen's script could not be changed (seemingly by Wisberg's territorial insistence). Instead, Edgar concentrated on performances and visual tone while Shirley worked as the script supervisor, her primary profession. She was talented in that capacity and eventually penned a manual called The *Role of Script Supervision in Film and Television*, with C. R. Seville, used for instruction for many years.

A Bleak Visionary

Like Hawks and Wise, Ulmer managed a variety of genres, from horror to comedy, from Westerns to science fiction. But unlike them, Ulmer's early affair while making *The Black Cat* made many of his professional decisions for him, landing him frequently on "Poverty Row," a collection of marginal, third rate "studios" like PRC. (At one point, he even directed a "nudie" called *The Naked Venus* in 1958 to make ends meet.) However, with limited time and budgets, Ulmer seemed to do his best work. He'd isolate himself during a production, sleeping in a separate room and concentrating on bringing a vision to life with few resources. "His work was his most important thing," recalled Cipes. "Not his wife, not his family, not his friends. He wanted to communicate through his art."

Ulmer eventually became a cult icon of sorts for French New Wave and American New Hollywood directors because of this capacity to work within limits but also due to the potency of his moody noir films. "Edgar was a bleak visionary,'" Shirley Ulmer once remarked. "'The moors. Bronte. Brooding. This was Edgar. He always, always had to go emotionally to the most serious places'" (qtd. in Skotak 210). As a result, Ulmer became a master of noir. He coaxed his audience into dark and uncertain worlds with compromised and ambiguous characters, foggy, dimly lit sets, and arresting images echoing his German Expressionist roots—all of which would serve *The Man from Planet X* exceedingly well.

A BLEAK VISION

Remarkably, *The Man from Planet X* has gotten almost no critical attention compared to Ulmer's other films. This may reflect its status as an early sci-fi flick or a slap-dash cheapie reliant on borrowed sets, fog machines and canvas backdrops. However, the noir elements cited above—fog, ambiguity, compromised characters—emerge early in *The Man from Planet X*, giving it uncanny potency at times and successfully tying the coming era of space age science fiction to traditional Gothic horror films like *The Black Cat*.

This mixture of noir, Gothic horror and the space age science fiction emerges in the first five minutes of the film. The opening titles feature a contrast of stormy skies and lightning strikes reminiscent of a *Frankenstein* sequel, but utilize industrial lettering connected with nuts and bolts. The Charles Koff theme hammers urgently like a teletype over blasts of horns and sawing strings. As the credits conclude, the music rises briefly to a light, hopeful phrase to accompany the first shot of a sunny seaside… but quickly downturns as the scene cross-fades to a foggy Scottish moor. The camera pans right and pulls in slightly until it settles on a lonely, distant tower framed between the branches of a dead tree, rapidly shifting the mood 180 degrees.

We can just make out a tiny lighted window in the tower, cross fading again to a closer view of the archaic tower for less than three seconds (barely enough time to register it as a model), and then finally inside where reporter John Lawrence, played by Robert Clarke, grapples with a coming task. From behind, we see him pace a shadowy room in a low angle shot, emphasizing his solitude. As he arrives at a desk to write his account, we get a glimpse of his old bomber jacket. His hand pushes a pencil across a sheet until the lead snaps.

While this goes on, Lawrence provides a moody, desperate narration, orienting us to the conflict and plot while letting us know he has both personal and global concerns affecting his action:

> I don't know if she's still alive or not. They've had her for the past 24 hours. I am equally uncertain as to the fate of her father, Professor Eliot. Both are probably dead. The odds are 100-1 I too will be finished before another sun rises. But tonight, I'm going to try to fight for my life, and those larger issues so perilously at stake affecting all mankind. If I fail, as seems most likely, the consequences to humanity defy the imagination. As the only trained reporter who has been in a position to observe the terror from its inception, and as one of the few living humans who has actually met face to face a man from Planet X, I will try to set down the strangest story a newspaper man ever covered.

Throughout, we never get a good glimpse of his face, which remains in the shadows as he walks to the desk. We see his hand instead—writing, then gripping his weary face. He is an embodied emotion, a problem with no good solutions, a man who could be anyone.

Consider what happens in this short space. We move from sunlight to darkness, from exterior to interior, from innocence to crisis all in a matter of seconds, becoming invested in a mystery. Visually, the castle on the moors isolates us, the bomber jacket tells us our narrator is a war veteran (thus both sympathetic and fit for the task) and his broken pencil reveals the tension. We leave a world of light dominating darkness for its polar opposite as if to say that, just beyond our experience, just a step or two away in the dark places of the world, mystery and danger lurk, and momentous events may shape the future without us ever knowing. This encapsulates what Ulmer could do on a shoestring.

From there, the scene fades to black momentarily before resolving to an iris shot of a planet amid the stars. We hear Lawrence's voice again cluing us into the flashback that takes over the story. Now, we finally see the hero, dapper in a tailored suit, kerchief in the breast pocket, smart tie, pencil thin mustache. We follow Lawrence through the lab as he questions an astronomer, Dr. Blane (Gilbert Fallman), who soon cuts out the light to expose a photograph of the mysterious planet. We are again left in the dark momentarily to absorb the mystery through Lawrence's question, "What's it all about, Doctor?" As the lights return in stages and exposition unfolds, the camera yields shadowy subjects from a distance making viewers feel like a person who has arrived at a party too early to know anyone.

This is pure noir style in a sci-fi context (which we must remember was in development in 1951). Ulmer allows details to pile up using juxtaposition of image and dialog, largely propelled through questions, connecting our hero's confusion and curiosity to the audience. It presents a mystery through a character literally and figuratively in the dark. Moreover, this sequence moves from the misty tropes 1930s' Gothic horror to the film's contemporary realm of science seamlessly, establishing an abstract connection between the two necessary to pull off the content.

By the time Ulmer died in 1972, he had long faded from the public's eye but earned significant respect from American New Hollywood directors like Peter Bogdonovich and Joe Dante and critics like Roger Ebert, who honored and extended his aesthetic legacy. Ulmer, notoriously self-possessed and driven by uneven passions, ultimately left an equally uneven track record as a challenging director and person, but an unequivocal genius. For example, actor Robert Clarke told writer Gary D. Rhodes that Ulmer berated him during the production of *The Man from Planet X* for "ruining his film," a technique that probably came from one-part temperamental personality and another from his German cinema days. On the other hand, when Clarke needed a director to pilot *Beyond the Time Barrier* (1960), he went looking for Ulmer. "'Edgar's ability to get more out of a script,'" Clarke said, "and put more on the screen for less money (than anyone else) was already very well known. He'd already done that on *Planet X*'" (qtd. in Shotak 209-210).

ROBERT CLARKE

Robert Clarke became a sympathetic favorite for fans of 1950s B movies in no small part due to *The Man from Planet X*, but also because of his string of sci-fi flicks including *Captive Women* (1952), *The Astounding She-Monster* (1957), and *Beyond the Time Barrier* (1960). In 1958, Clarke wrote, produced, directed and starred in *The Hideous Sun Demon*, an inversion of the werewolf myth where the afflicted scientist (Clarke) transforms into the title monster when exposed to sunlight.

Planet X, like *The Thing from Another World*, featured a cast of virtually unknown actors, but Clarke had been in Hollywood since 1944 and had over 40 screen appearances in bit parts when he got the role of reporter John Lawrence. He got in at RKO playing in movies like *Zombies on Broadway* (1945), *Back to Bataan* (1945) and his first feature, *The Falcon in Hollywood* (1944). Clarke's ability and natural charm impressed actress Dorothy McGuire, a future Best Actress Oscar winner, who lobbied for his shot in the RKO's *Radio Stars on Parade* in 1945. But despite grabbing a dozen roles in that year, he was a long way from stardom. Florabel Muir wrote, "He's a mighty pleasant youngster and in case you want a glimpse of him off guard, go to Delores's Drive-In on the Strip. He'll hand you your change and flash you his smile" (6).

Clarke heard about auditions for the film through Malvin Wald, brother of producer Jerry Wald. He was taking a screen writing class under the former who suggested that both he and Margaret Field audition. After interviewing around 100 potential leads, Pollexfen and Wisberg settled on these two, who had starred together a few months before in *A Modern Marriage* and showed up as a pair for the audition (Clarke 28). They would share the screen again in 1952's *Captive Women*, another Pollexfen and Wisberg quickie, and remain lifelong friends.

The Only Trained Reporter

Neither too hard nor soft, Clarke comes over with some personal depth even if the roles in his hands were sometimes basically flat. Reporter John Lawrence, however, does have some complexity to match the delicacy of the situation established in the film and Clarke gives the character a thoughtful performance despite some clunky lines, cheap sets and difficult working conditions. He's marked for heroism with his bomber jacket and we learn he was with the 8th Air Force, a U.S. air wing largely responsible for attacks on northern European targets from 1942-1945. It was one of the first and longest deployed American units in the war and saw significant action and casualties. In 1951, most of the audience would know this and make the heroic association.

However, Lawrence never exhibits rash, gung-ho qualities, even in the midst of the crisis, representing a different type of hero, and perhaps a more seasoned, realistic one. Lawrence shows no propensity to look for enemies around every foggy crag and Lawrence's war years may have internalized the value of rational thought and goodwill. When he first meets the man from Planet X, he saves the alien by adjusting the valve on his failing air supply. He could have killed him there but rescues him in hopes of establishing contact. Whether he's driven by his reporter's desire for a story or a more general philosophy of outreach might merit debate, but the action does not.

Other positive qualities show early on as well. He acknowledges Enid's beauty without lechery, and more importantly, reveals a moral code in his distaste for Mears, who has done something unethical Lawrence thinks should have earned 20 years in prison. We never know the nature of Mears' transgression, but his greed and ego motivations suggest a betrayal of some sort—perhaps even an act of treason.

At the end of the film, the military has ordered a strike against the spacecraft and the villagers, including Enid and Professor Elliot, remain under the alien's mind control, prompting Lawrence's action referenced in the opening minutes. Since their mental state means they follow commands regardless of who gives them, Lawrence directs them away from the ship in the nick of time, but to accomplish this he must first disable the alien. Reversing the scene from earlier in the film, he cuts off the gas tank and subdues him. Even at this point, he's not a stone-cold killer. It is not even clear that he intends to do more than slow down the X man. We can say, however, that his moral code requires personal risk and sacrifice for others and that he looks for options before turning to violence. Lawrence acts based on a moral philosophy rather than a strategic one, separating him from most sci-fi heroes the age.

MARGARET FIELD

Margaret Field began life far from Planet X in Houston, Texas on May 10, 1922, as Margaret Morlan and grew up in Pasadena, California. According to her daughter, two-time Oscar winner Sally Field, Margaret fell into acting after being discovered while sitting in the Pasadena Playhouse (where Hugh Marlowe got started) one evening. Someone from Paramount recognized her physical screen potential and based only on her appearance (much like her *Thing* counterpart, Margaret Sheridan), she went under contract shortly after in January of 1945, signing a six-month option in May ("Options" 60). A few weeks later *Film Daily* sandwiched her alphabetically between Frank Faylen and Miriam Franklin in a list of recent Paramount sign-ons, citing the group of largely unknowns as "an eloquent testimony of the company's current eminence" ("119 Players" 4).

Despite the relative anonymity of the announcement, Field began her acting career studying under none other than Charles Laughton who ran the studio's internal acting school. In an interview with Darby Maloney for the Television Academy Foundation, Sally Field described her mother as a "working class actor," but also noted that Margaret Field developed high aesthetic standards and motivations under Laughton's guidance. "She looked at it as artistry, as a way of expressing human behavior," Sally Field recalled. "My mother's longings, I felt, strongly reverberated in me."

Margaret Field's premiere assignment was supposed to be *Masquerade in Mexico* ("Margaret" 96), but that did not transpire. Instead, her first screen appearance was as a nightclub entertainer in a Paramount musical short, "The Little Witch," the first of nine uncredited small roles from 1945 to 1947. She got her first screen lead in another Paramount musical short (this time with a Western theme), *Jingle, Jangle, Jingle*, in 1948, but still nabbed small and often uncredited roles in the next two years.

By 1950, Field's contract with Paramount had run out and she was taking work where she could find it. In that year, she played a number of strange roles including a 16-year-old girl (at the age of 28) in William Castle's exploitation film, *It's A Small World* (a drama about a never-say-die man with a growth hormone deficiency) and a brief appearance as a housewife in *The DuPont Story*, a 90-minute cinematic sedative extolling the trials and triumphs of America's favorite chemical corporate family. (Even Whit Bissell and Stacy Keach, Sr. could not coax real drama out of the ponderous propaganda.)

And, as mentioned above, 1950 also brought her first pairing with Robert Clarke in *A Modern Marriage*, a "social drama" in the general niche of Ulmer's *Damaged Lives*. Field plays a woman psychologically dominated by her mother's fear of abandonment, making her hesitant about both sex and marriage until a psychiatrist helps her through it. It would later be repackaged as *Frigid Wife* in 1962, an "adult content" bait-and-switch with clunky wrap around segments, but Harrison Reports declared the original "a top picture... suitable for the whole family" (Harrison 59).

NOT GIVEN TO HYSTERIA

Given these roles, when she tested for *The Man from Planet X*, this science fiction film rushing into production must have seemed much the same—a quirky character in a quirky film aimed at a quirky audience. However, Enid (like Nikki in *The Thing* and Helen in *Day*), prototypes a new role for women in an emerging genre. It will still be a couple years before the "lady scientist" becomes a true trope of '50s genre cinema, but Enid constitutes more than a wilting flower and proactively engages the situation. And in a strange way, she seems to transform from a child to an adult before our eyes.

Enid first appears as Lawrence's chauffeur and escort to the brock. Subtly, some traditional male and female roles reverse in this expository scene, framing up the romance implied at the end of the film. Enid drives the car (as she must), prompting Lawrence to say, "Drive on Macduff," referencing the *Macbeth* line, "Lay on, Macduff." In any case, she's in charge and he submits cheerfully. As they drive into the fog and Lawrence enters this unknown realm, the conversation quickly turns to their shared past, one he's not forgotten but had not registered. "Now, isn't that a fine example of how unfaithful men are," she remarks. "The last time I saw you I got your solemn promise that when I grew up, I could be your girl." We learn they last saw one another six years prior, most likely in 1945, at the end of the war, when she was just a schoolgirl. (This would make her somewhere between 21 and 24, and given Lawrence's Air Force service, he'd be close to 30, a short separation of years in the age of Bogart and Bacall.) After commenting on how Nature has filled out her legs, Lawrence quickly resumes his professionalism, (citing the "newspaperman" in him noticing her adult proportions), but the scene is enough to set up the implied romance forthcoming, and more importantly, show us Enid has assertive qualities, which we will see later.

Enid functions early on as the expositional key of the film, giving the audience missing background information, history and explaining why Mears lives with them. She's also portrayed as the domestic machinery of the household, cooking and caretaking for her father, a classically stereotypical academic aloof from practical realities. However, she makes no claim to like the role or even excel at it, remarking that "What I lack in talent for cookery, I make up in speed."

But Enid's character value doesn't end at average culinary skills and sex appeal, which it might very well have in 1951. She consistently advances the plot through independent action, propelled by curiosity and a sense of her own capacity to affect change. As Graeme Harper says, she is generally "sturdy, informed and unflappable" (234). She leads Lawrence out to the moors and essentially discovers the bomb-like beacon he carries back to the brock. After a flat tire strands her in the rather spooky wilderness, she sees a flashing light out on the moors which she investigates rather than flees. Seeing the craft, she draws closer until she has the first face to face encounter with the alien in the film. And while she comes back understandably shaken, she insists on accompanying her father back out to investigate—not because she doesn't want to be alone but because she's wondering "just what I did see."

Enid might easily have topped out as a tepid love interest for Lawrence, and all indications early in the film suggest she will. At the beginning, Field frequently delivers her lines in his presence with a somewhat fluttery tone, seemingly always on the verge of a nervous giggle. She employs this style in other productions with romantic counterparts reflecting something between girlish anxiety and sexual excitement. But as the film pushes on, she drops the affect and becomes more serious. In fact, the last time we will hear this quality comes when she describes her encounter with the spacecraft and the X man, a true crisis moment that would make anyone breathless. But at the end of the film, she calmly discusses Lawrence's imminent departure for America, no longer the sobbing schoolgirl who can't bear to see him leave. She's downright philosophical, questioning the meaning of the events and wondering if they can really be suppressed, showing an evolution into maturity beyond the boundaries of a simple romantic foil.

WILLIAM SCHALLERT

With nearly 400 screen appearances on film and television, and one of the most recognizable faces in entertainment, William Schallert ranks high among the great character actors of the age. And yet, the man who played the nefarious Dr. Mears in *The Man from Planet X* never developed name recognition with the general public. He may be best recognized as the dad from the *Patty Duke Show*, but he appeared in dozens of popular shows. In fact, when he spoke to crowds, he would often challenge audiences to name a show he wasn't in. His career lasted more than 60 years until the age of 91, including a stint from 1978-1981 as the President of the Screen Actors Guild.

The Man from Planet X was Schallert's first significant screen role and it would lead to more opportunities, including the next Pollexfen/Wisberg production, *Captive Women* (1952) reuniting him with Clarke and Field. Prior to *Planet X*, he played uncredited in seven films including a brief role as the gas station attendant in *Mighty Joe Young* (1949). He'd done a great deal of stage work in Los Angeles, however, working extensively with Sydney Chaplin (son of Charlie Chaplin) at the Circle Theater as one of its founding members. That's where he met actress Leah Waggner, his wife from 1949 until her death in 2014.

People Don't Just Drop In Here

In a film replete with shadows and fog, Mears is the most shadowy and foggy of all the characters. In fact, the Jungian concept of the psychological "Shadow" archetype makes a good tool for reading Mears, especially since Carl Jung saw a reflection of the human psyche in literary characters throughout history. Literary (and cinematic) villains embody the Shadow, the dark side of the human personality filled with repressed urges, similar to the Freudian Id. However, where the Id is theoretically the product of individual trauma and history, the Shadow adds cultural and perhaps even genetically transmitted dark or destructive urges. For Jung, these urges—like the greed and power lust Mears embodies—must be acknowledged within ourselves and channeled in positive directions or consciously contained. Failing that, these urges will fester in the unconscious to become dangerous to others, eventually externalizing into evil. Thus, the dark archetypes of literature--tyrants, witches, monsters and other villains--constitute cultural archetypes for the unmastered Shadow. Mears, clearly, does not master his Shadow-self, but rather indulges it secretly, barely hiding it behind a thin social veil as necessary.

No doubt, the filmmakers saw the symbolic potential of Mears, and give him an aesthetic treatment reflecting his dark ambitions. He wears a trimmed and slightly pointed beard long associated with Satan in literature, art and film. He clearly embodies the greed and power lust associated with Satan as well, so the beard comes over as sinister rather than professorial. In fact, Schallert told Tom Weaver in 1992 he thought having a beard helped him get the villainous role (57). He also wears a gray suit that blends into the fog each time he stalks behind someone. It's a subtle and but effective touch. Even his name lends to his shady, untrustworthy character. Mears is an anagram of "smear," a homonym of "mere" (as in minimal and without depth) and very close to "mar," to harm. It's an easy name to drag out in disdain as well and comes over without much honor.

The film begins its disclosure of his shady character upon his introduction. When Lawrence reunites with Professor Elliot, he's shocked to see Mears, who says he'd "forgive" Lawrence if he didn't remember him.

Lawrence's terse and bitter reply, "Frankly, I hadn't given it much thought," tells us an unpleasant history exists and his look of bitter distrust suggests he knows more than the others regarding Mears' character. The scene shows some subtle direction as Mears watches Lawrence leave the room for just a second or two before returning to his work, long enough for us to feel Mears does not like being discovered.

In the next scene, Mears' Shadow qualities start crystallizing. As Enid and Lawrence talk over tea, we learn Mears has a sordid past. Enid mentions that Mears stays in a room below (symbolically relevant it would seem) and reveals that he "dropped in on us two weeks ago. Pleaded he was ill and broke and jolly well looked it, too." But as Lawrence points out, the place is too remote for someone to just drop in, suggesting Mears came specifically to find them, probably to take advantage of Professor Elliot's "soft heart," as Enid calls it. She says he was in Scotland in "seclusion since that trouble he got into." Lawrence says, "He should have gotten 20 years," to which she replies, "He did go to prison for a while, didn't he?" just before Mears, who has overheard the conversation while lurking in the doorway, interrupts. It's a quick and cryptic exchange but it establishes that the trouble between Lawrence and Mears exceeds a personal injustice and extends into a matter of ethics. Mears violated moral and legal (and thus cultural) codes somewhere and somehow got off easy, implying both a lack of full payment and rehabilitation. It also demonstrates Mears' tendency to play things to his advantage. If the conversation had offered him information, he'd have remained quiet, no doubt. However, it serves him better to interrupt and keep Enid somewhat in the dark. These actions bespeak the Shadow at work.

The scene additionally establishes Mears' pattern of eavesdropping, clandestine observation, suspicious behavior. He frequently lurks behind or away from the other characters, gathering exploitable information unnoticed. For example, he slips into the foreground shadows when he sees Enid running from the moors (as opposed to seeing what's wrong and offering to help as most would). She runs into the brock but before entering behind her, Mears taps on the doorway to see if he can follow undetected, again, a subtle note of Ulmer's direction. Mears then listens as she reveals her terrifying encounter with the alien, becoming a nearly perfect black silhouette at one point before he follows them to the spacecraft. He witnesses the ray strike Elliot, robbing him of his will, but does not step in to aid them.

This can't surprise an audience too much, since Mears has already expressed his basic Shadow tendencies toward greed and power lust after inspecting the alien metal. When his analysis reveals the unique qualities of the material, Mears immediately interprets the discovery in terms of personal financial gain:

> It could mean millions—millions—if that formula could be reproduced. Do you realize what this metal could mean? Why, it's harder than steel, it has tremendous tensile strength, and it weighs only a fifth as much as steel. The man who controls this formula controls the industry of the world.

Until this point, Mears' history and behaviors have suggested his Shadow character, but from here forward we know what motivates him—power over others. Consequently, Mears is a Faustian mad scientist in the model of Claude Rains' Dr. Griffin in *The Invisible Man* (1933).

Mears' worst qualities emerge fully when he isolates himself with the alien on the premise of initiating communication and then abuses him to extract information regarding the otherworldly metal. He reasons that geometry might open the doors of communication and suggests he should work without distraction. Professor Elliot quickly consents but Lawrence begins to object to leaving Mears alone with the alien. Mears deftly manipulates the situation saying, "I presume your concern arises from fears for my safety, Mr. Lawrence," and assures them all will be well. But of course, this is just to get them out of the room. The moment they leave, he says to the alien, "I'll have the world in my pocket... with your help."

Once Mears has the formula, he burns his notes in front of the unsuspecting alien and gloats over his good fortune. He casually wanders over to the alien and says to the unsuspecting visitor, "And now, I'm going to tear out every secret you have," before suddenly attacking him, cutting off its "air" supply. He plans to ration the alien's air to control him but is interrupted by Enid. Mears claims he has failed and the alien is resting. But when Enid goes in to look, she closes the door and screams, signaling her abduction. This demonstrates the danger of the Shadow, which conceals its intentions publicly in order to exercise them privately, and in the wake, innocent people like Enid become victims. The alien's behavior most certainly results from Mears' mistreatment, and in theory, has potentially endangered the entire planet.

In the end, Mears gets what's coming to him, but like so much of the movie, his demise rings with ambiguity (a trademark of Ulmer's direction in other films). Having been freed from the alien's mind control near the end of the film, he turns around and heads back toward the ship, seemingly realizing the army has begun shelling it. Mears says emphatically, "No. They can't destroy him. They mustn't!" before racing off and ultimately catching a bullet as the attack begins. When Dr. Carrington makes a similar plea at the end of *The Thing*, it reflects his consistent desire to learn from a superior life form. But, for Mears? It's difficult to believe he's had either a sudden awakening to the humanity of the alien, or to his own inhumanity toward the spaceman. Oddly enough, Mears' tone seems to express some level of genuine concern, but since he's spent the film concerned only for himself, such a reversal of character would mean an instantaneous understanding and rejection of his own Shadow qualities, which doesn't seem very likely.

A Horrible Grotesque Imitation of a Face

If Mears makes an easy read as a villain, the same cannot be said for the man from Planet X. In fact, this film's extraterrestrial is arguably the most complex of them all. His civilization cannot be too far ahead of our own, unlike Klaatu's or the Thing's. Granted, the cheapness of the production limits the spacefaring technology to hardware store gadgetry and electrically enhanced matte paintings, but the alien's spacecraft looks like "a big diving bell" (Lawrence's estimation) rather than a flying saucer. Consider for a moment our own human and robot landings on the moon and Mars thus far. Essentially, these are diving bell style drops on to a surface and far beneath the kind of mastery suggested by flying saucers. Additionally, the man from Planet X never seems to control a situation for more than a moment or two. Indeed, the man and his planet are painfully vulnerable and his behavior shows human-like thinking and desperation. Of the three aliens examined in this book, only this one inspires pity.

Where *The Thing from Another World*'s early press releases proudly touted James Arness as their creature and Michael Rennie's name appeared in *The Day the Earth Stood Still*'s publicity materials, more mystery surrounded the man from Planet X. That may have been tactical or simply a function of a quick production, but a syndicated article printed on January 14, 1951, called "Flying Saucers Land in Hollywood" remains the only source to reveal his name. A five-foot tall, 49-year-old Russian immigrant known as Pat Goldin took the role, along with its uncomfortable suit and lack of screen credit.

Goldin would never go on to be a star like James Arness (or for that matter, Robert Clarke or Margaret Fields), but the man in the X suit was not his first or last uncredited role. Goldin, a vaudevillian, had a minor but long film and TV career taking screen roles up to 1970, a year before he died at the age of 68. His diminutive stature was a blessing and a curse. It meant that when certain types of work became available, only he and a handful of others could fit the bill. But it also meant a limited career. The solitary time Goldin got a true starring film role was in a kid's flick called *The Half Pint* (1960) in which he plays a nameless hobo--and even then, he shares equal billing with a one hit wonder child actor, Tommy Blackman, and Dinke the Chimpanzee. There's no indication that this was anything more than filler work and he seems to have spent most of his career in live performance instead.

Goldin's most visible work came between 1945 and 1950. He had a regular run playing Dugan in the Monogram Pictures' *Bringing Up Father* series, a.k.a "Jiggs and Maggie," originally a comic strip. Forever in formal evening wear, the absurd Jiggs and Maggie have a Mutt and Jeff quality visually, with most plots revolving around Maggie's social ladder climbing and henpecked Jiggs' embarrassing attempts to avoid his wife. The look and feel of the films reflect Goldin's vaudeville past. Dugan never speaks, playing out variations on the same gag--getting the short end of the stick as a nearly invisible schlimazel surrounded by bigger, more opportunistic men. Each temporary smile ends down-turned and each hopeful gleam dissolves in a flattened, dejected gaze. With his long nose, clamped mouth and disconsolate eyes, one wonders if the oversized mask for the man from Planet X isn't based on Goldin's own features.

According to Arianné Ulmer Cipes, the head was designed and created by Edgar Ulmer and art director, Angelo Scibetta. The two friends had worked together years before on *Isle of Forgotten Sins* (1943) and *Bluebeard* (1944), and in fact, Scibetta created the paintings so important to the plot of the latter. The eerie, expressionless alien face emerged from Ulmer's design based on the script, but he wasn't particularly enamored with the creature's appearance. "Dad always talked about the fact that his head looked like a douche bag" (Cipes).

Still, the head comes over in a genuinely alien way through a combination of facial underlighting, artificial fog and black and white photography. A strange Gestalt experience can happen for viewers as a result. The creature can look absurdly phony at one glance and unsettling, disturbing and nightmarish at the next. Wisely, the camera never gives us too much close-up time with the alien—just enough to process some of the details and ponder them.

The rest of the space visitor's costume clearly bespeaks the budget, with most of the elements probably coming from a local hardware store. The primary poster art depicts him in a green body suit, but lobby card variations show him in maroonish red. According to the Mosby piece, however, he wore "skin-tight, dark gray tights and a large, bald rubber head with thin lips, thin eyes, and a thin nose," an accurate description (Mosby 4). The expressionless head came sealed in a clear plastic, egg-shaped bubble with an antenna mounted on the left toward the rear. Small gas tanks attached to the back of a light-colored harness with corrugated rubber tubes connecting the gas to an adjustment valve before running to an illuminated circular mount directly below the mouth. The tanks contained no actual pressurized oxygen so Goldin could not remain in the mask for long. Not surprisingly, Robert Clarke remembered him as complaining a lot. "I can work in this only seven minutes," Goldin lamented to Aline Mosby. "Not much air" (4).

The alien also wears heavy duty, cuffed welder's gloves and stacked rubber boots, both in white (or perhaps yellow if one takes the poster as a guide). On his chest sits a rectangular box with a glass panel revealing some cylinders and other mechanical apparatus within, visible thanks to an interior light. The box holsters a "ray gun" connected with an electrical cord. In the Blu-Ray commentary track, Tom Weaver seems to have correctly identified the prop as prostate relief device known as a "Dila-Therm" (which he politely pronounces "dial-a-therm"). In 1950, after the manufacturer fell under scrutiny for its medical claims, the Federal Trade Commission ordered the company to discontinue its averment of any therapeutic or treatment value—meaning they probably went for a song in 1951 ("Dila-Therm" 28).

The X man first appears after Enid suffers a flat tire (or at least the noise a popped tire makes) after dropping Lawrence off at a hotel. While walking back to her father's lab, she investigates a flashing light on the moors, discovering a truly unique space craft. Shaped something like a small rocket with a spherical center, the craft lies at a slight angle in the marshes amid slowly drifting fog. As she draws up to the glowing glass (a "greenish color" as she narrates later), the alien leans down at an angle that dramatically exposes his face but he does not look directly at Enid or move his head to watch her run off. In other words, it's a static image framed up for the audience to get their first shocking look at the creature.

Because the eye-line does not match, it leaves us with two intriguing possibilities. The fast and cheap production suggests Goldin, essentially blind inside the mask, simply guessed where to position his head. However, he pulls into a perfect full view for a few seconds. Ulmer may very well have wanted that image to strike the audience and coached it, especially given his reputation for purposeful visual direction. Either way, it is effective, especially when seen the first time. It's not hard to imagine the original audiences getting a jump scare when he first pops into frame as they behold "a ghastly caricature, like something distorted by pressure, a horrible, grotesque imitation of a face."

The second time we see the visitor, Professor Eliot and Lawrence go to investigate the ship and he comes from behind with his weapon drawn. As Lawrence and Elliot try to establish a peaceful exchange, his "air" (presumably his planet's equivalent to oxygen) fails, and Lawrence revives him by adjusting the valve. This stands as a critical scene, revealing something about the compassionate qualities of the hero, Lawrence, and the limitations of the visitor. At this point, we should consider what we've seen, or perhaps more accurately what we have not seen (and will never see in the film). The alien never acts destructively. The ship's light ray zombifies people--robs them of their will and essentially enslaves them as a work force—but it does not kill. If the alien had hostile intent, he could have shot Lawrence and Elliot before they ever saw him, but in truth, we don't even know that it would harm them. Perhaps it would act as the ship's ray, affecting them mentally, a likelihood based on the creature's general lack of violence. In fact, the alien race may not even have destructive power—in which case, destroying the ship and dooming the alien planet at the end of the film becomes tragic.

It's difficult to know, of course. Near the end of the film, while still under the influence of the ray, Mears fills in the gaps for the audience—an "invasion" is coming from Planet X, a dying world turning to ice. The visitor has arrived in advance to establish "a wireless directional beam" as a homing beacon for the efforts to occupy Earth. Mears also says that "if his people do not escape from his planet before it swings back along its route through space, they will be doomed." "Escape" is an interesting word here, a verb applied to refugees, not military conquerors, undermining the idea of a hostile "invasion." If his people are very much like him, they would not constitute the "concrete menace" Mears warns against earlier in the film. In the end, the X man and his people are more pitiable than formidable.

PRODUCTION/EFFECTS

Edgar Ulmer would never have helmed the project without Ilse Lahn, his agent and a fellow Austrian. She was Ulmer's first love from Vienna during the Reinhardt days (Rhodes) and the two reconnected in the United States. Though her name doesn't appear on screen, she's considered an associate producer for bringing Ulmer and Wisberg/Pollexfen (whom she also represented) together as well as aiding in other production arrangements.

The assignment came with the script in hand which, as noted above, was written with a small budget in mind. By comparison, its competitor films boast much more attention to technical detail, but Pollexfen attested to purpose in the generalities. One advance notice in Erskine Johnson's column mentions the distances from Earth to Planet X never find hard numbers in the movie. "'We did that on purpose,' Pollexfen said with a grin. 'If we had mentioned the distance, some 12 year old with a slide rule would have proved we were bums'" (7). Meanwhile, of course, 20th Century Fox was a few weeks away from hiring an astrophysicist to do their math for them.

Production officially began on December 13, 1950--though some advance word of the film hit the press a couple weeks before, with Louella Parsons noting on Dec. 2 that writers Aubrey Wisberg and Jack Pollexfen had "rented space at the Hal Roach Ranch to make their eerie epic" (7). Shot on a six-day schedule with a publicized budget of $50,000, the film came in at even less, $41,000 (Isenberg 244). Initially, the pair intended to sell the script and pocket what they could, but with the other well publicized, high budget cinematic alien encounters grabbing headlines, they quickly decided to produce it themselves and ride the wave.

The quick production schedule reflected not just the finances and drive to arrive first in the alien invasion race. The Ulmers had also accepted a trip to Europe to produce movies for Harry and Edward Danziger in Spain (which would ultimately result in *Babes in Bagdad* in 1952). So, with just a week to shoot and little money to invest in effects, the project demanded creativity… and parsimony. In an article published just after shooting started, Wisberg clarified that as a writer with money in the film, the production strategy consciously minimized expenses:

> This kind of set up has the advantage of making a writer con-
> scious of costs. I recommend this sort of screen training to all
> writers in an industry which is increasingly yelling for econ-
> omy. As writers, we recognized and anticipated the time and
> budget limitations in our script in advance and are now able
> to cut corners on the set. (Goodman 28)

And cut corners, they did, with varying results.

Wisberg openly promoted their use of the existing *Joan of Arc* sets from Victor Fleming's 1948 high-dollar production featuring Ingrid Berg-man as evidence of underlying quality despite the paltry budget. Located on the Hal Roach Studios grounds, these serve beautifully as atmospheric castle interiors and moors around the isolated Orkney broch. In fact, that particular setting seems so tailored for the film, it is tempting to think Wisberg and Pollexfen wrote the script expecting to get access to these sets. Robert Clarke wrote in *To "B" Or Not to "B"* that Ulmer's creativity made the most of the castle sets. "To give the scene a more eerie effect, they had one of the grips hose down the walkway with water so that there would be a sheen, so that the lights would reflect and it would shine" (124). The great majority of the work took place on these sets. The brief observatory scenes were shot locally at the Griffith Park facilities and ac-cording to Robert Clarke only one or two shots of the film actually took place outdoors.

On the other hand, the limitations required audience imagination to keep the illusion. The studio was so small that when an automobile pulled into frame, it had to be backed out because there was no room to move forward, let alone turn around. And creating a convincing moor required a smoke and mirror strategy... or at least the smoke. The Nu-Gel (i.e., tetrachloride) fog permeating the film served a dual purpose as Ben Mankiewicz noted once in an introduction of the film for Turner Classic Movies: "Ulmer used fog machines not only to create atmosphere, but also to fill in the space where the set didn't exist." The downside? The ac-tors struggled to keep from coughing and removed themselves whenever possible... a luxury not afforded to most of the technical staff. Everyone who ever commented on the film's production, from Shirley Ulmer to Robert Clarke to Jack Pollexfen, all recall getting sick from working on that soundstage.

And then there were the painted backdrops completed just before shooting by the director himself and art director Angelo Scibetta (Cipes).

When the hero first arrives at the Scottish port, it's hard to miss the theatrical drape posing as a seaside village. In fairness, sci-fi hungry audiences may have ignored this since mid-century B movie expectations resided well below 21st Century standards and the line between stage and screen was not so sharp in the early 1950s. Reviewers don't directly comment on it and of course, curtain seams and folds appear in several undisputed horror classics of the 1930s including, no less, *Frankenstein* (1931) and *Bride of Frankenstein* (1935). Precisely at the time *The Man from Planet X* hit the theaters, Realart was making a mint re-releasing Universal's Gothic classics for the big screen, so 1951's audiences still expected to use their imaginations and swallow canvas scenery for the thrill of a weird tale.

Director Edgar Ulmer got in on the set design in other ways as well. This was not uncommon for him, especially given his work as an artist in a few Weimar era classics. Robert Clarke noted in *Starlog* that when he and Margaret Field first came to Ulmer's house for a pre-production rehearsal, they were rather stunned to see Ulmer had started work on the scenery.

> We were so impressed by what we found just inside the door: Here in the foyer of his home was the glass painting of the "broch" (Scottish for "castle") that would be seen in the movie. Edgar had painted it himself and Maggie and I were quite amazed; neither of us knew he had been a fine art director. (28)

The final product, a crisp depiction of the broch as a stonework cylinder pushing out of the foggy landscape with one lighted window, appears only for a moment in a low angle shot when Lawrence first arrives. It feels (like so much of the film's atmospheric elements) like it belongs in a Universal Frankenstein picture and might even remind one of the mad scientist's lonely tower in the first film. In other words, it registers as a painting, but doesn't break the illusion so much as enhance the film's dreamy, otherworldly quality.

Elsewhere, the broch is a model which Ulmer crafted as well (Pollexfen 275). In the opening sequence, it resides centered in a foreground miniature of the moors, shot with cross fades moving the audience inward. The model appears again in the middle of the film as well. The scale in the foreground seems a little off, especially in the second shot, but because the camera moves and cuts quickly (only a couple seconds), it contributes to the illusion aptly enough in context to serve the film.

Ulmer also designed the spaceship, which doesn't really match Enid's description. When she comes back to the broch, shaken by her experience, she reports: "The light flickered on and off. It wasn't very bright. A ghastly greenish color. When I got close to it, it looked like a giant glass ball, girdled with something like a steel belt. Three of them I think." This sounds like a transparent sphere, but beyond the basic shape, it doesn't match the image we see on screen. Arianne Ulmer Cipes believes the discrepancy between Enid's lines and the final product reflects a gap between the completion of the script, Ulmer's revision of the spacecraft concept and the realities of a quick shooting schedule. "I think that may be why you have this mix up about what the darned ship looks like," she said. Ulmer would assign some work and do some himself and everyone was working as fast as possible. In the end, he just made the change and didn't worry about the script, especially since the subtleties of English escaped him. "He didn't like that glass globe thing," she said, so he just made the change himself and ran with it.

The uniquely shaped ship remains one of the positives of the film. The lower half is a sphere with a pair of windows (Professor Elliot's diamond ring won't cut it, so it beats glass for hardness). The upper part looks like the steel tip of a modern arrow. It resembles Christmas ornaments popular at the time and as we've seen, Lawrence compares it to a diving bell. Significantly, it looks dropped into the moors at a slight angle, suggesting lack of control. Also, it seems designed for landing but not for takeoff—which means the alien doesn't expect go to home. Again, perhaps his civilization just doesn't have that level of technology. We only see inside the ship a couple times through the window. The interior gadgetry is essentially a painted backdrop, wisely illuminated for only a moment or two by a flashing light (green, presumably, based on Enid's dialog). A critical eye will reveal the illusion, but for a theater audience seeing it quickly and only once, it works.

The sound design for the film plays an important role in creating the spooky tone as well. When Enid approaches the spaceship, first alone and then with her father, the spacecraft emits a low electrical hum that pulses with the rise and fall of the interior lights as though it has a leaky, limited or compromised power source. The intention probably goes no further than to create an eerie theater experience, but it plays into the theme of the X man as a denizen of a desperate planet on its last hope. The ship never projects cultural might the way Klaatu's does (or even the Thing's for that matter) and this power surging contributes subtly to our feeling that the ship's technology is limited.

Another interesting application of sound in the film comes when the alien tries to communicate. When Lawrence and Elliot first encounter him he holds his "weapon" on them but quickly collapses when his breathing apparatus fails. (Perhaps the stress or exertion requires more gas than anticipated). The alien does not speak so much as project sound waves in a low register. J. J. Johnson noted that by the 1950s, separate sound recording (as opposed to recording directly on film) allowed a sound mixer to "take a strong droning hum and mix it just 'underneath' or below the voice of an alien as William Randall did in *The Man from Planet X* (1951). Those same sound effects, by the way, were used for the 1979 classic *Alien*" (47-48).

Special effects are less convincing elsewhere. When Lawrence gets a look through Dr. Blane's (Gilbert Fallman) telescope early in the film at the mysterious Planet X, a painting of the sphere amid a generous smattering of "stars" stands in. Later, in Scotland, Lawrence gets a second, closer look at the planet, again a painting, but this time a little clearer. Both images linger on the screen for about five seconds, too long for modern audiences to accept the illusion, but perhaps enough for generous theater goers of 1951. He will look a third time as the film nears its climax revealing the surface of the dying world. Ulmer may have painted these as well, but there's no documentation for that.

In any case, the special effects passed the general test in 1951. Hollywood reviewer Lowell Redelings didn't think much of the film as a whole when he reviewed it in April 1951, but he did single out the special effects crew. "Andy Anderson and Howard Weeks rate special mention for their special effects, a definite (and pleasing) highlight of the film" (6). Ironically, Anderson never received another film credit, and it was only one of a handful for Weeks. Much of the art crew, in fact, had little experience before or after, which partially explains why Ulmer and Scibetta did a good deal of the artwork themselves.

The photography department, however, featured three artists who would have long, successful careers. John L. Russell, the director of photography, began his film career in 1948 and would act as DP on many films and television shows. Most impressively, he was nominated for an Oscar for his work on Hitchcock's *Psycho*. Jack Glass (photographic effects) and Jack Rabin (optical effects) had extensive sci-fi resumes. *The Man from Planet X* was Glass's first screen credit and he would quickly turn his talents to television, guiding the effects on *The Adventures of Superman* with

George Reeves. Rabin had only worked on four films before *Planet X*, but immediately before coming to the Ulmer production, he plied his craft on *Rocketship X-M*. His career would last through the early 1980s and feature dozens of science fiction films including *Invaders from Mars* (1953), *The Beast from Hollow Mountain* (1956) and the cumbersomely titled *The Saga of the Viking Women and Their Voyage to the Waters of the Great Sea Serpent* (1957). He would also work with Pollexfen, Wisberg, Clarke and Fields again on *Captive Women* (1952).

ACE HIGH MERCHANDISING

Unlike *The Thing* and *The Day the Earth Stood Still*, no major studios stood behind *The Man from Planet X* to help in promotion or distribution. To solve that problem, Wisberg and Pollexfen struck a deal with exhibitor Sherill Corwin, who formed Mid-Century Films for that purpose. Corwin paid the pair $100,000 for 75% of the returns on it (they kept the remainder), In turn, Corwin arranged for United Artists to release the movie which did exceedingly well in ticket rentals (see below). A review in *Motion Picture Daily* for March lauds the arrangement on Corwin's behalf so gushingly he might well have written it himself (or perhaps Wisberg, since it has his earmarks). Citing the response from an advance screening, it says "Out of all this attention came the consensus of opinion that Exhibitor Corwin had dealt himself ace-high merchandising product" [sic] ("The Man" 6).

On March 4, five days before the film premiered in San Francisco at the Paramount, the pair ran an advertisement in the San Francisco Examiner disguised as an "Allied Press" news release entitled, "Visitors from New Planet Held Possible." With a Mt. Wilson dateline, the article describes a mysterious planet hurtling in our general direction at a "miraculous rate of speed" in a "'very alarming'" manner. In an acrobatic display of passive voice and convoluted writing, the item suggests the inhabitants of Planet X intentionally target Earth before revealing this as the plot for the upcoming film (20). Appearing in the "Pictorial Review" section of the paper likely cued readers to the disguised advertisement, but someone could have easily read the release out of context and been taken aback.

Along those same lines, the May 22 issue of *Motion Picture Daily* reported that "United Artists is developing a special pre-selling approach for 'The Man from Planet X,' by arranging pre-views and extra publicity originating with leading scientists who have specialized in inter-planetary phenomena." The intention was to "lend authenticity" to the film "by stirring up scientific discussion of the eventualities of such a thing, which has never actually happened, but is said to be still within the realm of possibility" (Brooks 3). There's no indication this ever took place anywhere.

Apparently, the famed Mayfair theater on Broadway, the East Coast premiere site, had second thoughts about their planned ballyhoo for the film. Dorothy Kilgallen reported in her "Broadway Bulletin Board" column that at the last minute, after some serious debate, the management "decided against dressing its ushers in weird space suits" while the film played there, "afraid some customers might be scared stiff in the dim light and sue" (11). The Mayfair did, however, have someone in quite a get-up walking the streets and making public appearances to promote the film. A man in a reasonably close costume--complete with bubble head and Dila-Therm-style body box--pulled people in and even appeared at the Brooklyn Red Cross Donor Center to give a pint and take a publicity shot ("Donors and Volunteers" NT-3). It paid off nicely. The film did quite well at the Mayfair, pulling in $20,000 the first week ("Business Average" 7) and $13,500 the second week ("B'way Grosses" 10).

The man in a suit gag wasn't particularly original or uncommon. In Tacoma, Washington, The Blue Mouse theater sent a staffer to stalk the streets in a black tights, a cape, long cuffed gloves and a paper mâché mask that bore some general resemblance to the Planet X refugee... if one could ignore the big eyes and mustache ("Things You Meet" 50). The Strand in Milwaukee pulled a similar stunt with a spaceman walking around town trying to drum up ticket sales ("Milwaukee" NT-2). In Indianapolis, Lyric Theater manager Frank Paul and United Artists' field manager Wally Heim arranged for a dramatic eye grabber: "the landing of a helicopter, bearing "The Man from Planet X," before 40,000 spectators at the Indianapolis Speedway" ("Indianapolis" NT-2).

Another strange item noted Kenyon and Eckhardt's decline to cross promote *The Man from Planet X* with *Tom Corbett, Space Cadet*, a popular TV show also distributed through United Artists. Essentially, the distributor hoped to get some airtime during the program in exchange for publicity at the theater, but the K and E advertising agency balked. The reason? "'Space Cadet' is scientific stuff based upon a peace-loving world of 2351, whereas the film is blood and thunder, with nightmare overtones for moppets" ("Space Promotion" 7).

RECEPTION

The Man from Planet X not only beat its competitors to theaters, but it also beat them in terms of profitability. In an article announcing Pollexfen and Ulmer teaming up for *Daughter of Dr. Jekyll* in 1956, Edwin Schallert (William Schallert's father, incidentally) reported that their first collaboration earned $1.2 million versus a budget of $51,000 (Schallert Part II, p. 11). That's a staggering profit of nearly 2253%. And it was likely higher. Pollexfen told Tom Weaver that Ulmer brought it in at $41,000 (274). In any case, those box office numbers rival both Hawk's and Wise's efforts in terms of ticket sales and far and away out stretch both in profit versus expense.

In this context, *The Man from Planet X* may have had more direct impact than *The Thing from Another World* or *The Day the Earth Stood Still* on the next decade of science fiction as well. *The Thing* and *Day* both commanded A picture budgets and advertising, garnering more critical acclaim with superior production values and more attention to detail. But that didn't translate into profits, the real engine that moves Hollywood. As a result, few big budget sci-fi films came out in the 1950s. As Bradley Schauer notes, in 1953, a black and white Ray Harryhausen effects film, *The Beast from 20,000 Fathoms,* actually out-grossed George Pal's technicolor extravaganza, *War of the Worlds* on a tenth of the budget. He says this suggests two things: "First, that audiences for SF films did not especially privilege the higher production values of the A films. Second, that SF A films did not successfully appeal to a general audience as studios had hoped" (74). In other words, the financial success of *The Man from Planet X* against its budget probably encouraged more science-fiction productions than its competitors because sci-fi obsessed audiences willingly exchanged art for thrills.

Harrison Reports' overview (targeted toward exhibitors) understood this principle: "This is primarily an exploitation picture. The story is not very substantial but it should please the majority of picture-goers, for millions of people have shown interest in anything that travels through space." It called Ulmer's direction and the acting "good" and noted that the photography "is clear but not overbright" (55). *Film Bulletin*'s anonymous reviewer's less generous pen still saw good reason for a theater owner to grab the flick:

> Although from the viewpoints of production quality, story and acting, "The Man from Planet X" is inferior to most of the pseudo-scientific yarns that have come to the screen in

the past season, the subject is, nevertheless, well worthy of the exhibitor's attention as a valuable exploitation film. The title is good and the basic gimmick of a visitor from space is a provocative sales angle. (12)

The review goes on to compare it to *The Thing* and even laments the way modern monster movies lose "the chilly gore of the first Frankenstein flickers" (12).

Ezra Goodman's review of the film (printed right next to a large ad for *The Thing from Another World* in the Los Angeles paper, *Daily News*) called the X man "quite an extraordinary guy" in an otherwise "rather ordinary" film and gave the reviewer "the impression he was watching 'The Man from Planet B'" (16). He credited John Russell with "first rate fog-bound photography," and noted with a parting shot, "On the same bill is 'Saddle Legion,' a Tim Holt horse opera in which nobody wears a glass globe on his head."

In contrast to the "blood and thunder" appraisal Kenyon and Eckhardt had for the film, writer Dorothy Masters thought it was "Too Tame For Modern Kids." She lectured that the film just did not compare to pulp magazines and Frankenstein flicks and all the ticket buyers got for their investment is "a spaceship, a zombie ray and a compression helmeted visitor from parts unknown." She further warned that adults could expect their impertinent progeny to spend the film critiquing the lack of thrills and realism, and to skip the whole affair to discourage future tepid terrors. "If producers Aubrey Wisberg and Jack Pollexfen don't get their 10 bucks back maybe they will be discouraged from future operations along these lines" (BL 10). Little did she know the film would make them both very well off.

Interpretations

Given the ambiguity of *The Man from Planet X*, it has inspired surprisingly little interpretation compared to other Ulmer films, particularly his iconic modernist horror film, *The Black Cat* (1933) and noir classic, *Detour* (1945). The general cheapness and rapidity of production accounts for this, but much of the criticism generally applied to Ulmer illuminates *Planet X* as well. For example, as Noah Isenberg notes, much of Ulmer's work reflects "the art of outcasts." While he doesn't specifically discuss

Planet X in this context, the concept applies at several levels. Mears stands as a clear outcast, hiding in Scotland due to some undefined past offense, signifying his criminal nature since he seems incapable of obeying society's moral codes. Professor Eliot and Enid also live in isolation, cut off from society by the nature of his work. This similarly applies to Lawrence, who, as a reporter, constitutes something of a professional outsider—someone who enters and exits the lives of others but never stays after the story ends. We might even see the visitor as a *de facto* outcast, an explorer with a lonely, unique and ultimately tragic experience.

Vera Kropf sees a similar underlying framework in the film, writing in her article "Agent with a Typewriter" that the film "can be seen as a metaphor for immigration and alienation: the Immigrant Alien becomes the 'Weird Visitor' from Outer Space (i.e., the other side of the Atlantic Ocean) and encounters suspicion, fear and resentment because of its Otherness." That certainly describes the alien in the film, who never really shows aggression. Elliot, Enid and Lawrence show some restraint in this regard, but the villagers and military demonstrate both suspicion and fear with little variance. Mears resents the alien's technical knowledge, wanting to acquire and exploit the visitor's "secret" for himself. In turn, he's happy to cultivate fears of the outsider as a "concrete menace." Given Ulmer's status as both immigrant and Hollywood fringe, he may have had some sympathy for the alien who gets remarkably humane treatment by the director if not Mears.

Writer Graeme Harper notes that the remote and mystical Scottish setting would remind the film's original audiences of *Brigadoon*, a post-war play and film about an earthly stranger stumbling into a village that only appears once a year in our realm. The visitor's presence "might threaten the stability of a mythical place of happiness and contentment," leading Harper to ask who really plays the role of the disruptive outsider in *The Man from Planet X* (229). The obvious answer is the X Man himself, but it might just as well be Lawrence, or Professor Elliot and Enid, none of whom really belong in Scotland. In that sense, the inquisitions of journalism or science threaten security and/or illusions (which may, in fact, be the same thing). Dr. Mears embodies the unexpected visitor role too, and his greed, selfishness and dishonesty constitute classical external corruptions. Maybe the awareness of other worlds alone is enough to dismantle our reality. In any case, Ulmer seems to exploit the "outsider" theme in several films, giving it an ominous global twist here even in the isolated, personal nature of the story.

Harper also observes that "Ulmer's *Planet X* presents faith as one of the lynchpins of human existence" (233). He doesn't develop the idea in depth but it's easy to see in action in the film. Lawrence represents the principle of good faith in this context. He initiates his journey based on his faith in the professor's promise to "give him a crack at" anything of real importance. He further establishes good faith with the alien by initially rescuing him when his pressure tank fails (though ironically, he later disables the alien to save Enid and the others). Mears, naturally, represents the opposite in his deceptions, aggression and self-interested actions. And to some degree, the film resolves with a question of faith. As Lawrence and Enid ponder the true intentions of the alien, they've essentially doomed another civilization to destruction without fully knowing if it is a justified act of self-defense. They don't even really know that they will see one another again as Lawrence prepares to go back to Los Angeles. All they have is faith.

THE X FILES

With all this emphasis on symbolic Otherness and facing "alien-ness," it is worth taking the discussion back to the face value question of just how Earthlings would treat an extraterrestrial who presents no clearly defined threat. And this may not be a purely theoretical question. Early in 2019, videos of UFOs haunting U.S. Navy fliers surfaced, unleashing a series of questions and admissions regarding the subject. In June of 2021, the Office of the Director of National Intelligence released a nine-page preliminary report stating unequivocally that some UAPs (Unidentified Aerial Phenomenon) were not only physically real, but in 18 of the 141 cases reviewed, the observers reported unusual UAP movement patterns or flight characteristics (United States 5). No official United States entity has said these have extraterrestrial origins, but the document doesn't refuse the possibility. Therefore, the question of how we might deal with extraterrestrials with superior technology (even marginally superior technology as this film suggests) echoes outside the thin walls of science fiction and into nuts and bolts, day to day reality.

In that context, we might consider a line from Lt. Col. Philip J. Corso's 1997 book, *The Day After Roswell*. Corso was a high-ranking career intelligence officer with a distinguished career in World War II and Korea. Supposedly, he had the task of parsing out recovered alien technology from the Roswell UFO crash to American industrial entities for the development of defense and commercial applications. In his book, he specifically mentions *The Man from Planet X*:

> Flying saucers did truly buzz over Washington, D.C., in 1952, and there are plenty of photographs and radar reports to substantiate it. But we denied it while encouraging science fiction writers to make movies like *The Man from Planet X* to blow off some of the pressure concerning the truth about flying disks. This was called camouflage through limited disclosure, and it worked. If people could enjoy it as entertainment, get duly frightened, and follow trails to nowhere that the working group had planted, then they'd be less likely to stumble over what we were really doing (117).

In the context of Corso's assertion, the last lines of the film have much more potency. Enid asks, "Is it true that no one will ever know what happened here?" to which Lawrence replies that it would only add to the fear and confusion of the world. She then wonders if it can really be kept a secret. "No," says Lawrence, "but it can be reduced to gossip." This matches nicely to Corso's assertion that keeping the public fed with carefully constructed rumors of half-truths anchored the plan: "A secret this big about flying saucers was bound to get out and cause untold panic among the civilian population unless an elaborate camouflage was established" (103). In other words, just as the film suggests, the moment anyone began asserting that the Roswell crash was true, someone would surely turn around and say, "you've been watching too many movies."

It's hard to know exactly what to make of the claim, especially since Corso was a counter-intelligence officer who speaks about his role in disinformation campaigns throughout. However, we know *The Thing from Another World* got no cooperation from the Department of Defense and Robert Wise remembered resistance to *The Day the Earth Stood Still* (at least initially), so, if *The Man from Planet X* did have some secret guidance, why would Ulmer's film garner different treatment? It may come down to messaging. *The Thing* and *Day* both suggest advanced civilizations might overtake or destroy us, but *Planet X* says we've got the situation under control and overcome the danger. It also suggests alien civilizations simply are not too far ahead of us, especially since a few artillery shells eliminate the threat. The Pentagon might feel very differently about that kind of film, especially if it reinforced a "camouflage" campaign as Corso suggests. Unfortunately, Corso gives us little else to go on and died in 1998 without referencing the film elsewhere. But for what it is worth, the "Weird Visitor" very closely resembles the aliens associated with the Roswell story with its bulbous head, thin lips, expressionless eyes and small body.

CONCLUSIONS

Almost any modern audience coming to this film for the first time would have a hard time seeing beyond its limitations. Today, we experience film very differently from the audiences of 1951. We have the advantage of piecemeal viewing with home video. We can distort the flow of time, stopping and starting, slowing and speeding as we like. We can blow up an image to inspect it on a 4K television that takes up most of a wall. We also see and quickly process sophisticated video images all day long on monitors, laptops, cell phones and even while shopping for fresh vegetables. This alone has made our eyes more astute and critical, and our experience more dependent upon convincing special effects and unconscious expectations.

This was not the experience in 1951. Television was tiny and certainly not on demand. If you wanted to see a movie, you went to the theater, immersing yourself in the dark with strangers in a strange land. You entered invested in enjoying the show and expected to engage your imagination as part of the film. Many genre films of the period now come over as unconvincing because their task of creating illusion demands more than the budgets and technology would allow. But a mid-century cinematic thrill-seeker expected to look past some of these limitations for an alien invasion plot that was both new and suddenly plausible. This helps explain why audiences could enjoy and even feel exited by a film like *The Man from Planet X*, despite its painted backdrops, borrowed sets, short sound stage and alien in a rubber mask holding a bogus prostate relief device in his hand.

Works Cited

"119 Players on Roster." *Film Daily*. 9 July 1945, p. 4.

"Arnie's first flick was no Herculean effort." Daily News. 11 December 1991, p. 43.

Bergan, Robert. "Shirley Ulmer." *The Guardian*. 3 September 2000. https://www.theguardian.com/news/2000/sep/04/guardianobituaries3

Brooks, Walter. "National Preselling." *Motion Picture Daily*, 22 May 1951, p. 3.

"Business Average in Broadway Sector." *Exhibitor*. 11 April 1951, p. 7.

"B'way Grosses Still Hit Average." *Exhibitor*. 18 April 1951, p. 10.

Cipes, Arianne Ulmer. Personal Interview. 5 October 2021.

Clarke, Robert. "The Actor from Planet X." *Starlog Magazine 219*. October 1995. pp. 27-31, 66.

——, "Robert Clarke." *Interviews with B Science Fiction and Horror Movie Makers. Writers, Producers, Directors, Actors, Moguls and Makeup* by Tom Weaver, McFarland & Company, Inc. pp 75-92.

Clarke, Robert and Tom Weaver. To "B" Or Not To "B." Midnight Marquee Press, 1996, pp. 115-139.

Corso, Philip J. with William J. Birnes. *The Day After Roswell*. Pocket Books, 1997.

"'Dila-Therm' Firm Told To Stop False Claims." The Gazette and Daily. York, PA. 25 July 1950, p. 28.

"Donors and Volunteers" (photo). *Exhibitor*, 25 April 1951, NT-3.

Goodman, Ezra. "Film Review: The Man from Planet X." *Daily News*, 21 April 1951, p. 16.

Harper, Graeme. "Meeting the Man from Planet X." Edgar G. Ulmer: Detour on Poverty Row, edited by Gary D. Rhodes, Lexington Books, 2008, pp 225-238.

Harrison, P. S., ed. "'A Modern Marriage'" with Robert Clarke, Margaret Field and Reed Hadley." *Harrison Reports*. 15 April 1950, p. 59.

——. "'The Man from Planet X'" with Robert Clarke and Margaret Field'" *Harrison Reports*. 7 April 1951, p. 55.

"Indianapolis." *Exhibitor*. 6 June 1951, p. NT-2.

Isenberg, Noah. *Edgar Ulmer: Filmmaker at the Margins*. University of California Press, Berkley and Los Angeles, CA. 2014.

Johnson, Erskine. "Ho Hum! Garland Now Leans on Arm of Luft." The La Crosse Tribune, La Crosse, WI., 6 January 1951, p. 7.

Kalat, David. "*Detour's* Detour." *The Films of Edgar G. Ulmer* edited by Bernd Herzogenrath, Scarecrow Press, 2009, pp. 137-158.

Kilgallen, Dorothy. "Broadway Bulletin Board." *The Record-Argus*, 12 April 1951, p. 11.

Kropf, Vera. "The Agent with the Typewriter – Ilse Lichtblau Lahn and the Émigré Network in Mid-20th-Century Hollywood." *Quiet Invaders Revisited: Biographies of Austrian Immigrants to the United States in the Twentieth Century*, edited by Gunter Bishof, Studien-Verlag, 2017.

Mankiewicz, Ben. "Ben Mankiewicz Intro - *The Man from Planet X* (1951)". *TCM.com.* https://www.tcm.com/video/1323613/ben-mankiewicz-intro-the-man-from-planet-x-1951

"Margret Field to Contract." Box Office. 20 January 1945, p. 96

"Milwaukee." *Exhibitor*. 11 July 1951, p. NT-2.

Mosby, Aline. "Flying Saucers Land in Hollywood." *St. Petersburg Times*. 14 January 1951. p. 4.

Muir, Florabel. "Miss Montez Balks at Universal Role." Los Angeles Evening Citizen News. 17 April 1945, p. 6.

Parsons, Louella O. "Myrna Slated to Play Character of Sob Sister." The Cedar Rapids Gazette, 27 January 1942, p. 7.

Parsons, Louella O. "Stars Cast for Movie about Lotta Crabtree." *San Francisco Examiner*. 2 Dec. 1950. p. 7.

Pollexfen, Jack. "Jack Pollexfen." *Interviews with B Science Fiction and Horror Movie Makers. Writers, Producers, Directors, Actors, Moguls and Makeup* by Tom Weaver, McFarland & Company, Inc. pp 273-283.

"Options." Box Office. 12 May 1945, p. 60.

Redelings, Lowell E. "Man from Planet X a Formula Movie in a Scientific Vein." *Los Angeles Evening Citizen News*. 21 April 1951. p. 6.

Rhodes, Gary D. "Audio commentary by Gary D. Rhodes and Arianne Ulmer Cipes." *Man from Planet X* Blu-Ray. Scream Factory, 2017.

Schaefer, Eric. *"Bold! Daring! Shocking! True!" A History of Exploitation Films, 1919-1959*. Duke University Press, 1999, p. 419.

Schallert, Edwin. "Monroe Specifications Named for 'Karamazov'; Lean Offers Ford Film." Los Angeles Times, 22 October 1956, Part II, p. 11.

"Space Promotion." *Exhibitor, Vol 45*, Issue 23, 11 April 1951, p. 7.

"The Man from Planet X." *Motion Picture Daily*, 13 March 1951, p. 6.

"Things You Meet on the Streets in Tacoma!" Motion Picture Herald, 22 December 1951, p. 50.

Ulmer, Edgar. "Nothing Was Impossible." Interviewed by Peter Bogdanovich. *Who the Devil Made It?* pp. 560-603.

Ulmer, Shirley. "Shirley Ulmer." Interview by Tom Weaver. *I Was A Monster Movie Maker*. McFarland & Co., 2001. pp. 227-249.

United States, Office of the Director of National Intelligence. "Preliminary Assessment: Unidentified Aerial Phenomenon." 25 June 2021, https://www.dni.gov/files/ODNI/documents/assessments/Prelimary-Assessment-UAP-20210625.pdf

"Visitor From Another Planet Held Possible." *San Francisco Examiner*, Pictorial Review Section, 4 March 1951, p. 20.

Weaver, Tom. "Science-Fiction Dad." *Starlog Magazine*, vol. 184, Nov. 1992, pp. 57–62.

The Cinematic Legacy

7

THE THING FROM ANOTHER WORLD

If we think about these three films as engendering a new genre, the influence of *The Thing from Another World* is best seen in its basic elements. Many of the films influenced by Hawks' creation contain most of its basic story anchors expressed in varying degrees in alien invasion films after 1951. The alien force is generally small, something of an advanced guard seeking to get a foothold in an isolated area before a full-scale attack. The success of the plan relies on avoiding detection and failing that, squelching opposition early. (That could be said of *The Man from Planet X* as well, but most of the time the alien's technology and powers dwarf our own.) The adversary has one weakness that, once discovered, offers the key to human salvation. A combination of scientists and military personnel working in concert derive a solution and set a plan in motion, typically matching wits with the monster. Finally, small scale combat heroics save the day and humanity goes forward cautiously, wary against more hidden threats.

The list of films that utilize the basic pattern in the decade following *The Thing* range in quality from the respectable to the laughable. *Invaders from Mars* (1953) and *Invasion of the Body Snatchers* (1956) rank among the better films. Both add in an element of mind control (which will become popular in 1950s science fiction film reflecting fears of Soviet propaganda) and while not in *The Thing*, does link to the source material at least tangentially. Both films provide small town settings, hidden aliens and invasion plans that rely on spreading unseen. A British film, *The Trollenberg Terror* from 1958 (a.k.a. *The Crawling Eye* in the United States) gives us the same basic blueprint—an alien invasion begins in a clandestine way in the isolated Swiss Alps and must be thwarted by the heroics of regular people, fighting the giant one-eyed, tentacled Lovecraftian creatures with Molotov cocktails until a military firebombing finishes them off.

We might consider *The Blob* (1958) here too. It lacks the intentional invasion aspect, but in other ways fits the pattern of spreading out of isolation. Its monster absorbs animal life seemingly for its blood and flesh and in theory could spread unchecked across the world. It seems completely invulnerable until a blast from a fire extinguisher reveals the weakness. Ironically, this alien cannot bear cold and once contained, gets dropped in the Arctic to ensure it remains contained.

Somewhere in the middle of the pack (perhaps generously so) are *The Brain from Planet Arous* (1957) and *The Beast with a Million Eyes* (1955) which fall into the "watchable" category. *Invasion of the Saucer Men* (1957), a sci-fi comedy, uses the basic formula and works well enough if the viewer understands the spirit of the film. However, the bulk of *Thing* inspired films are unintentional comedies with poor writing, acting, direction and effects. *Robot Monster* (1953), *Killers from Space* (1954), *Night of the Bloodbeast* (1958) and the infamous *Plan 9 from Outer Space* (1957) head that list.

It Conquered the World (1956), a Roger Corman cheapie, compares to *The Thing* in a few ways, though quality is not one of them. It features the work of Paul Blaisdell, a special effects man and suit creator who produced some of the most interesting (if not convincing) monsters of the era on minuscule budgets. Two glaring similarities are the monster's vegetable composition and its relationship to a scientist, Dr. Tom Anderson, a Dr. Carrington type played by Lee Van Cleef. Anderson's fascination with the Venusian blinds him to the peril that comes with helping it. The film mixes and matches many sci-fi movie elements that came before it and the invader stops all earth electricity a la *The Day the Earth Stood Still*. Unfortunately, despite the talents of Peter Graves and Beverly Garland, its monster looks much more like a space-carrot than Graves' half-brother, James Arness, ever did and it's hard to take seriously, especially since it must hide in a cave and dies fairly easily.

The Thing from Another World inspired John Carpenter's 1982 version, *The Thing*, which comes much closer to *Who Goes There?* since its invader is essentially a viral copycat. The action takes place at an American arctic research base, beginning when the scientists hear a helicopter and shots ringing out. A "dog" runs through the snow as a pair of Norwegians try to shoot it, ending with the dog escaping and the Norwegians dead. The dog harbors a viral copycat, the Thing, which wants to take over humans and escape to civilization where it can take over everything. The rest of the film centers on MacReady (Kurt Russell) trying to locate and destroy the copies through a process of elimination until only he and Childs (Keith David) remain as the camp burns down around them.

The Carpenter version remains a masterpiece for most critics today, though it struggled at the box-office and got high profile reviews that pegged it as dark, depressing and lacking humanity in 1982. But many of the points of original criticism have become the film's strongest elements for fans. Its gory practical effects hold up and it falls into the "horror" category for many viewers, tying it back to the original film's qualities. The low, pulsating soundtrack maintains a nervy tension and the distrusting characters thrown together with little in common peels back the veneer of civility disguising what lies just below the surface of society. Likewise, the ambiguous ending gives the film a haunting power and realism. Viewers do not know for sure if the Thing has invaded either MacReady or Childs.

In 2011, a prequel, also (confusingly) titled *The Thing*, tells the story of the events taking place before Carpenter's film. It begins in the Norwegian outpost and ends with a lead into the 1982 film. In January 2020, Blumhouse and Universal Studios announced a collaboration on a remake combining elements of *The Thing from Another World*, Carpenter's film and the full text of *Who Goes There?* (discovered in 2018) embodied in the illustrated novel, *Frozen Hell* (Squires). Significant additional information has not come out since the original announcement. Carpenter's *Thing* has also inspired a trove of games, comic books, toys and other merchandise that would likely never have happened without the original film, which appears, incidentally, in a clip from Carpenter's 1978 breakthrough film, *Halloween*.

THE DAY THE EARTH STOOD STILL LEGACY

Not surprisingly, far fewer films try to emulate *The Day the Earth Stood Still*. The "Us vs. Them" plot of *The Thing* precedes that movie by a few thousand years and for better or worse, human beings respond instinctively. However, outside of satire, very few stories point the finger at humanity as the cause of its own woes with an alien standing in judgment.

A British offering, *Stranger from Venus* (1954), tried to replicate the story, going as far as nabbing one of the stars. Also known as *The Venusian* or *Immediate Disaster,* the tale concerns a Venusian ambassador who lands in rural England (rather inconsequentially as opposed to London). The lights and noise from his spaceship cause a car to crash, driven by none other than Patricia Neal in the role of Susan North, perhaps an interesting homage to Edmund North, *Day's* screenwriter. The stranger, the titular Venusian (Helmut Dantine), saves her off camera in the opening credits and soon appears at a local pub and inn. The villagers discover he has no money, no name and no pulse, rousing suspicions. The story begins to unfold when Susan appears at the pub, completely healed from her accident and the stranger reveals he has arrived on a mission very similar to Klaatu's. His people worry that a large-scale nuclear war would upset Earth's rotation and thus affect all the other planets. He's treated with suspicion and deception causing him to finally conclude that Earth is not ready for interplanetary assistance and he's proved right when the ambitious U. K. War Department wants to trap his landing craft which will descend at a specific time and place.

In the meantime, the alien manages to share a kiss with Susan, fulfilling more of the implied romance from *The Day the Earth Stood Still.* However, while he's discovering love on Earth, his communicator gets swiped by a police officer. Not long after, Susan's fiancée--the Undersecretary to the Ministry of State incidentally--learns that the Venusian's "mothership" (an early use of the word in cinema) will incinerate the atmosphere over Britain if they attack the ship in anyway. Walker retrieves the communicator and the alien averts the conflict at the last second, dooming himself in the process. As it turns out, he can only stay on Earth for so long before he dies, which for his people means essentially blinking out of existence. Dozens of elements mimic *Day,* but the end differs in its reversion to a romantic subplot. The alien leaves without any important message or speech. In the end, his shuttle departs without him and he sacrifices his life to avoid an interplanetary disaster. The stranger imparts no great thoughts or ultimatums to seal the drama. Instead, he offers only a personal, rather corny message: "Susan, I'm proud of your man." As Patricia Neal, who self-admittedly only took the role for the money, put it: "this was no *Day the Earth Stood Still*" (183).

The film has a few positives and is worth a viewing for sci-fi aficionados. Helmut Dantine's alien behaves with a distance and awkwardness sharply contrasting Klaatu's ability to fit in and he seems almost robotic at times, which serves the character more than one might think. And the other performances are generally solid, though Patricia Neal's character never makes an important decision and her role amounts to a plot pawn. A viewer can catch a tear in her eye in the final scene, however. Overall, though, the film moves slowly, taking place mostly in three rooms and generic outdoors settings, and has a predictable British reserve about it with no meaningful soundtrack to propel the tension.

A second film of an even lower budget casts John Carradine in the Klaatu-inspired title role in *The Cosmic Man* (1959). A strange extraterrestrial sphere about seven feet in diameter appears in the mountains near the fictional Pacific Institute of Technology. Scientific tests driven by military interests fail to dent, puncture or move it. The Cosmic Man (Carradine) poses as a scientist when in human company, arriving mid-film. He gets a room at a local lodge run by a Korean War widow, Kathy Grant (Angela Greene) and her wheelchair-bound son, Ken (Scotty Morrow). His message echoes Klaatu's, stating his people are not concerned with our "international politics" but rather our "philosophy." As in *The Day the Earth Stood Still*, we must learn to live together before we can join the intergalactic community.

Cosmic Man (as he's actually called in the movie) appears as a shadowy black silhouette (in a cape) at the lodge to address some military men and the scientist-hero, Dr. Sorenson (Bruce Bennet), whom he says must continue his search for truth because our planet depends on it. Like the Venusian, he must leave by dawn or die. Naturally, the military behaves with pigheaded aggression and in the final reel, the Cosmic Man kidnaps the boy as a hostage to negotiate a return to his ship. He is seemingly killed while trying to leave by an ambitious scientist but the boy has miraculously recovered and can walk and its clear Cosmic Man planned this all along. Soon after, the sphere absorbs Cosmic Man's body and departs. The interplanetary peace message, the power of healing, and a death and resurrection of sorts all play into this film.

The best-known recycling of the original film was the 2008 remake by the same title featuring Keanu Reeves as Klaatu in a movie that changed many of the basic elements of the first film and left few fans (if any) happy with the results. In this version, Helen Benson (Jennifer Connelly) is a scientist called into action when Klaatu's ship, misinterpreted as an interstellar asteroid, seems destined to impact the Earth. Instead, the ship, a sphere resembling a stormy Earth, lands in New York's Central Park, shifting the content from the political capital of the United States to its economic capital. Like Michael Rennie before him, Reeves gets shot immediately but utters the famous line, "Klaatu barada nikto" to stop Gort's impending rampage. When he arrives, Klaatu does not have true human form but using harvested DNA "grows" into his form. He's essentially captured and sent for interrogation, but with the help of Benson, escapes. Much of the film then focuses on the search for Klaatu while he, Benson and her stepson, Jacob (Jaden Smith) try to avoid authorities with varying results.

This time Klaatu's message is environmental, an updated crisis for the time, and he decides to eradicate Earth's human life to save the rest of the planet. To discourage that, Benson takes him to see Professor Barnhardt (John Cleese) who urges Klaatu to acknowledge that like his own species, we need a chance to recognize our crisis moment. Gort eventually breaks from his military captors by transforming into a swarm of particles that destroy everything in their path. In the end, Klaatu finds enough hope in Helen and Jacob to stop the destruction, but leaves Earth without its electricity functioning, perhaps as a warning, perhaps as a new condition of existence.

The remake lacks the charm of the original and replaces much of the thematic development with action sequences. It suffers from having essentially no likable characters with the possible exception of Helen (here and there) and Professor Barnhardt, whose role has been reduced to one scene—though Cleese plays him with convincing style. Reeve's wooden alienness fits the re-envisioned Klaatu, but also makes him something between boring and cold. The relationship between Helen and Jacob, who blames her for his father's death, grates the audience through much of the film. As opposed to the cheerful and relatively innocent Bobby in the first film, the viewer must endure a petulant, obstinate and unsympathetic child. His repaired relationship with Helen at the grave of his father inspires Klaatu to save humanity, but by the time we get there, it is hard to swallow.

In this version, GORT gets his name from the researchers studying him rather than Klaatu. The "Giant Organic Robot Technology" now resembles the original concept of the robot. In "Farewell to the Master," it is made of a flexible green metal that shows human musculature and operates as an independent biomechanical entity. In the remake, GORT seems composed of a flexible blackish metal, but the finale of the film reveals that it can reorganize and replicate its own matter. The relationship between GORT and Klaatu in this film may also be more like the source material in that the robot is really the master, but if that message is intended, the viewer must make the connection with little help from the film.

Like John Carpenter's 1982 remake of *The Thing*, the 2008 remake of *The Day the Earth Stood Still* made a conscious attempt to rewrite its scientists for a more contemporary audience by humanizing them, moving away from the stereotypes and the "hero-scientist" coding palatable in the 1950s. Astronomer Seth Shostak, the senior scientist at the SETI Institute (Search for Extraterrestrial Intelligence), came on board to advise the remake. According to David Kirby, he "'tried to wean the filmmakers from the cliché image of scientists as clipboard carrying, lab coat-wearing ciphers'" (68). Shostak also wrote out the mathematical equations Klaatu conjures in the film. The actor merely traced over them in chalk, with editing enhancements creating the illusion of rapid action (Kirby 69). Shostak, incidentally, was only one of several math and science consultants used to add scientific believably to the film (the others being Hector Calderon, William Hiscock and Marco Peluso).

On paper, many of the film's updates make sense and reflect our times. Women have risen to positions of power and social worth, and families operate dysfunctionally on the surface as opposed to the 1950s' public illusion of domestic harmony everywhere. Additionally, trust in the American government and military has eroded steadily since Watergate and the Vietnam war. Given the prevalence of stories about clandestine government installations probing wayward aliens for secrets, that too reflects 21 Century cultural expectations. And of course, human indifference toward other species and the general health of the planet plays out more each year.

In fairness, modern remakes of classics have major obstacles to overcome. A remake must court fans of the original films, who often resent changes. They also need to capture the attention of younger audiences who frequently value big budget action sequences over character and theme. Not surprisingly, given that problem, the 2008 film never feels like it has a cohesive vision and the final punch fizzles out compared to the original which seemed much more honestly invested in its own message. Much in the same way fans of the original *Star Wars* trilogy reject the prequel episodes as inferior despite improved effects, fans of 1951's *The Day the Earth Stood Still* tend to respond to this remake with disdain.

One final note: the idea of environmental crisis as the catalyst for Klaatu's arrival was not original to the 2008 film. Fox considered a sequel to *The Day the Earth Stood Still* as early as 1981 and none other than Ray Bradbury outlined an updated tale. Called *The Day the Earth Stood Still II: The Evening of the Second Day*, Bradbury's story begins on Christmas Eve and features Klaatu's daughter (Klaata) arriving to meet a rather random NASA employee, Chris Atkins. Klaata tells Atkins that humanity has done some good things in the 30 years since her father issued his warning, but we need to do more. We must heal the environmentally ailing planet or face the consequences. "Where Klaatu warned humanity to abandon its violent ways, Klaata mostly wants us to end our dependence on oil. Before she leaves, she gathers military officials and world leaders to witness a demonstration of solar power, implying that Atkins should help lead them all into an era of alternative energy" (Davis). Somehow oil dependency simply didn't ring with metaphoric power in 1981 and not surprisingly, the project never made it past Bradbury's rather romantic outline.

THE MAN FROM PLANET X

On the surface, it would seem *The Man from Planet X* had few imitators and certainly no remakes, but its basic plot line does get reworked by other movies. This film introduces a few unique themes that help identify the films in its family tree more easily. Unlike the Thing, Planet X's alien lacks an overt conqueror's motive and has limitations that allow for human domination and exploitation. The film's structure explores the darker sides of human nature in that context since, in Dr. Mears, it offers us the only true human villain in any of the 1951 offerings. Also, the X man is by far the most isolated of our aliens and the only one inspiring pity from the viewer. Additionally, the film introduces the concept of a dying planet which will appear in other films as well. Through that lens, we can see the impact of *The Man from Planet X* more clearly.

As a stand-alone plot element, the trope of aliens coming from a dying world finds expression in many films. *This Island Earth* (1955) uses this basic premise and gives us mysterious big-headed humanlike aliens recruiting (and eventually abducting) Earth scientists to help them win an interplanetary war. Similarly, Roger Corman's 1957 film, *Not of This Earth*, features an alien who appears hostile but has come to extract human blood in an effort to cure a blood disease on his home planet.

The Man Who Fell to Earth (1976) featuring David Bowie as the alien, adopts the Earth name Thomas Jerome Newton. His planet needs Earth's water, and to accomplish that he needs to make a spaceship capable of transporting it, which requires money. He teams up with a patent attorney and forms World Enterprises Corporation, making millions rapidly. On the surface, the alien appears superior, but the more he experiences human culture, the more he declines. Thomas becomes obsessed with television, especially images of violence and sex (linked throughout the film) screened on multiple TVs simultaneously. He's soon dependent upon alcohol as well, which he consumes to the point of madness. He also develops a relationship with Mary-Lou (Candy Clark), a hotel maid who rescues him after faints in an elevator. She clearly loves him, but he has left a family behind and seems incapable of processing his dualistic reality, becoming abusive to Mary-Lou. Somewhere far away his people are dying without water while he indulges in Earthly pleasures.

The Mears character of the film, Dr. Nathan Bryce (Rip Torn), spends the first part of the film sleeping with his college students and following the rise of World Enterprises Corporation until they finally hire him. Bryce eventually pins Thomas as an extraterrestrial and before he can return home and complete his mission, Thomas is abducted in a paramilitary raid initiated by a corporate competitor. Languishing in a luxury prison, Thomas can fulfill any indulgence but mourns his failure, communicated through images of his family that end in their deaths. Ultimately, Thomas leaves the prison, still wealthy but ageless in a world that has moved forward. Near the end of the film, drunk at an outdoor cafe, he meets Bryce again who asks if he's bitter about everything that happened. "Bitter?" he replies. "No. We'd have probably treated you the same if you had come over to our place."

The Man Who Fell to Earth reflects the world of the 1970s and makes a nice metaphor for the life of a rock star as inherently alien, especially since David Bowie, the quintessential rock star, explored space travel thematically and invented a lost alien character as a stage persona. Fame, money, sex, drugs all at one's fingertips yet always isolated, never understood. At the same time, its *Man from Planet X* elements make great clay for sculpting that kind of story. As a film, it seems disjointed and artfully indulgent and has no real climax or resolution, requiring the audience to fill in gaps. That's not a bad quality but it is less science fiction and more art film.

As a final note, Showtime's episodic version of the story starring Chiwetel Ejiofor was set to air beginning in late spring 2022, after the completion of this book. Undoubtedly, the story and execution will receive criticism by fans of the original, but how it reworks the Planet X themes should be fascinating.

CONCLUSIONS

Most alien visitation/invasion films after 1951 freely mix and match the elements of *The Thing*, *The Day the Earth Stood Still* and *The Man from Planet X* to tell new (if not completely original) stories. *E. T.* (1982) and *Starman* (1984), for example, reflect *The Man from Planet X* in their sympathetic aliens who would be captured or even killed for their secrets, but the pursuers line up more with the government forces in *The Day the Earth Stood Still*. The confused *Plan 9 from Outer Space* has *The Thing*'s theme of a hostile invader spreading outward from a small starting point (this time with corpses), but it uses the rationale that humanity will soon become too dangerous for the rest of the galaxy *à la The Day the Earth Stood Still*. However, the blueprint established by these first films makes up most of the color palate of the alien-on-Earth movies to come. This might reflect a general lack of creativity or courage, but it probably also indicates the main ways we can see "aliens" and ourselves.

So, what does this say about us? Our paranoia emerges in all three films, taking different forms in each. Subsequent alien contact films have generally followed these basic themes laid out in each: aliens are hostile, aliens are superior and/or aliens cannot be understood. In all three cases, humans default to a defensive posture and work on the assumption we may—and perhaps must—prepare to fight an enemy. In the 2008 remake of *The Day the Earth Stood Still*, Kathy Bates plays Regina Davis, the Secretary of Defense. She orders that Klaatu undergo a drug enhanced interrogation, rationalizing it with the following lines: "History has lessons to teach us about first encounters between civilizations. As a rule, the less advanced civilization is either exterminated or enslaved." It's a truthful statement, but perhaps only for human beings. Is it impossible to believe that a civilization powerful enough to master time and space may just not have the same aggressive way of thinking?

WORKS CITED

Davis, Lauren. "Ray Bradbury's Bizarre 'Earth Stood Still' Christmas Sequel." Gizmodo, 9 December 2008, https://gizmodo.com/ray-bradbury-s-bizarre-earth-stood-still-christmas-se-5105075. Accessed 15 November 2021.

Kirby, David. *Lab Coats in Hollywood: Science, Scientists and Cinema.* MIT Press, Cambridge, MA., 2011, p. 69.

Neal, Patricia, with Richard DeNuet. *As I Am.* Simon and Schuster, 1988. p. 183-184.

Squires, John. "Universal and Blumhouse Developing New Version of 'The Thing' That Will Adapt Long Lost Original Novel!" *Bloody Disgusting*, 27 January 2020, https://bloody-disgusting.com/movie/3602436/universal-blumhouse-developing-new-version-thing-will-adapt-long-lost-original-novel/. Accessed 8 November 2021.

Invasion '52...
and Beyond

8

ON APRIL 7, 1952, exactly one year and one day after the release of *The Thing from Another World*, the most captivating woman in America made an unintentional appeal to the nation to start taking the whole flying saucer thing seriously. Marilyn Monroe, the 25-year-old "bombshell" in the dead center of her film career found herself sharing her first *Life* magazine cover story with visitors from outer space. She exemplified sex appeal in a quickly changing Hollywood but just in case that couldn't entice a person to fish out 20 cents at the newsstand, the top right corner offered a teaser: "There Is A Case for Interplanetary Saucers."

The article, entitled "Have We Visitors from Space?" devoted more than 6000 thoughtful words to reviewing and discussing the best UFO cases to date, drawing five specific conclusions. They were not psychological phenomenon, they were not the Russians, they were not atmospheric anomalies, they were not Skyhook balloons, and they were not the product of U.S. experimental research. While *Life* never masqueraded as a hard news journal, it commanded respect and the article demonstrates careful research. Millions of Americans read that article, which never breaks its earnest tone and gave people good reason to take the phenomenon seriously.

1952 was a banner "flap" year, featuring interesting and highly publicized cases, some of which reflect elements of the films of '51. The event that jarred America most happened on the last two weekends in July when objects were sighted and detected on both commercial and military radar over Washington D. C., causing jets to scramble and reporters to ask uncomfortable questions. Headlines across the country warned in one way or another that saucers were buzzing the nation's capital and our best jets and pilots were helpless to catch them. The nation anxiously waited for Klaatu, or perhaps worse yet, the Thing. "Soon the federal government was fighting the UFOs with the most powerful weapons in the Washington arsenal -- bureaucracy, obfuscation and gobbledygook" (Carlson). The official conclusion held that atmospheric "temperature inversions," a known phenomenon detectable on radar, accounted for everything. Well, almost everything. Experienced pilots chased objects traveling several thousand miles an hour and reliable witnesses saw them with their own eyes (Carlson).

A MODERN MYTH

The word "myth" tends mean "baloney" in mainstream culture, particularly when applied to UFOs, but it shouldn't. A better definition revolves around the concept of a deeper symbolic reality, one that need not be objectively proven to be "true." In this case, a myth defines cultural codes and values through storytelling for past, present and future generations. The narratives can change over time and new ones can evolve out of old ones, or in the case of UFOs, out of new experiences and technologies. Myths provide patterns for behavior and moral problem solving and offer examples of strength, courage and ingenuity that inspire faith. That requires defining the dark side of reality and humanity as well, since virtue and vice have no meaning without one another. Cinema acts as mythology in these ways and the UFO phenomenon provides substantial raw material.

The Thing from Another World, The Day the Earth Stood Still and *The Man from Planet X* come along essentially four years after flying saucers became major news. Sightings and odd experiences (including hoaxes and misidentifications) did not dissipate after 1947. With few reliable concrete answers, cinematic stories evolved to fill in the gaps and wrestle with the anxieties produced by the growing idea that we are not alone in the universe. The motivation may have been purely commercial but the underlying issues were not. Beginning in 1951, cinematic myths regarding alien visitation and invasion have shaped our expectations, concepts and attitudes in ways that will condition whatever first contact we may make... or have made.

CINEMATIC CASE STUDY: GEORGE ADAMSKI AND THE SPACE BROTHERS

On November 20, 1952, in the California wilderness, "Professor" George Adamski made contact with Klaatu's spiritual cousin, a tall "Nordic" looking alien with a good tan and long blond hair from Venus named Orthon. Adamski, a Prussian immigrant who served in the U.S. Cavalry just prior to WWI, was a self-styled philosopher, astronomer and the founder of the Royal Order of Tibet, a religious front for winemaking during Prohibition (Bennet 18-19). His obsession with outer space surged around 1947, seemingly inspired by the Kenneth Arnold sighting, and to his credit he advocated for an expanded consciousness that unified the world and looked toward other planets as potential neighbors. In a letter to the editor of *The Weekly Times-Advocate* on June 4, 1948, Adamski wrote passionately that the new 200-inch telescope at Palomar would help bring the heavenly bodies "closer to the realities of man as though it was his neighbor next door" (4).

Before long, Adamski's interest turned into a profession of sorts. He began giving lectures, conducting tours to UFO hot spots, taking photos of saucers and after 1952, he became the center point of what would become the "Contactee" movement, a group of generally average people who were somehow special in the eyes of alien visitors and chosen to help spread the word in advance of formal, widespread contact. Step for step, the Contactee playbook came from *The Day the Earth Stood Still.*

Adamski claimed that when he met the Venusian alone in the desert (one of several meetings over the next few years), they communicated primarily through hand gestures and telepathy. Adamski's level-headed and critical biographer, Colin Bennet, wrote:

> There then follows a familiar exchange. Orthon "says" that the coming of the extraterrestrials is in friendship. He indicates they are worried about nuclear bomb tests in the atmosphere and says "Boom Boom" without being prompted by Adamski. The images communicated then become religious, and the thoughts of Orthon on this subject are curiously similar to Adamski's own on "Natural Law." (34)

The basic elements of *The Day the Earth Stood Still* jump out at any objective thinker. A friendly, socially evolved alien arrives. He expresses concerns for our planet and our propensity toward war in a nuclear age and, with religious overtones, offers a pathway to peace that includes joining an interstellar community. As obvious as the connection is, surprisingly none of Adamski's followers or detractors seemed to make the direct link with *The Day the Earth Stood Still*. Perhaps that's because prophets and charlatans, psychics and faith healers had made similar claims for hundreds of years about angels and occasionally even other planets. The important distinction with Adamski is the UFO element, something that did not happen before 1951 in any meaningful way.

In 1953, to document this experience and open the world's eyes, Adamski published the first of three books with Desmond Leslie, a British writer and pilot who could decipher Adamski. *The Flying Saucers Have Landed* became an international bestseller, transforming Adamski from a passionate crackpot with barely two coins to rub together to globetrotting guru garnering attention (both positive and negative) from scientists, military figures and heads of state as well as hopeful and wayward souls anxious to become part of something important.

In that book, Adamski uses the blueprint provided in *The Day the Earth Stood Still* to make a buck, but in fairness, it also sends a positive appeal for world peace. Like the film, it offers a de facto counter-nationalist, counter-racist, counter-materialist message. Furthermore, consciously or unconsciously, Adamski seems to tap into the spiritual cosmology of the film to support that appeal. The Venusian (the name Orthon was divined by one of Adamski's followers) spoke of the "Creator of All" similarly to the way Klaatu refers to the "Almighty Spirit." Adamski wrote that humanity's "shallow" understanding of that Creator paled in comparison to the other planets, explaining why we struggle with war, crime and injustice while our so-called Space Brothers do not. On the other planets, "they live according to the Will of the Creator, not by their own personal will as we do here on Earth" (Leslie).

In Adamski's lore, the "Space Brothers" correlate to Klaatu and the unseen inhabitants of his cosmos. In short, Adamski's solar system boasted civilizations on nearly every planet, all physiologically human and spiritually enlightened, all benevolent (and all rather boring and humorless). Like Klaatu, they had learned to live in peace and wanted Earthlings to join them, but we backwards Earth folks had to abandon violence if we wanted to enter the cosmic community. Unlike Klaatu, the Space Brothers apparently eschewed politicians, social leaders and scientists and others with societal clout. Instead, they gravitated to relatively invisible people like Adamski who were ready for the message and willing to spread it. But they saw more than just receptiveness in Adamski. In him, saw a kindred soul, making him no less than a formal member of their interplanetary council.

The shared element of a perfected interplanetary society bears some consideration here. Klaatu's civilization exemplifies both the hopes of the period and our history of imposing human social ideals and structures on the cosmos in our myths. Just as the European idea of the Kingdom of Heaven or Chinese concept of the Jade Emperor reflects the world order of their times, Klaatu's society of distinct but peacefully interacting planets reflects an idealized United Nations longed for in the 1950s. It's a cinematic concept that stuck and evolved to reflect changing and often less innocent times (*Star Trek*'s Federation of Planets comes to mind, for example). However, even so, the underlying notion of differences resolved through a consciously created social structure motivated by a common good remains. When Adamski began projecting his personalized version to the world, the U. N. was facing its first major challenge in the Korean War, and Adamski's vision, primed by *The Day the Earth Stood Still*, offered hope.

While the vast majority of astronomers in 1952 would have discounted humanoid life on other planets in the solar system, the thought of life on Mars or Venus registered in the general public's imagination. However, Adamski's accounts extended beyond the improbable and into the absurd, especially as continually adding to the story maintained interest and support. "During the year 1958, I had the pleasure of attending a meeting comprised of people from Mars, Venus, Saturn, Jupiter, Uranus, and Neptune," Adamski once claimed.

> It was a friendly get-together, devoted mainly to discussions of some of our everyday problems. The subject of eating was introduced, and I asked for more specific information, since so many questions regarding this topic are coming to me. Their answer was simple and precise. They told me they usually purchase the cheaper cuts which can be boiled with vegetables like my mother used to cook when I was a boy. (49)

As foolish as it seems to swallow this, Adamski's Space Brothers mythology had a logic to it for true believers. After all, if you had conquered war, poverty, disease and the like, maybe all you have to talk about is your dinner plans.

Naturally, Adamski never mentions seeing *The Day the Earth Stood Still*, but given his early flying saucer preoccupations and the ubiquity of the film in the months preceding his first contact, no doubt Adamski knew the plot. And given the number of followers he attracted and copycats he inspired, one has to wonder if the film had not been made, would the contactee movement have ever taken place?

THE MAN FROM PLANET X AND/OR
FLATWOODS, WEST VIRGINIA

About a month before Adamski began his philosophical exchanges with the Nordic Venusian, Kathleen May of Flatwoods, West Virginia, found herself face to face with two horrifying monsters. One seemed to be a lost space traveler sputtering around the woods and fields after its spacecraft came down in distress. The other was public mockery in the press.

On September 12, 1952, Edison and Freddie May, two young boys were playing with friends in a nearby schoolyard when they witnessed an object descend on a nearby farm seemingly in flames. They ran home and went back to the site with their mother (Kathleen), uncle (Eugene Lemon), three other boys and a dog. Armed with only flashlights and curiosity, the group eventually came across a crashed vehicle and its wayward occupant. The vehicle emitted a foggy gas that made everyone sick and seems to have killed the dog a few days later. The occupant, now known as the Braxton County Monster, the Flatwoods Monster and various other names, stood 10-12 feet tall inside of what appeared to be a mechanical contraption.

Elements of the story connect to *The Man from Planet X*, though it should be noted that there's no evidence anyone in the party saw the film. "They found an object crashed into the earth and sticking out; it appeared to be pulsing in brightness. A strange sound like whining or hissing filled the air. There was a violet hue to the air. After their arrival, a mysterious foglike mist began to blanket the area" (Guiley 65). The pulsing light, the object sticking out of the ground and the mysterious fog echo the film as does the whining sound. Moreover, Kathleen May described a creature in a contraption with a strange hood-like frame around the head shaped like an ace of spades. She reported a green body and red face and eyes and said the creature moved about in a bouncing motion hovering above the ground.

The person who spent the most time researching the event in the immediate aftermath, Gray Barker (a colorful and enigmatic Mountain State native), took most of his account from Neil Nunley whom he considered the most impartial, detailed and clear spectator. That version of the story holds more Planet X connections than what most newspapers ever printed. In that account, the Nunley and Lemon lead the party and came across a large "globular mass," either a sphere or a hemisphere lodged in the ground pulsating with a fiery light. To their left, the so-called Flatwoods Monster loomed (Barker 23-24). Nunley told Barker that the figure was basically humanoid with a red face. "No one noticed a nose or a mouth, only eyes, or eye-like openings, from which projected 'greenish-orange' beams of light" (24). The beams of light cut through the mist seemingly created by vapors released in the crash. Nunley said the beams were aimed over their heads, very similar to images from *The Man from Planet X*, and to no small degree, suggestive of Gort's disintegration ray eyes as well. Barker also notes that Kathleen May thought it was illuminated from the inside, again evocative of the X man. As viewers will recall, Enid makes remarks about the greenish lighting in the ship and the X man seems to rely on his illuminated body box to manage the Earth's atmosphere.

Accounts in the press got less reliable with each telling and within days the description became absurd and insulting: "Frankenstein monster with B. O.," "a half-man, half-dragon," and a "fire-breathing monster" ("Monster" 1). Things did not get better for poor Kathleen May when she appeared on the CBS television show *We the People* on September 19. "On the show, an artist drew a sketch based on May's description, but took some dramatic license. The resulting sketch was so outrageous that it caused many to immediately denounce the whole thing as a hoax" (Jessee). Mrs. May, earnest and hoping to clarify what happened, ended up being the object of mockery, unfortunately.

Less well known is an incident that happened about 20 miles away near Frametown the following evening. A couple from Queens, New York, had car trouble in the area and not only suffered from the same noxious gasses but when driver George Snitowsky got out to investigate, he saw "a luminescent spheroid that looked like a giant frosted streetlamp" (Guiley 69). Fans of the film will recall Enid first describes the spaceship she encounters as a giant glass ball, not too far off Snitowsky's initial impression. Not long after sighting this, Snitowsky's wife, Edith, let out a scream and he turned back to the car. "He saw a huge figure illuminated in the light from the spheroid. It was about eight to nine feet tall and shaped like a man but with a reptilian head. It had shoulders, a weirdly bloated body, and a lower torso that seemed to be a solid mass of some sort" (69). The creature moved forward, extending "a spindly arm that ended in a soft, bi-sected fork of 'fingers'" that it used to examine the hood and windshield before retreating (69).

Certainly, a great deal differs in these accounts from *The Man from Planet X*, but similarities exist as well. Even skeptics agree that something happened that night, even if it was just a downed meteor emitting gasses upon impact. Believers suggest that a spacecraft landed with mechanical trouble, its occupant came out to inspect the damage using a device with mechanical arms and skirt that enabled it to hover. When people investigated, it was forced to quickly relocate and may have taken some time to repair or been rescued by others of its kind. At bare minimum, people were violently sick for days and investigators could confirm the toxic smell in the air. No impact was found, but strange skid marks and an oily substance which apparently got on Kathleen's dress were witnessed the next day.

THE THINGS FROM HOPKINSVILLE, KENTUCKY

At least one famous case from the 1950s bears a resemblance to *The Thing from Another World,* if not in its title character, then in its horrific attack on an unsuspecting isolated group fighting for their lives against space aliens.

The story goes that the Sutton family was hosting friends, the Taylor family, in their rural Kentucky home located near the town of Hopkinsville. On August 21, 1955, around 7 PM, Billy Ray Taylor went out to get water from the well and came back with a sighting of a flying saucer. "It was large with dazzling lights that beamed toward the ground, illuminating its undercarriage and the meadow" (Lovern 113). He was not believed initially but something certainly had frightened him. Not long after, perhaps an hour, they began hearing unidentifiable noises outside and the family dog started barking wildly. By the time Billy Ray Taylor and Elmer Sutton got out to investigate, armed with a .22 and a shotgun respectively, the dog was hiding under the house and would not budge.

As they crossed the yard, the men noticed three (some accounts say two) creatures not of this earth. "The men described the aliens as each being approximately four foot tall, having large solid eyes, short legs, large ears, long arms and hands that appeared to be claws" (114). The story begins to take on elements of the Thing the moment they opened fire. The shells and bullets seemed to have no effect. They ran back to the house and panic set in. The creatures came up and when one peered into the living room window, someone fired a blast right through it. They supposedly rapped at doors and windows, leapt up on the roof, swiped at the men and loped around in a bizarre swaying fashion in some kind of silver, close fitting clothing. After a few hours of torment, the family made a mad dash for their automobiles and headed to get the sheriff.

When law enforcement arrived (as many as 20), they could find no sign of space monsters, but saw plenty of firearms damage in the home. Then, soon after the police departed around 2:15 AM, the harassment continued off and on until dawn. UFO investigators discovered that other area residents did see strange lights in the sky that night, but no one outside of the two families saw the creatures, now known as the Hopkinsville Goblins. The family was not known as troublemakers, lunatics or pranksters and it's hard to imagine someone shooting up their own home for no good reason. Whatever set off the Taylors and Suttons was very real to them and as the Sutton's property became a local tourist attraction, the family moved away, never to return.

Clearly, this is a case where hysteria might explain things. Consider how quickly situations can escalate with a snake or spider in the presence of a group of people. There were several children present and mothers trying to protect them from something unseen, so in that environment, irrationality might just have taken over. It would be hard to claim *The Thing* played into this directly since there is no evidence that anyone in these two families had seen it. However, by 1955, most alien films were of the "space monsters attack small town" variety, featuring small groups defending their homes and towns, frequently with gunfire that had no effect. It would have been very hard to not know the basic story, and even if extraterrestrial goblins walked that old Kentucky home one night, the psychological reaction of anyone seeing them would have been tempered by such a plot line.

CONCLUSIONS

There is an old (likely apocryphal) story about Captain Cook's encounter with some island natives in the South Seas who asked where he came from. Through an interpreter, he tried to explain that he came from the sailing vessel out in deeper waters. Supposedly, the natives literally could not see the ship because their word for boat (used by the interpreter) and what Cook pointed to did not match up.

Putting the veracity and cultural attitudes of the story aside for a moment, it demonstrates the psychological gap that occurs when new experiences affect us, but we don't have language or concepts to anchor it down. In moments of psychological crisis or confusion, we instinctively fall back to mythology (social constructions, literary sources, or religious dogma, for example) to make sense of the world and direct our actions. By the middle of the last century, cinema was clearly part of that mythic nexus, the primary source of shared experience across the United States and in many ways, much of the world.

Given that, assume for a moment you did see something so unique and different from anything you'd known before that it challenges your most basic and unquestioned pillars of reality. You really can't explain what you saw and you struggle to make sense of it, to even describe it, as you try to talk out your brush with the paranormal. And then, suddenly, there's a reporter with a microphone in your face angling for a description, hopeful for a good story. Would it be such a surprise if your account came out like a black and white sci-fi thriller from 1951?

WORKS CITED

Barker, Gray. *They Knew Too Much About Flying Saucers.* University Books, 1956, pp. 11-36.

Bennet, Colin. *Looking for Orthon: The Story of George Adamski, The First Flying Saucer Contactee, and How He Changed the World.* Cosimo Books, 2008. Kindle Version.

Carlson, Peter. "50 Years Ago, Unidentified Flying Objects from Way Beyond the Beltway Seized the Capital's Imagination." *The Washington Post,* 12 July 2002, https://www.washingtonpost.com/archive/lifestyle/2002/07/21/50-years-ago-unidentified-flying-objects-from-way-beyond-the-beltway-seized-the-capitals-imagination/59f74156-51f4-4204-96df-e12be061d3f8/. Accessed 14 November 2021.

Darrach, H. B. Jr. and Robert Ginna. "Have We Visitors from Space." *Life Magazine,* 7 April 1952, reprinted on http://www.project1947.

com/shg/articles/lifemag52.html. Accessed on 13 November 2021.

Guiley, Rosemary Ellen. *The Monsters of West Virginia: Mysterious Creatures in the Mountain State*. Stackpole Books, 2012.

Jessee, B. "The Flatwoods Monster: A Tale of the Atomic Age." Medium. com, 24 November 2019. https://medium.com/the-mysterious-miscellany/https-medium-com-the-mysterious-miscellany-close-encounters-of-the-feathered-kind-the-flatwoods-monster-e519e1b9ce6b. Accessed 15 November 2021.

Leslie, Desmond and George Adamski. *Flying Saucers Have Landed*. Kindle Edition. Original 1952 copyright expired.

Lovern, Kyle. *Appalachian Case Study UFO, Vol. 2*. Woodland Press, 2009, pp. 113-118.

Index